VOCATIONAL HABILITATION OF SEVERELY RETARDED ADULTS

VOCATIONAL HABILITATION OF SEVERELY RETARDED ADULTS

A Direct Service Technology

G. Thomas Bellamy, Ph.D.
Director, Specialized Training Program, University of Oregon

Robert H. Horner, Ph.D.
Research Associate, Specialized Training Program, University of Oregon

Dean P. Inman, Ph.D.
Research Associate, Center on Human Development, University of Oregon

Illustrated by
Arden Munkres

University Park Press
Baltimore

UNIVERSITY PARK PRESS
International Publishers in Science and Medicine
233 East Redwood Street
Baltimore, Maryland 21202

Composed by University Park Press, Typesetting Division.

Manufactured in the United States of America by The Maple Press Company.

Library of Congress Cataloging in Publication Data

Bellamy, G. Thomas.
Vocational habilitation of severely retarded adults.

"The habilitation efforts described in this text have evolved over the last five years in the Specialized Training Program at the University of Oregon."
Bibliography: p.
Includes index.
1. Mentally handicapped — Rehabilitation — United States — Handbooks, manuals, etc. 2. Vocational rehabilitation — United States — Handbooks, manuals, etc. I. Horner, Robert H., joint author. II. Inman, Dean P., joint author. III. Oregon. University. IV. Title.
HV3005.B44 362.3 78-10161
ISBN 0-8391-1296-3

contents

figures

acknowledgments

The habilitation efforts described in this text have evolved over the last five years in the Specialized Training Program at the University of Oregon. During this time we have tried to integrate the available research with our own thinking to provide a group of severely retarded adults with meaningful vocational opportunities. In this process, substantial contributions have been made both to our service and research efforts by the excellent staff of the Specialized Training Program, representatives of agencies purchasing habilitation services, our colleagues at the University of Oregon, and the retarded adults with whom we have the privilege to work.

In our service efforts we have been fortunate to work with students and staff who blend personal concern with technical skill and seemingly inexhaustible energy. On more than a few occasions our assumptions of the vocational potential of severely retarded individuals were realized only because of the ingenuity and determination with which our expectations and suggestions were translated into daily program practice.

The University of Oregon has been one of the most supportive environments imaginable for our work. Dr. Robert H. Schwarz, Director of the Center on Human Development, has been instrumental in arranging this environment. He has combined an understanding of our work with timely guidance and support. His efforts provided us with a research environment in which the demands of daily university living did not preclude service commitments to the community or prevent careful attention to daily details of ongoing research. The Rehabilitation Research and Training Center at the University of Oregon also has been an important resource. Through collaboration on a variety of research projects, we have gained considerable awareness of vocational rehabilitation issues that extend beyond our interest in service to severely retarded adults.

We have been extremely fortunate to enjoy support from various state and federal agencies whose assistance has made our program operational. Foremost among these is the Bureau of Education for the Handicapped, the Developmental Disabilities Office, Region X, and the Oregon State Mental Health Division. Each has contributed both monetarily and professionally to the services we have provided for retarded adults and the development of our thinking about service technology.

Perhaps our greatest debt is to the severely retarded adults who have participated in the Specialized Training Program. They have been our best teachers. Their successes have maintained our behavior and their failures have reminded us that we have much to learn about habilitation procedures.

Finally, we would like to give our thanks to Pam Whaley and Mary Freer for their patient manuscript typing and retyping, and to Arden Munkres whose graphics and design skills add immeasurably to the text. Shawn Boles, Thomas Schwartz, Rick Brennan, and Frank Bertrand read earlier drafts of the book, and their critical comments assisted greatly in clarifying many suggested procedures and ideas.

Dedicated to
John and Dennis

VOCATIONAL HABILITATION OF SEVERELY RETARDED ADULTS

PART I

A CONCEPTUAL BASIS

chapter 1
INTRODUCTION

Vocational rehabilitation involves development or restoration of individual productivity, so that both personal and public earnings are increased, individual independence is enhanced, and future public service costs are minimized. Vocational rehabilitation is distinct from most other employment programs in its focus on remediation of employment barriers associated with the individual, rather than barriers associated with broader issues of unemployment, economic trends, and job creation (Levithan and Taggart, 1977).

Vocational rehabilitation services in the United States have been closely identified with the state-federal vocational rehabilitation network, which for fifty years has combined federal policies and financial backing with state program administration. Four important characteristics of the rehabilitation process are closely associated with the history and operation of this agency. The first is a clear emphasis on *individualization* of services. Based on the judgment of the rehabilitation counselor and the desires of the service recipient, medical, educational, prosthetic, counseling, or other services are tailored to the unique needs and job aspirations of each individual. An emphasis on *employment* outcomes is the second characteristic. The success of rehabilitation efforts traditionally has been indexed by the number of individuals who entered gainful employment, and the costs of services typically have been evaluated by comparing individual earnings and public service costs before and after rehabilitation (Conley, 1969).

A third characteristic of vocational rehabilitation in this country has been the *selectivity* with which services have been made available. By law and by agency policy rehabilitation efforts have focused on individuals for whom remunerative employment was a feasible service objective. More severely handicapped individuals, whose potential for increased productivity was less certain, frequently have been excluded from services. However, a fourth characteristic of vocational rehabilitation agencies has been the trend toward *extension* of services. Increasingly, individuals with severe disabilities have been included, as techniques for providing effective services became available and as the service need became apparent to policy makers.

Such an extension of vocational rehabilitation services is now occurring. In 1973 Congress applied to rehabilitation the civil rights philosophy that has permeated various education and service programs during the last two decades. Discrimination on the basis of handicap was expressly forbidden for federal contractors. Further, the vocational rehabilitation network's own resources were allocated with the stipulation that service priority be given to severely disabled individuals for whom employment was a feasible goal (Rehabilitation Act, 1973). While this severely disabled group includes a number of previously served individuals, it also encompasses many heretofore excluded groups (Levithan and Taggart, 1977).

One of the groups likely to be affected by this extension of rehabilitation services is severely retarded adults. Actually, the term "rehabilitation" is a misnomer when applied to most severely retarded individuals. Since services are designed to assist in entry, not re-entry into the labor force, we have chosen the term vocational *habilitation* as more descriptive. Although previously viewed as unlikely to succeed in competitive occupations, individuals in this group increasingly are receiving vocational services. This reflects both an increase in the need for community services and an expanding set of procedures for helping severely retarded individuals develop vocational competence. Severely retarded adults, like many other traditionally institutionalized groups in our society, are experiencing a radical shift in service availability and location (Paul, Stedman, and Neufeld, 1977). Community residences and community support services are replacing large residential institutions as the preferred and primary treatment strategy. It is hardly surprising, therefore, that advocacy for vocational services in the community has expanded (Gold, 1973; Laski, 1977). Techniques for providing effective vocational services to severely retarded individuals also have been developing rapidly during the last few years, making it more likely that these individuals will be found eligible for vocational rehabilitation services (Bellamy, Inman, and Schwarz, 1978; Karan, Wehman, Renzaglia, and Schutz, 1976).

The purpose of this text is to describe the procedures that are currently available for vocational habilitation of severely retarded adults. Although procedural information has been accumulating for the last two decades, little effort has been made to compile this information in a practical, inexpensive handbook for persons responsible for service delivery. In preparing such a procedural guide, our intent is twofold: to increase the efficiency and success with which vocational services are provided to severely retarded persons and to expedite the extension of habilitation services to these individuals nationwide.

The specific procedures that we have chosen to emphasize reflect our assumptions about characteristics of those labeled severely retarded and the behavioral model (Ullmann and Krasner, 1965) from which we have approached service problems in vocational habilitation. To facilitate our communication with readers who may or may not share our views, each of these influences is discussed in this and the following chapters before any procedural recommendations are made.

SEVERELY RETARDED ADULTS

Mental retardation, according to the *Manual on Terminology and Classification* of the American Association on Mental Deficiency, refers to "significantly sub-average general intellectual functioning existing concurrently with deficits in adaptive behavior and manifested during the developmental period" (Grossman, 1973, p. 11). Severe retardation, the manual continues, refers to a level of intellectual and adaptive behavior of four to five standard deviations below the population mean. This corresponds to Stanford-Binet IQ scores of 20 to 35 with similar deficits in adaptive behavior. For adults, vocational and social functioning are identified as critical aspects of adaptive behavior.

In this book the terms retarded and severely retarded will be used according to the recommendations of the Grossman (1973) manual. Much of the research to be cited and much of our own work has involved adults who have been labeled severely retarded on the basis of normal diagnostic information. From a practical perspective, however, the focus of the book is not restricted to any particular set of intelligence or adaptive behavior test scores. Rather, the group with which we are concerned might be better defined by the difficulty encountered in changing individual behavior or developing vocational competence with commonly used teaching and management procedures. It is this difficulty that the procedures described in later chapters are designed to remediate, regardless of the label with which an individual enters the habilitation setting. The bulk of our supporting data has derived from individuals labeled severely retarded who have experienced considerable difficulty in learning vocational and other skills. Individuals labeled severely retarded remain our primary concern in the text.

Four important assumptions about severe retardation have guided our research on rehabilitation and our reflection about procedural needs in vocational programs. We assume that: 1) current skill deficits do not imply limited learning ability; 2) habilitation goals for severely retarded persons should be socially equitable; 3) habilitative behavior changes should not be expected without direct treatment and training; and 4) accommodation to individual differences is an integral aspect of service to severely retarded individuals.

Assumption 1: Current Skill Deficits Do Not Imply Limited Learning Ability

The level of behavioral complexity and adaptation that severely retarded individuals may attain remains largely unknown. What is clear, however, is that as treatment and training strategies have improved during the past few decades, views of what severely retarded persons are capable of learning have been revised repeatedly toward more optimistic projections. Nevertheless, a robust belief persists in our society that severely retarded individuals possess little potential for learning new skills, working productively, or adapting to complex community demands. Our view is that this belief is unfounded, and that, for all practical programming purposes, severely retarded adults can be assumed to have the potential to learn a variety of complex skills and perform these in socially acceptable ways in work, living, and social environments.

The optimistic note of this assumption reflects our uncertainty about what limits may be experienced when sophisticated intervention procedures are used systematically and longitudinally. Research and demonstration efforts during the last few years have provided so many illustrations of competence obtained through structured training that any presumed limitation of potential seems unwarranted without additional data (see reviews by Berkson and Landesman-Dwyer, 1977; Dokecki, 1964; Gold, 1973).

This assumption has three important implications for our view of the vocational habilitation process. The first is that habilitation and remunerative employment are seen as feasible objectives for most severely retarded individuals. Indeed, an imposing collection of research and demonstration reports now support this view. More than two decades ago, Loos and Tizard (1955) demonstrated that adults who would now be labeled severely retarded could learn vocational tasks performed in an institution's sheltered workshop. Furthermore, after learning the tasks, these workers produced them as rapidly as other workshop employees during normal workdays with no additional supervision. The apparent difficulty of the tasks, which involved nine separate movements in constructing cake boxes, and the efficiency of performance argued strongly for the potential vocational competence of severely retarded persons. A continuing series of research and demonstration projects since that time extended the optimistic findings of Loos and Tizard (1955) to more severely handicapped individuals (Crosson, 1966; Williams, 1967; Hunter and Bellamy, 1976) and to more difficult tasks (Clarke and Hermelin, 1955; Gold, 1972; Bellamy, Peterson, and Close, 1975). These projects demonstrated that severely retarded adults can master such diverse tasks as bicycle pumps (Clarke and Hermelin, 1955) and bicycle brakes (Gold, 1972); oscilloscope switches (Bellamy, Peterson, and Close, 1975); wiring harnesses (Hunter and Bellamy, 1977); nursery specimen cans (Karan, Eisner, and Endres, 1974); ballpoint pens (Martin and Flexer, 1975); chain saw blades (O'Neill and Bellamy, 1978); agricultural gleaning (Jacobs, 1976); and use of power equipment (Crosson, 1966).

More evidence of the potential vocational competence of severely retarded adults was reported by Cook, Dahl, and Gale (1977) after a national survey of exemplary vocational rehabilitation practices. Rehabilitation agencies responding to printed survey materials indicated that severely retarded adults were currently employed in the following occupations in sheltered or competitive employment: order clerk, collator, sorter, duplicating machine operator, sewing machine operator, maid, cafeteria and fountain attendant, orderly, assembler, baker's helper, sandwich maker, auto mechanic helper, racket stringer, silkscreen printer, drill press operator's helper, printer, eyelet machine operator, porter, farmhand, woodworking shophand, painter's helper, and hand packager. Certainly, the variety of these jobs supports our contention that many severely retarded adults have remarkable work potential.

The second important implication of the assumption that skill deficits of severely retarded individuals do not imply limited learning abilities is the relatively minor role we assign to evaluation of work potential in the rehabilitation process. Assessing whether or not a severely retarded adult has the potential for work and thus is or is not eligible for vocational habilitation services is directly contradictory to our assumption of learning potential. Although vocational rehabilitation agencies may well be forced to serve only a fraction of the individuals who could benefit, it is our assumption that the resulting service denials would be more appropriately attributed to such practical issues as availability of funds, access to needed services, and skill of the service providers than to presumed lack of potential on the part of a severely retarded individual (Bellamy and Snyder, 1976; Gold, 1973). This is not to say that other assessment issues are not important. Critical decisions about the treatment and training process require refined assessment skills. The purpose of this needed assessment, however, is to facilitate immediate treatment decisions, not to predict whether treatment will be successful.

Finally, the first assumption leads to a useful interpretation of treatment or training failures in habilitation. If it is assumed that severely retarded adults have the potential to learn and perform vocational skills, failure to do so can be attributed to the intervention program or to the treatment specialist, rather than to the severely retarded individual. Consequently in our view, vocational habilitation procedures should incorporate systematic review and modification of procedure as an integral part of all treatment. From this perspective, failure to progress simply signals to the treatment specialist that some procedural modification is in order. Certainly, we claim no distinctiveness for this position. In discussing his educational attempts with Victor almost two centuries ago, Itard commented on an unsuccessful teaching strategy by writing "...if I had not been understood by my pupil, it was my fault rather than his" (quoted by Ball, 1971, p. 31).

Assumption 2: Habilitation Goals for Severely Retarded Persons Should Be Socially Equitable

Our second assumption is that no special ideology is required to establish service goals for severely retarded individuals. Treatment goals can and should be derived from the same values that are applied to other persons in society. Some of the most influential professional writing during the last decade has focused on this issue of values and objectives in treatment programs. Particularly important in our approach to vocational habilitation of the severely retarded are the concept of normalization as described by Nirje (1969) and Wolfensberger (1972), the emphasis on development of personal competence suggested by Edmonson (1974), Perske's (1972) defense of the dignity of risk, and Roos's (1975) interest in application of a developmental or learning model throughout lifetime services.

From the value perspective that these writers provided, we assume that coordinated services should result in improved quality of life for severely retarded adults by increasing their opportunities to participate competently in the mainstream of community life. This participation is multi-dimensional, involving the opportunity to make individual choices; to participate in defining one's own lifestyle; to have access to normalized experiences, as well as experiences that enhance individuality and uniqueness; and to be viewed by others as competent citizens in areas of mutual importance.

These value positions posit a critical role for vocational habilitation in coordinated community services for severely retarded adults. It is difficult to imagine a normal lifestyle or a significant level of community participation without work responsibilities and the economic opportunities that result from work. We feel that adult programs that perpetuate "prevocational" training indefinitely and those that eschew vocational goals for day care, recreational, and educational services unnecessarily prevent participation in an important aspect of community life. Work is a valued and normal activity in our society, and there seems little socially equitable basis for denying work opportunities to individuals who perform poorly on standardized tests.

Assumption 3: Habilitative Behavior Changes Should Not Be Expected Without Direct Treatment and Training

The third assumption underlying our approach to vocational habilitation of retarded individuals is that direct environmental intervention is the most efficient method of producing changes in vocationally relevant behaviors. In this regard our approach is similar to the emphasis on direct instruction of Becker, Engelmann, and Thomas (1975) and to Brown's (1973) concept of "instructional determinism." Behavioral gains, these authors have argued, should be expected as a result of specific instructional activities, rather than maturation, experience, or exposure. In short, it is our position that in developing vocational competence of severely retarded adults, one should expect no incidental learning, no generalized behavioral effects of periodic counseling sessions, no spontaneous remission of symptoms, and no maintenance of behavior changes without planned, systematic intervention procedures.

The primary effect of this assumption on our view of the habilitation process is the importance that we assign to *direct services.* For several years sheltered workshops have relied on counseling, work evaluation, and work adjustment experiences to produce generalized changes in the work behaviors of handicapped adults (Brolin, 1976; Rosen, Clark, and Kivitz, 1977). To provide these services, a cadre of support service professionals has evolved, and the roles of program coordinator, counselor, and evaluator have become central to the rehabilitation process in most vocational facilities. Professional research, university personnel preparation programs, and most inservice training opportunities reflect this emphasis on support services in rehabilitation.

In contrast, the direct service staff of these facilities, who have actual day-to-day responsibility for management of handicapped workers, usually have received less attention, less remuneration, and less status than support staff. Nevertheless, it is the direct service staff person who typically is charged with implementation of habilitation programs for severely retarded individuals. Successful demonstrations of vocational involvement by severely retarded per-

have involved continuous intervention throughout the learning or performance period, not episodic treatments from which a trainee was expected to generalize. Therefore, as more severely retarded adults enter rehabilitation facilities, the role of the direct service staff should assume greater importance than in the past. To provide effective habilitation, facilities will rely increasingly on the skills of direct service staff persons who can plan and implement structured, consistent, and individually appropriate intervention programs in day-to-day interactions with trainees.

Assumption 4: Accommodation to Individual Differences is an Integral Aspect of Service to Severely Retarded Individuals

Severely retarded adults are not a homogeneous group. Rather, the label severely retarded is applied for a variety of reasons and describes individuals with quite different skills and skill deficits. Because of this diversity we have specifically avoided a cookbook approach to vocational habilitation, which would advocate the use of identical techniques with all trainees. Rather, the coherence of our approach rests upon the general application of basic principles, from which several alternate procedures usually can be derived for any given individual and situation.

These basic principles have been defined in the experimental analysis of behavior (e.g., Skinner, 1953). Our interest in individual accommodation follows directly from the *functional* approach that has characterized this line of behavioral research. Rather than attempting to identify specific environmental events that have predictable effects on the behavior of all individuals or organisms, behavior analysts have sought to define basic learning principles, inductively, through study of the relationship between environmental events and the behavior of single organisms (Sidman, 1960).

Environmental events of importance in this analysis were those that changed the probability of an individual's subsequent responding, regardless of the specific nature of the event or its effect on other people. Events were thus defined *functionally* in terms of their effects on the behavior of a single individual. The principles of learning that have resulted from this effort relate to the functional effect of events on behavior rather than to properties or attributes of the events themselves. Because of its particular influence on our work, this functional or behavioral approach to habilitation is described in more detail in later chapters. Suffice it to say for the moment that this approach does allow us to accommodate wide individual differences in the procedures we associate with the habilitation process. We assume that each severely retarded individual enters habilitation with a unique learning history that determines the function of various environmental events or intervention procedures. Trainer behaviors that effectively reinforce, assist, or correct the work behavior of some individuals may well have the opposite effect for others. These individual differences are accommodated in effective habilitation, as basic behavioral principles are applied to different individuals by selecting different reinforcement, assistance, and correction procedures. The availability of basic behavioral principles allows us to avoid suggesting the use of a single set of techniques with all trainees. Rather, our procedural recommendations outline a pragmatic, problem-solving approach in which the trainer or supervisor uses available information to identify events that may function as effective reinforcers, corrections, and assists for an individual worker; s/he then incorporates these events into procedures that apply general learning principles and modifies either the events selected or the procedures used if the desired performance does not result.

THE VOCATIONAL HABILITATION PROCESS

Two conclusions should be apparent from our assumptions about severe retardation. First, we believe that vocational habilitation is both desirable and possible for most severely retarded adults. To exclude these individuals from services on the presumption that they have no vocational potential ignores both general research on learning abilities and specific demonstrations of vocational competence. The second conclusion that follows from our view is that critical characteristics of traditional rehabilitation practice need not be changed as services are extended. Traditional emphasis on individualization of services, remunerative occupational outcomes, and restriction of services to those likely to become employed, all are possible as habilitation is extended to severely retarded individuals. To change the criteria for service provision or to limit the objective of habilitation efforts to development of independent living skills could needlessly restrict vocational opportunities.

The vocational habilitation process for severely retarded individuals no doubt will center in sheltered workshop programs. Sheltered workshops in this country are not-for-profit organizations that provide employment for disabled individuals, typically at subminimum wages under special Department of Labor certification, and that attempt to increase non-sheltered vocational opportunities through individual counseling, evaluation, work adjustment, and job placement efforts (Brolin, 1976). Workshops have developed with potentially conflicting roles and funding sources. As parts of a local service system these programs are expected to provide organized daily services that lead to employment of handicapped individuals. Workshops are also expected to function as effective businesses, supporting part of their operation with commercial income. The potential conflict among these roles, which is highlighted by Scott's (1967) historical review, has led in many cases both to underfunding as a service program and to competitive disadvantage as a business. Nevertheless, workshops have continued to expand to meet growing service needs, and for many handicapped individuals they remain the only service option that emphasizes vocational development.

Because of the central role of sheltered workshops, the immediate vocational outlook for most severely retarded individuals depends on the ability of these organizations to provide extended employment at high wage levels or to develop placements in competitive employment. Unfortunately, data from several recent surveys provide little evidence of successful habilitation of severely retarded adults in either extended employment or placement efforts. Severely retarded adults are often totally excluded from sheltered work programs (Greenleigh Associates, 1975; Lynch and Graber, 1977); the moderately and mildly retarded individuals in workshops earn very low wages and often are employed only intermittently (Whitehead, 1978); and the public cost of subsidizing sheltered employment has led some authors to question whether welfare would not be a more attractive policy alternative for the severely disabled (Levithan and Taggart, 1977). While these results are not surprising in light of the multiple objectives of workshops, they do raise serious questions about the utility of workshop programs in providing habilitation services to severely retarded individuals.

However, these national survey averages conceal a significant group of workshops that have successfully offered employment opportunities to severely retarded adults (Bellamy, 1977; Cook, Dahl, and Gale, 1977). Because of these programs it seems unwise to conclude from the survey data either that workshops are inappropriate service options or that severely retarded individuals lack work potential. Rather, an analysis of successful habilitation efforts should be made in order to identify common characteristics of successful programs. If such characteristics were identified, they could provide the basis for planning, evaluating, and modifying procedures in workshops that extend services to the severely retarded.

Although published studies of vocational habilitation efforts with the severely retarded represent a diversity of service locations, theoretical positions, value perspectives, and methodology, two features of the rehabilitation process are encountered repeatedly. First, successful habilitation has typically meant remunerative employment in a sheltered setting, rather than individual placement in a competitive job. Because of the low wages associated with sheltered employment (Whitehead, 1978), this characteristic of successful habilitation efforts appears critical. However, the dichotomy between sheltered and competitive employment may now be fading as various intermediate employment opportunities are defined (Horner and Bellamy, 1978a). Sheltered workshops that function as factories with minimal public subsidy (DuRand and Neufeldt, 1975), workshops that contract to perform jobs in normal work situations, and enclaves with industry represent a growing trend toward more normal and more remunerative employment for individuals with significant disabilities. In providing vocational habilitation services to severely retarded adults, it will be important for agencies to assist workshops in developing these intermediate employment options and to design habilitation efforts to ensure individual success in intermediate employment.

The second common theme in reports of successful vocational habilitation of severely retarded individuals was noted earlier: a focus on direct services rather than support services in developing vocational competencies. Critical components of the direct service process are readily apparent in much of this demonstration literature. These are: 1) task analysis (i.e., precise definition of the behavioral requirements that the worker is expected to meet); 2) direct training of skills required by vocational tasks; and 3) continued supervision of production, using deliberate arrangement of social and physical aspects of the work environment.

The vocational habilitation process for severely retarded individuals will be similar in many ways to services for other groups. Client identification, definition of individual service need, purchase or provision of services, and employment apply to severely retarded adults just as they do to other rehabilitation clients. As habilitation is provided, however, emphasis should be placed on direct service activities, and intermediate employment options should be identified as service objectives.

STRUCTURE OF THIS BOOK

The need for procedural information is apparent if sheltered workshops are to provide effective habilitation and employment for severely retarded adults. In particular, the roles and responsibilities of the direct service staff of these facilities should be defined in a way that applies current research information. The purpose of this book is to provide that definition, to begin bridging the gap between research results and service needs with a practical but empirically based technology for the direct service activities of task analysis, vocational training, and production supervision. The book integrates available procedural information to define specific *guidelines* for direct service activities. In selecting and formulating these guidelines, our interest has been in communicating effectively both with individuals now responsible for direct service and with other professionals involved in habilitation and behavioral research. To facilitate this communication we have attempted to meet four criteria in the definition of guidelines: that they be *practical, comprehensive, empirically valid,* and *experientially sound.*

Our *practicality* criterion for the procedural guidelines reflects a general recognition of the constraints of normal staff and equipment resources in vocational facilities. Thus, the guidelines avoid reliance on expensive mechanical equipment, which has been used successfully in some research. To evaluate the practicality of our suggestions in the area of staffing, we have relied on the report of Greenleigh Associates (1975) that the national average ratio of *total* facility staff to clients in sheltered workshops is one to five. Of course this ratio includes administrative, professional, direct service, and all other staff. Implementing our suggestions should not require any increase in this total staff to client ratio. However, a re-allocation of staff resources in facilities serving severely retarded adults may well be in order, so that greater emphasis can be placed on direct service responsibilities.

It may well be that the suggestions made in this book are beyond the current skill levels of direct service staff in some facilities. Since we have found it necessary to present somewhat technical information for adequate coverage of some procedures, the practicality of our suggestions may be limited to a degree. We feel, however, that technical competence is required for effective direct service. In facilities where this poses difficulty, it is hoped that it will also create motivation to enhance direct service personnel resources, because without minimal staff competencies in these procedures the failure of the facility to serve severely retarded individuals is practically ensured.

Comprehensiveness has been our second criterion in selecting and defining procedural guidelines. The responsibility of most direct service staff persons is quite broad, ranging from design of production methods to production supervision, training, and behavior management. We have attempted to match this breadth in our procedural suggestions, believing that the choice of procedures for use in one service area is affected greatly by the utility of approaches to all others. A focus just on training or task analysis or behavior management would be of limited utility, except for direct service employees who are already highly skilled in each of the other areas.

Our third criterion was that the suggestions have a clear *empirical basis*. When professional research is used to define rules for direct service habilitation staff that are both practical and comprehensive, the extensiveness of the professional literature proves more apparent than real. There are indeed several studies relevant to task analysis, training, and production procedures, but they leave many direct service questions unanswered. For example, it is still unclear whether procedures reported in the research can be practically applied with *most* severely retarded adults or *most* industrial tasks that a workshop might encounter. The typical academic response to such a situation is to rely on qualifications and limitations that often make resulting suggestions either incomprehensible or impractical. (For example, according to so-and-so, such-and-such a procedure may work for some persons, but the research setting in which the work was done makes generalization to service situations somewhat questionable.) Little wonder that research utilization remains a perplexing national problem in rehabilitation. It is not the case that the complexity implied by such hedging is incorrect or unnecessary. Instead, this academic response simply provides an inadequate basis for dealing with the practical problems that habilitation facilities are facing as they attempt to serve more severely retarded individuals.

Many of our guidelines have clear empirical support in research on habilitation of the severely retarded. To provide a comprehensive account, other rules are presented that rely on extrapolation from basic research or applied research in other areas. As a result, future applied research on habilitation of the severely retarded will no doubt demonstrate that some of our suggestions were imprecise, incomplete, or even inaccurate. The risk of such error, however, seems warranted by the pressing current need for a comprehensive guidebook for direct services in habilitation.

Our final criterion in defining procedural guidelines is that they be *experientially sound*, i.e., consistent with our own professional experience in providing vocational habilitation services to severely retarded adults. Since 1973 the authors have assisted in operating the Specialized Training Program, which is a small habilitation workshop and a research project designed to demonstrate the feasibility of vocational involvement with severely retarded adults. Our approach was to select newly deinstitutionalized adults who were thought to be representative of some of the difficult cases likely to be referred to vocational programs during the next few years (Bellamy, Inman, and Horner, 1978). Work tasks with economic value in the Pacific Northwest were obtained, and efforts to develop vocational competence on these tasks ensued. The available research provided a first approximation for our procedural efforts. Refinement of these early efforts has been a continuing process of studying service problems and trying a variety of new approaches until success was achieved with each individual. The guidelines presented in this text are no doubt greatly influenced by the experiences that we have had in this demonstration and research program. For more complete descriptions of the Specialized Training Program, see Bellamy (1976), Bellamy, Horner, and Inman (1977), Bellamy, Inman, and Horner (1978).

SUMMARY

Vocational habilitation is a process through which an individual is helped to develop work skills relevant to the job market and then to secure remunerative employment. Extension of vocational habilitation services to severely retarded people is consistent with current legislation, with the growing need for service by these individuals, and with the expanding technology for delivering effective services.

Four assumptions about severe retardation affect the way habilitation procedures are defined in this text. These are: 1) that skill deficits of retarded adults do not necessarily imply limited vocational potential; 2) that habilitation goals for severely retarded adults should reflect the same values that are applied to other individuals in society; 3) that important behavior changes should not be expected without direct intervention; and 4) that accommodation to individual differences is a critical aspect of habilitation service. These assumptions lead to a definition of the vocational habilitation process that preserves the traditional occupational emphasis of rehabilitation while emphasizing the importance of direct services. Critical components of effective direct service are task analysis, vocational training, and production supervision. In this text specific procedures for integrating each of these components into workshop operations are presented through guidelines for staff behavior.

chapter 2
A BEHAVIORAL APPROACH TO HABILITATION

It was noted in the preceding chapter that task analysis, direct training, and production supervision have been common procedural elements of programs in which severely retarded individuals have achieved vocational competence. Our emphasis on these procedures reflects not only this historical utility but also the behavioral model from which we approach practical issues in vocational habilitation.

One purpose of this chapter is to describe our behavioral perspective and to discuss implications for vocational habilitation of severely retarded individuals. The chapter is not intended as an introduction to applied behavior analysis, since several texts provide excellent overviews (Bandura, 1969; Kanfer and Phillips, 1970; Kazdin, 1975). The discussion focuses instead on the issues that arise when basic behavioral concepts are applied to vocational habilitation. A second purpose of the chapter is to describe research on operant chains, which we feel is particularly relevant to task analysis, vocational training, and production supervision. Although the research provides an incomplete empirical basis for habilitation efforts, it nevertheless offers a useful conceptual framework for procedural development. Although readers who are primarily interested in the practical application of direct service procedures may find the discussion of chaining somewhat technical, we feel it is useful to clarify the research tradition on which our suggestions are based.

IMPLICATIONS OF THE BEHAVIORAL MODEL

During the last decade the behavioral model has been applied to the study of an increasing array of human service concerns. Now, systematic approaches have been defined for such diverse areas as management of community service programs (Davidson, Clark, and Hamerlynck, 1974), treatment of individual problems of personal, social, and sexual adjustment (Goldfried and Davison, 1976), and management of classroom environments in which children acquire basic skills (Becker, Engelmann, and Thomas, 1975). In each case, the behavioral approach provides both a set of techniques and a way of looking at broader issues related to the service context, goals, and accomplishments (see discussions of Browning and Stover, 1971, and Krasner and Ullmann, 1965).

Similarly, applying the behavioral model to the vocational habilitation of severely retarded adults has implications that extend beyond the intervention setting. Also affected are the way the habilitation objectives are analyzed and defined, the way the habilitation process is conceptualized, and the way habilitation procedures are evaluated.

Response Analysis

A defining characteristic of the behavioral model is that both treatment problems and objectives are stated in terms of what an individual does. In habilitation, the discrepancy between an individual's current condition and the desired vocational competence is defined in terms of the responses, or behaviors, that s/he is expected to produce in vocational (and other) settings.

This interest in behavior is also an interest in public verification. Responses are defined as behavior that can be observed or otherwise reliably and publicly measured. Such a clear definition of behavioral objectives in habilitation settings establishes a basis for scientific study of both work behavior and habilitation procedures.

The empirical emphasis of response analysis contrasts rather sharply with the way habilitation goals and problems are typically defined. Brolin (1976) and Neff (1968), in important accounts of rehabilitation and work behavior, define the goals of habilitation efforts primarily in terms of a worker's personality. That is, the development of enduring personal characteristics or traits, which are seen as important to an individual's adaptation to work environments, are the primary focus of habilitation efforts. Of course, the presence or absence of such traits is always a matter of inference from an individual's behavior, either in real work or test situations. The behavioral approach, in contrast, focuses on these behaviors themselves, not the underlying personal characteristics that are often inferred from them (Mischel, 1968).

Nothing about the behavioral approach contradicts the importance in habilitation of the outcomes emphasized by Neff (1968) and Brolin (1976), because the behavioral model is essentially content free. It specifies how objectives and problems should be defined, not what constitutes an important objective. In our application of the behavioral model to vocational habilitation, goals have been defined on the basis of our assumptions about severely retarded individuals (see Chapter 1). In general, the resulting objectives have much in common with more traditional rehabilitation approaches, except for an added emphasis on behavioral measurement. Thus, instead of focusing on an individual's work readiness or work tolerance, objectives in this text are defined in terms of the skills and responses from which readiness and tolerance are inferred.

Response analysis holds several implications for habilitation of severely retarded individuals. First, the behavioral requirements of work situations should be defined, so that the objectives of individual habilitation efforts are clear. This includes not only the identification of specific responses involved in performing a work task, but also delineation of aspects of the work setting that affect how and when these responses should be performed. In this text such an emphasis on response analysis is evident in our description of procedures for task design and analysis (Chapters 3 and 4) and in our attention to additional requirements of various work settings. For further discussion of this area, the reader is referred to Brown and Belmore (1978) and Davies (1973).

A second important implication of response analysis is the focus that it provides for habilitation efforts. Once the behavioral requirements of a work setting are identified, these can be objectively compared with an individual's current behaviors. Habilitation efforts can then be directed toward any discrepancies that might exist. It is useful to distinguish between two classes of these discrepancies (Bellamy, Inman, and Schwarz, 1978). The first class includes behavioral *deficits.* An individual may not be able to perform a required response, either because the behavior is not in the individual's repertoire, or because s/he has not learned to discriminate relevant stimulus events that are critical to correct performance. These behavioral deficits are usually remediated through training procedures, discussed in Chapters 5 to 10. The second class of discrepancies between an individual's behavior and that required in a vocational setting can be labeled *performance* problems. That is, the individual can perform the required responses in the appropriate settings, but does so either too often or not often enough. Procedures for changing how often behaviors are performed in vocational settings are emphasized in Chapters 11 to 13 on production supervision issues.

Experimental Basis of Procedures

Together with its emphasis on response analysis, the behavioral approach to habilitation has been associated with treatment techniques that are derived from the experimental analysis of behavior (see Skinner, 1953). Extensive study with literally thousands of human and infra-human subjects has led to the identification of a few principles of behavior on which habilitation procedures can be based. These principles describe a set of relationships, which have been observed time and time again, between an individual's behavior and the nature of the surrounding environment. In particular, environmental events that precede and follow a response may change the probability that the response will be emitted in similar situations in the future. The principles — reinforcement, stimulus control, discrimination, extinction, punishment, shaping, etc. — catalog the lawful relationships between environmental events and the probability or frequency that a response will be emitted (Honig, 1966; Honig and Staddon, 1977).

Because these principles relate behavior to environmental events, rather than to an individual's personality, they have immediate relevance for habilitation. To help an individual develop vocational competence, the habilitation specialist need not change presumably enduring individual characteristics or traits. Rather, individual differences are simply accommodated as the client's work or training environment is modified in accordance with established principles of behavior. This environmental change continues, systematically, until the desired behaviors are performed in appropriate settings and at acceptable rates. Environmental changes suggested in the experimental literature usually involve altering immediate social or physical consequences of an individual's behavior. Thus, applying behavioral principles to habilitation necessarily focuses attention on direct service staff persons and the details of their daily interactions with trainees.

An additional impact that the experimental analysis of behavior has had in our treatment of habilitation is upon the language that is used in describing intervention procedures. As ongoing research has classified relationships between individual and environmental events, rather common words have been used to refer to precise processes and events. Thus, although terms like behavior, reinforcement, punishment, and shaping are familiar to most individuals, they are used in very specific ways in describing behavioral procedures. We feel that the drawbacks of adopting this unusual language system are offset by the benefits that accrue, because we can more precisely describe specific habilitation procedures. This is not to say that other perspectives and other vocabularies fail to promote clear understanding or effective services. Rather, the language of behavioral analysis is particularly well suited for these purposes, because it has inherited much of the rigor and precision associated with the older and more basic tradition of experimental analysis of behavior. Throughout the book we strive to use thorough explanations. Nevertheless, the reader should be familiar with basic concepts and vocabulary of behavioral analysis (cf. White, 1970b).

Vocational Habilitation as a Technology

One of the most important legacies of the experimental analysis of behavior has been its emphasis on behavioral measurement. As principles of behavior were applied in natural settings, continuous measurement of target behaviors became the basis through which intervention procedures were evaluated and modified (Johnson and Bolstad, 1973). This behavioral measurement now provides the methodological basis for a *technology* of habilitation, an applied science in which laboratory methods are used in the study and treatment of practical vocational problems.

From a behavioral perspective, therefore, habilitation involves more than simply changing vocationally relevant behaviors through the application of experimentally established principles of behavior. As a technology, vocational habilitation also involves independent scientific inquiry, as various procedural possibilities are evaluated in terms of their effect on vocational behaviors. This technology of vocational habilitation has several important features.

First, vocational habilitation is not just the practical application of previous findings from more basic research endeavors. New techniques and approaches can be developed, tried, evaluated, and incorporated into habilitation practice with or without basic research support. Of course, many of the techniques that are tried do relate to previous laboratory research. The important feature of a technology is that this need not always be true; advancement in application can occur independently of advancement in basic research.

A second feature of the technology of vocational habilitation is its pragmatic eclecticism. Workshop staff can choose from among many program options in an attempt to identify procedures that result in improved performance. A successful technology is one that *works,* in a practical sense, not one that remains theoretically pure. To the extent that intervention procedures based on these or other areas of research produce reliable changes in vocationally relevant behavior, they are useful elements in a technology of habilitation. Therefore, a technology of habilitation based on measured outcomes can incorporate findings from any area of research. Findings with particular relevance for vocational habilitation have been reported in research on social learning (Bandura, 1977), discrimination and concept learning (Zeaman and House, 1963; Becker, Engelmann, and Thomas, 1975), cognitive functioning (Meichenbaum, 1977), and organizational effectiveness (Steers, 1976).

A third feature of the technology of habilitation is its service accountability. It provides objective measurement of outcomes that are central to the habilitation process to consumers of habilitation services — clients, funding agencies, legislative groups, and the community at large — with a clear view of what service dollars are accomplishing. Application of the technology of habilitation in any vocational context involves an analysis of responses required for competent performance in that setting. This behavioral analysis of job requirements provides the standard against which an individual's current behaviors can be compared to identify treatment needs. The following section will illustrate a method of defining these response requirements.

ANALYSIS OF VOCATIONAL BEHAVIOR

At the heart of a technology of habilitation is the definition of behavioral competencies in terms of how a person responds to various situations in the work environment. Even casual observation reveals that people at work do not behave in random ways. Quite the contrary, most workers perform complex series of behaviors that affect and in turn are affected by changing characteristics of the work environment.

Conceptually, it is useful to regard the interaction between an individual's behavior and his or her environment as a continuous stream of events (Barker, 1963). Segmenting the behavioral stream into discrete behavioral or environmental events is necessarily arbitrary, and different schools of thought have chosen to concentrate on different aspects of it. The response analysis involved in a behavioral model involves dividing the stream into discrete, measurable units, referred to as responses, or behaviors. For each of these responses, objects or events can be identified that serve as consequences and antecedents.

Responses

Responses are the basic units in an analysis of vocational behavior. To illustrate, let R refer to a response, or a behavioral unit, in which a worker picks up and places a completed product into a storage bin for inspection.

R (pick up and place product in bin)

As was noted earlier, such a behavioral unit should be publicly verifiable, i.e., its occurrence must be potentially subject to external verification. Of course, several other aspects of the behavior may also be of interest, such as its topography (how it was done), duration (how long it lasted), intensity (what force was used), and latency (how much time elapsed before the behavior was exhibited). Each of these characteristics can be treated as a variable affecting rate of occurrence. That is, it is possible to observe a behavior over time that is defined by a particular topography, latency, intensity, and duration. The rate of the behavior then simply refers to the frequency of occurrence divided by a measure of time. In the example, the pick-up-and-place response might be considered an instance of vocational competence only if it were done in a way that did not damage the part, and only if it were performed at a rate that was high enough to meet normal production expectations.

The size of the behavioral unit is a matter of definition. At one extreme a response might be defined as a single instance of a pincer grasp — or perhaps even the contraction of a single muscle (Inman, 1978). At a molar or general level one could define a worker's assembly of a complete product as one behavioral unit. The decision of how to "chunk" behavior, that is, divide the behavioral stream into discrete responses, depends on the purpose of the analysis. For example, when the purpose is to teach someone a new skill, smaller response units are usually more useful. Such a fine-grained analysis can provide the trainer with a precise definition of behaviors to be taught and the order of performance. The trainer then can monitor the success of training by noting mastery of each small behavioral unit. On the other hand, if the purpose of the analysis is to provide a means to monitor work rate on a task which an individual already can perform, it would probably be more useful to define larger response units. Such a coarse-grained analysis could provide the needed basis for measuring performance while avoiding the cost required to collect data on smaller behavioral units.

Other practical factors are also important in deciding the size of response units. The skill with which a worker enters a vocational training situation affects the size of responses that should be defined for training. Experienced workers can often learn complex responses with minimal instruction, so a fine-grained analysis of vocational behaviors is somewhat superfluous in many situations. Our research with severely retarded workers, on the other hand, has led us to define quite small behavioral units. As an illustration of this point, the reader is invited to compare the small response units that we have used in this text with those described by Davies (1973) in his excellent discussion of task analysis with respect to industrial jobs. Application of these considerations in analysis of workshop tasks is discussed in Chapter 4.

From a vocational perspective a response not only must be performed correctly, but also must be performed at the right time and at a high enough rate to earn a significant wage. Two important variables affecting these response dimensions are the stimuli immediately following a response, consequences, and the stimuli immediately preceding a response, antecedents.

Consequences

Stimuli (i.e., objects, sounds, and events) that follow a response are referred to as consequences. Much experimental work has focused on describing the effects that consequent events have on the future probability or rate of response units. Briefly, research has shown that stimuli following a response hereafter symbolized as

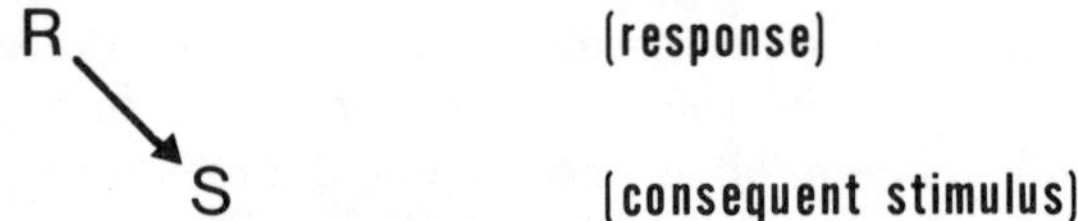

usually fall into one of three categories. One class of consequences increases the future probability of occurrence of R, in which case the stimulus is called a *reinforcer* (symbolized S^{r+}). The actual process of delivering a reinforcer is called *reinforcement.* Another type of consequent stimulus is labeled a *punisher,* and its contingent application is called *punishment.* A third class of consequences is regarded as *neutral* because they have no noticeable affect on the future probability of occurrence of R. It is important to note that reinforcers, punishers, and neutral stimuli are defined functionally, i.e., in terms of their effect on the behavior. Moreover, how an event will affect the behavior of any given individual in any given situation can only be determined after the fact by measuring changes in the behavior.

With regard to the example behavior (R_1), several events might function as reinforcing consequences (S^{r+}) all of which increase the future probability of the response. These could include, for instance, periodic paychecks or compliments from a supervisor for a job well done. We refer to these events as reinforcers since, if these consequences were eliminated altogether, the

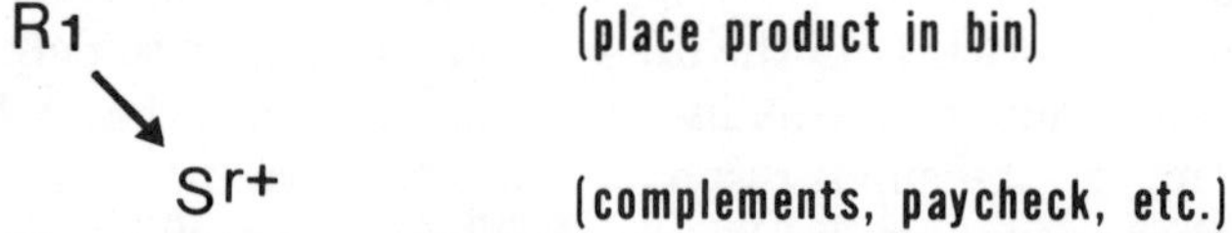

frequency of R_1 probably would drop rapidly to zero for most workers. Other stimuli following R_1, such as changes in the general noise level in the work environment and proximity of the supervisor, should function as neutral consequences for the behavior of competent workers in most vocational settings. (For a technical account of research on consequent events, the reader should consult Dunham, 1977.)

Research on the effects of consequences of behavior provides two important tools to the habilitation specialist. First, it suggests a set of procedures for changing how often a behavior is performed by changing the environmental events that follow work-related behavior. The learning or performance environment often can be arranged so that events that are likely to function as reinforcers or punishers for an individual's behavior occur after the behavior is performed. Second, analysis of consequences in natural work settings can identify events that are likely to follow work-related behaviors in natural vocational settings. As is described in later chapters, treatment procedures can then be designed to facilitate performance with such consequences.

Antecedents

Clearly, vocational competence cannot be related just to the *frequency* with which defined responses are performed. A competent worker seldom performs work behaviors such as R_1 (placing completed products in the bin) when the products are defective, during work breaks, or when s/he is critically ill. The response (R_1) is appropriate only in the presence of a specific set of circumstances, or antecedent stimuli. To describe vocational competence in terms of behavior frequencies, therefore, it is necessary to define the desired behavior in terms of a particular antecedent stimulus or situation.

An antecedent stimulus is said to control a response if, in the presence of that stimulus, the probability of the response is changed. When this stimulus control exists, the antecedent is called a *discriminative stimulus* (S^D). For example, if an antecedent condition (S_1, a completed product) is a stimulus in the presence of which R_1 is reinforced,

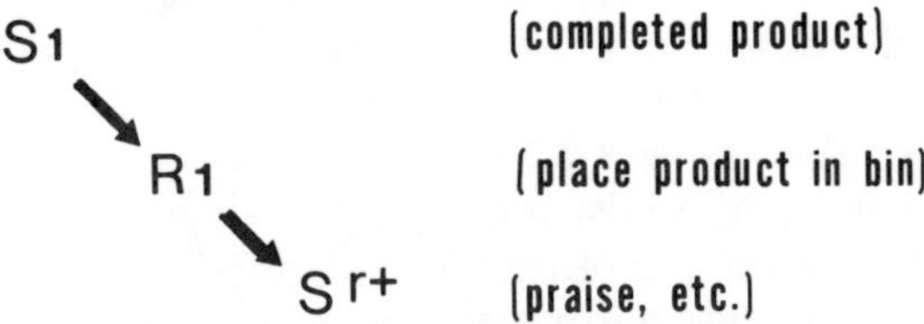

then the probability of R_1 increases in the presence of S_1. If S_1 controls R_1, the worker will be more likely to stay employed than if such stimulus control does not exist. In analyzing the responses that comprise vocational competence in any given setting, therefore, desired

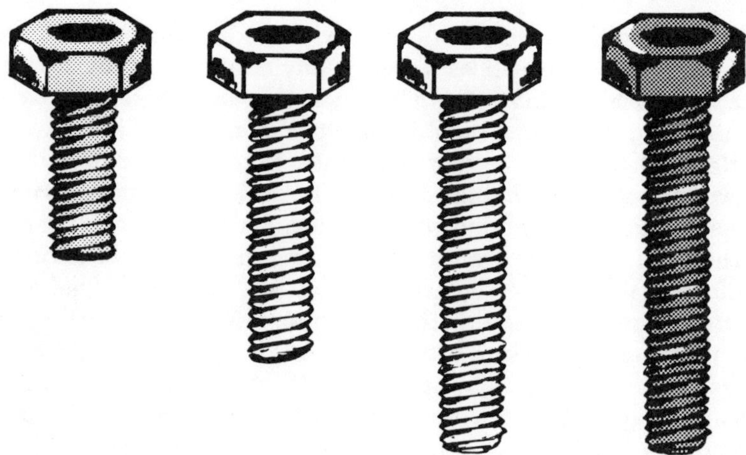

Figure 2.1. Hex bolts that vary in size and color.

performance should be specified in terms of both the frequency of various behaviors and the situations in which they should be performed.

Operant research and investigations of discrimination and concept learning (Becker, Engelmann, and Thomas, 1975) have provided some useful distinctions among functions of antecedent events. In any given context, some stimuli signal that a particular response is appropriate, others signal that it is inappropriate, and still others are irrelevant and as such should not alter the frequency of the response. More specifically, any stimulus has several dimensions on which variations can occur. For example, an object may be described in terms of its color, size, shape, weight, position, rotation, etc., and may be distinguished from other objects on all of these dimensions.

Distinctions among objects are made on the basis of differing *values* or *levels* on one or more of these dimensions. If a worker were asked to use only brass bolts from a bin containing both steel and brass bolts, s/he could do so by noting different levels on the color dimension, while different levels of shape, size, and position dimensions would provide no useful information. In this example, color would be called the *relevant dimension* and brass the *positive level* (S^+) on that dimension. All other colors, like silver, are *negative levels* on the color dimension. All other dimensions (shape, size, etc.) are *irrelevant* (S_i) in this context. In many behavioral contexts, the values along two or more stimulus dimensions are relevant. When this occurs, the two dimensions can be either *relevant and redundant* or *relevant and conjunctive.* To illustrate, assume that the parts bin noted above contained 1-in brass bolts, 1½-in and 2-in steel bolts, and 2-in blue-painted bolts. As can be seen in Figure 2.1, if the task required use of only the 1-in brass bolt, the worker could respond appropriately by noting *either* the color or length of each item in the bin. In this context, color and length are relevant and redundant. However, if the task required use of only the 2-in steel bolt, the worker could respond appropriately only if s/he noted *both* the length and color of each item, making length and color relevant and conjunctive.

The utility of this nomenclature is apparent in many vocational situations in which a worker must respond differentially to stimuli that are very similar. Especially important applications are described in Chapter 8 on procedures for teaching difficult responses.

OPERANT CHAINS

The many different behaviors that, taken together, comprise vocational competence are seldom single independent responses. More often work involves performance of a complex sequence or chain of responses. Operant chains differ from just a series of independent responses in that each response in a chain produces the discriminative stimulus for the next response (Gollub, 1977; Kelleher, 1966; Millenson, 1967). It has been generally assumed in the applied behavior analysis literature that chained discriminative stimuli also function as reinforcers for the preceding response, although some questions still exist on this aspect of chain performance (Gollub, 1977).

Thus, operant chains are linked fundamentally to concepts of stimulus control and reinforcement. An antecedent stimulus (S_1) comes to affect (control) the probability of a response (R_1) because it predicts a reinforcing contingency. In other words, S_1 informs the worker that if R_1 is emitted, a reinforcer (S^{r+}) is forthcoming. Since this is the case, S_1 becomes something that is desirable in and of itself because it provides the worker an opportunity to emit R_1. In other words, an individual will work, i.e., emit another response, R_2, to be in the presence of S_1.

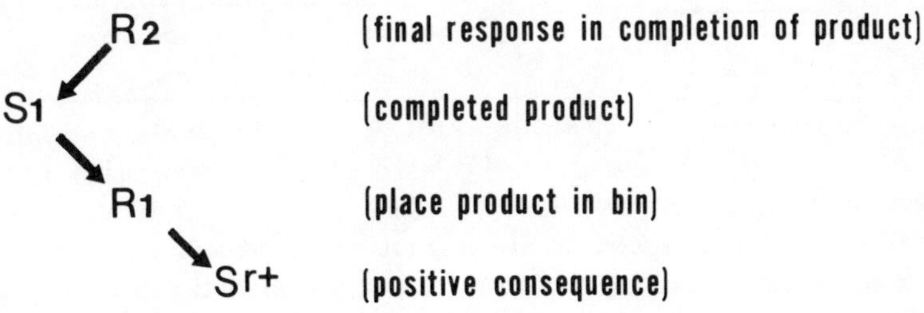

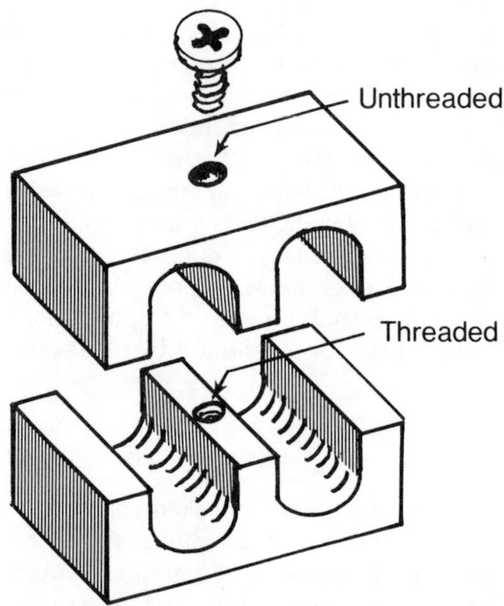

Figure 2.2. Exploded view of a heat sink.

Moreover, in the same way R_1 can be brought under control of S_1, R_2 can come under the control of another distinct antecedent stimulus condition, S_2. To explain, let us consider an example. In order to assemble the heat sink pictured in Figure 2.2, the threaded (lower) and unthreaded (upper) components are placed in correct alignment with each other, the screw is seated in the hole, and tightened with a screwdriver, then the completed product is picked up and placed in a parts bin for inspection. In this instance, S_1 and R_1 would be the same as described earlier: given a completed product, it is picked up and placed in the parts bin. R_2 then refers to using a screwdriver to tighten the screw that joins the two components. This response can only bring about S_1 when it occurs in the presence of S_2, which is having the screw properly placed in the product and a phillips screwdriver available.

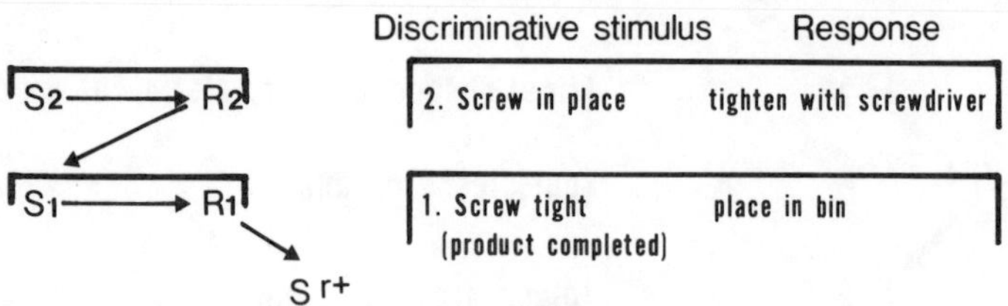

Moreover, S_2 is produced because another response, R_3, is emitted, which consists of placing the screw in the unfinished assembly:

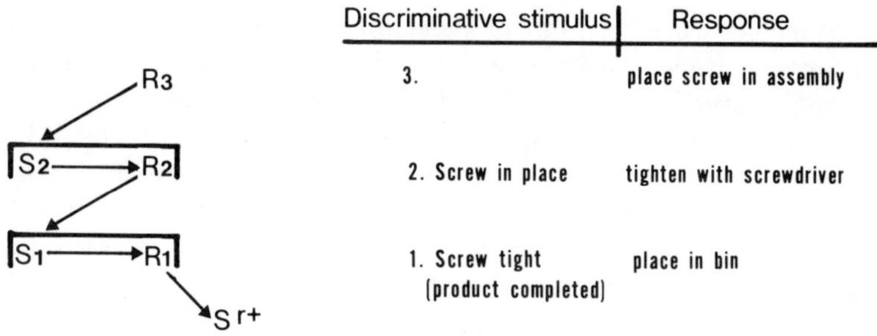

Discriminative stimulus	Response
3.	place screw in assembly
2. Screw in place	tighten with screwdriver
1. Screw tight (product completed)	place in bin

R_3, like R_2, comes under stimulus control of another antecedent stimulus, S_3, which consists of having the two disconnected parts correctly positioned:

Discriminative stimulus	Response
3. Two parts positioned	place screw in assembly
2. Screw in place	tighten with screwdriver
1. Screw tight (product completed)	place in bin

Similarly, S_3 is produced by the responses of placing the two parts (R_4 and R_5):

Discriminative stimulus	Response
5. Two parts in bins	place threaded sink, flat side down
4. Threaded sink in place	place unthreaded sink on top, with flat side up.
3. Both parts positioned	place screw in assembly
2. Screw in place	tighten with screwdriver
1. Screw tight (product completed)	place in bin

Of course, assembly of this small product could be conceptualized as a single response, rather than an operant chain. As was noted earlier, it would probably be useful to use a single response definition if one's purpose were to monitor assembly rate over a long time or to teach an experienced learner what to do. In many instructional situations with naive learners and/or difficult tasks, however, an analysis that employs fine-grained operant chains is much more useful. Consider, for example, the difficulty most individuals would have learning to pick a lock if it were described only as one response, with a locked door as the antecedent and an unlocked one as the consequence. Learning would likely proceed more rapidly if the response chain required by the task were also defined, as well as the relevant antecedent stimuli for each step. (Readers interested in picking locks should consult Becker, 1971.)

Defining operant chains in vocational contexts is useful not only when tasks are relatively difficult, but also when they are lengthy. Many jobs involve sequenced assembly of a large number of parts. Figure 2.3, for example, illustrates a cam switch assembled by a severely retarded adult in the Specialized Training Program. The switch has 18 separate components and takes industrial workers an average of 10 minutes to complete. By defining the assembly response as an operant chain, rather than as a single response, it is possible to plan training activities around smaller segments.

The definition of operant chains in analyzing vocational behaviors may also be relevant for planning supervision activities designed to increase performance rates. Although chains are usually treated as single responses when performance rate is the focus of attention, more powerful intervention techniques can sometimes be based on identification of chain components. Certain schedules of reinforcement, for instance, may be built into the chain, such that following completion of a particularly difficult component the worker would receive a reinforcer. Similarly, quality control procedures may need to occur after certain chain components. These possibilities are discussed in Chapters 11 to 13 on production supervision techniques.

RESEARCH ON OPERANT CHAINS

Studies in both experimental and applied settings have identified several characteristics of operant chains. These studies have typically focused on the acquisition of chains and their performance over time. Variables related both to acquisition and performance of chained behavior are relevant to an analysis of vocational behavior, and the operant research provides useful, although incomplete, information on both.

Figure 2.3. Exploded view of an 18-piece cam switch assembled by retarded adults at the Specialized Training Program.

Acquisition of Operant Chains

Much of the research addressing chain acquisition has used small animals as subjects. It is always impressive to watch non-verbal, relatively "unintelligent" animals exhibit long complex chains of behavior without error. For example, most beginning psychology students are astonished when they see a rat that has learned to climb a spiral staircase, negotiate a drawbridge, climb a ladder, pull a chain to move a car, peddle the car through a tunnel, climb a flight of stairs, run through a tube, step into an elevator, raise a Columbia University flag, which starts the elevator downward, and after reaching the ground, move to and press a lever, after which a food pellet is delivered. This type of demonstration almost always leads the students to ask how it is possible to teach a complex chain of behaviors to an organism that cannot talk or understand verbal directions. The answer, of course, is that the chain is taught one component at a time. As each component behavior is mastered another is added and taught to criterion. More and more behavior components are added until the whole chain can be performed as one smooth sequence of behaviors.

The student's next question is usually more difficult: how do you teach each component (for example, flag raising) so that it is performed correctly and at the appropriate point in the chain? The "answer" requires dissertations on both theory and technique and often constitutes a major portion of introductory classes in operant psychology. For the purposes of the present discussion, a practical presentation of the issues seems preferable to such a treatise.

When Pierrel and Sherman (1963) originally taught the now famous rat, Barnabas, to perform the operant chain mentioned earlier, they first placed the animal in the presence of the last discriminative stimulus (S_1) in the chain and taught him to perform the correct terminal response (R_1). That is, the rat was placed in front of a bar and taught to press the bar in order to obtain a food pellet. Then, when this response was very likely to occur whenever the rat was in that setting, the next-to-last response, riding down the elevator (R_2) was taught. Each time the rat correctly descended on the elevator, he received the opportunity to press the bar and receive a food pellet. Next, the flag-raising (R_3) response was taught, and so on, with each response introduced in reverse order.

Backward Chaining

The teaching procedure used with Barnabas has been labeled reverse or backward chaining and has found many applications in practical teaching situations (Bensberg, 1965). Moreover, several variations on this basic reverse chaining procedure have been used. For example, in teaching the self-dressing skill of pulling on a T-shirt, the shirt could be positioned initially with the learner's head and arms already placed through the appropriate holes, so that only the final response of pulling the shirt down remained. In the original reverse chaining paradigm, this final step would be repeated until it was mastered, at which time the next behavior would be added to the chain. In other variations of backward chaining the trainer might perform the entire task on each training trial, while the learner either observed or assisted passively (i.e., was physically guided through the required movements). On each trial, when the last step was reached, the learner would be expected to perform independently. Again, new components could be added to the end of the chain as the learner progressed. Thus, in later trials the trainer might assist in performance of only the first two or three steps, while the learner performed the rest independently. The advantage of this modification of the basic reverse chaining procedure is that it exposes the learner to the entire chain of responses, although independent performance is expected on the final steps. The disadvantage is that the time required for passive assistance on the initial steps of the chain on each trial can limit the total number of learner responses in any given training period.

Forward Chaining

Operant chains can also be taught in the order they are normally performed. Called forward chaining, this procedure involves initially teaching the first response that is to be performed in the chain, then adding the second after a criterion performance has been reached on the first, and so on, until the last response that produces the terminal reinforcer is finally taught. As is the case with reverse chaining, variations on this procedure exist. For example, it is possible to teach the initial responses while exposing the learner to all responses in the chain on every training trial. Crosson (1966) identified 103 sequential steps in the operation of a drill press. These were taught to severely retarded residents of a state institution in a forward chain, that is, they were presented in the order of final performance.

In another common variation of the forward chaining procedure, a learner is exposed to an entire chain (or a segment of a longer chain) in the order of performance and provided instruction on each step, while proceeding through the entire chain. Access to one step is not contingent upon acquisition of the preceding step. This procedure appears to have the advantage of maximizing the learner's independence early in training, especially if some steps are already familiar. This approach is exemplified in the reports of Gold (1972) and Bellamy, Peterson, and Close (1975).

Although research supports the efficacy of each of these forward and reverse chaining strategies in some training contexts, little is known to date about which strategy is most appropriate in any given situation. Whether one approach leads to more rapid acquisition, fewer errors, or fewer pauses in subsequent performance is still largely a matter of conjecture in applied vocational settings. Workshop staff, however, are currently faced with a need to conduct training *now*. The option of waiting for data comparing various training strategies and their possible interaction with worker characteristics is not a viable one. In lieu of adequate data, we suggest in later chapters that a forward chaining approach be used in which the entire chain is performed. The major advantages to this approach are that it 1) focuses on teaching response topography and response sequence simultaneously and 2) requires less task preparation than the backward chaining approaches. It must be emphasized, however, that we suggest this approach as one that we have found effective, not as the option of choice of all workers, tasks, and settings.

PERFORMANCE OF OPERANT CHAINS

Once a chain is learned, that is, after a learner can emit an entire chain without hesitating and without errors, questions arise about what rate and under what conditions the chain will be performed over time. This is a very real concern for habilitation specialists, because habilitation is not complete until vocational chains are performed over extended periods of time in the absence of immediate supervision. This is an especially difficult problem because it demands, at some level, that a worker come to "enjoy" working or at least the benefits associated with it. Clearly, if a person does not learn to value his or her work or its benefits regardless of how well the work can be performed, it is unlikely work performance will endure.

It is unfortunate that so little is known about the performance of operant chains, because there are at least three parameters of chain performance that are relevant to the vocational setting. First, the rate at which vocational chains are performed is of paramount importance. Individuals who work too slowly will not generate enough revenue to offset the costs of paying their salary, thereby selecting themselves out of the job market. Second, the accuracy with which vocational chains are performed is also critically important because most employers cannot afford inferior work. It doesn't matter how well a worker might have been trained; if his/her on-the-job performance is sloppy or inaccurate, it is unlikely s/he will remain employed for very long. Finally, it is important that work performance remain consistent over time. This means that rate and accuracy are unaffected by irrelevant environmental events or by duration of an employment period.

The majority of available data on the rate, accuracy, and consistency of chain performance come from animal research. A review of this literature reveals some basic relationships that are potentially relevant to vocational habilitation. Care must be taken, however, in extrapolating these findings to humans working in vocational settings. For one thing, almost all animal studies are conducted using primary reinforcement; i.e., the animals are deprived of food and work (emit chains) to earn food. This may not be analogous to the human situation, leaving open the possibility that variables affecting chain performance of people in work situations are inherently different from those affecting chain performance in hungry animals working for food (Spradlin, Girardeau, and Corte, 1965; Schroeder, 1972). In addition to this major difference between human and animal research, Rilling (1977) has urged that caution be used whenever the behavior of one species is used to predict that of another. Rilling has noted the impropriety of predicting pigeon behavior on the basis of observed patterns of rats. Even greater restraint must be maintained when animal research is applied to human performance. Nevertheless, the body of evidence on animal behavior is the best information available on chain performance. Therefore, the following discussion integrates what is known about chain performance and relates it to performing vocational chains in a work setting.

Operant Chains as Response Units

As was mentioned earlier, a response unit is a discrete, modifiable unit of behavior. A response unit can be the contraction of a single muscle, although usually we view a series of muscle movements (i.e., hitting, eating, waving) as a response unit. A response unit is modifiable in that all the muscle movements comprising the response are affected similarly by manipulation of the reinforcers or punishers that immediately follow the response. For example, eating with a spoon requires many different muscle movements. These movements can be treated as a single response unit and reinforced accordingly. Thus, reinforcement increases all the muscle movements involved in the response unit "eating with a spoon."

Operant chains can be considered to be discrete response units (Crossman, 1971; Inman and Cheney, 1974), and as such can be consequated with reinforcement like any other behavior. Therefore, the chain as a whole is modifiable because the probability of the entire chain is affected by the consequences following the terminal response.

These characteristics make it apparent that an operant chain can in fact be perceived as a response unit. This perception has substantial implications for maintenance of the accuracy and rate with which a chain is performed. It suggests that principles of reinforcement that aptly predict the frequency of individual responses may also be useful when applied to the performance of operant chains.

Reinforcement and Chain Performance

Reinforcement describes a functional relationship between contingent presentation of a stimulus and increase in the frequency of a preceding response. Reinforcers delivered after the terminal response in a chain effectively reinforce each response in the chain. Researchers working with both animal (Kelleher, 1966; Millenson, 1967; Gollub, 1977) and human (Crosson, 1966; White, 1970a; Horner, 1978) subjects, however, have demonstrated that responses within a chain are not equally affected by terminal reinforcers. Rather, the reinforcer has a greater effect on responses that occur later in the chain, i.e., the closer the proximity of the response to the reinforcer, the more effective the reinforcer will be. While all steps in a chain may be maintained by a terminal reinforcer, pausing will be more likely early in the chain than toward the end. This is due to the reduced effect of reinforcement on responses early in the chain. The longer a chain is the less likely a terminal reinforcer will maintain performance of early responses. As is seen in later chapters, this response pattern has major implications for both task design variables and schedules of reinforcement in production settings.

The schedule with which reinforcers are delivered has long been an area of study for researchers exploring the relationship between environmental events and behavior patterns (Ferster and Skinner, 1957; Schoenfeld, 1970; Staddon, 1977; Zeiler, 1977). The effects that different reinforcement schedules have on operant chain performance also have been studied. For the purpose of the present discussion we wish to emphasize only two points: 1) chain performance can be maintained with reinforcement schedules similar to those used to maintain single responses, and 2) the number of responses within a chain must be taken into account when defining a chain reinforcement schedule.

Both human and infra-human research strongly supports the fact that reinforcement schedules that require a subject to perform several repetitions of a chain can effectively maintain high, accurate performance levels. Schedule research adopted with human workers has generally focused on varying the number of repetitions of a chain the subject must perform before reinforcement is delivered. This literature suggests that a worker performing the chain of responses required for assembly of a bicycle brake or circuit board, for instance, might be expected to work rapidly even if reinforcement were delivered only after completion of two or three or more units. Schroeder (1972) and Crosson (1966) studied the performance of severely retarded workers who performed many chain repetitions before reinforcement was delivered. They demonstrated that consistent high performance rates were maintained. Schroeder's data indicated that in some instances production rates improved as workers were required to do more work (i.e., more repetitions of the chain) before a reinforcer was delivered.

Many variables affect the rate and accuracy with which a chain will be performed. The schedule of reinforcement is one such variable. A second is the length of the operant chain. When assessing schedules of reinforcement for chain completion, it is important to recognize the importance of chain length. If a worker needs to complete two chains before s/he is reinforced, the amount of behavior required would be substantially different if one chain contained only four responses and the other contained forty responses. The length of the chain contributes to defining a schedule of reinforcement. As such, schedule manipulations will need to focus on the overall amount of behavior (i.e., number of responses in the chain and number of chains) being reinforced. While a worker may maintain high performance rates on a short chain when 20 chains must be completed before reinforcement, s/he may need to be reinforced after completing every chain (or even one-half of a chain) to maintain the same high rate if the chain is exceptionally long.

While extensive research effort has focused on the performance of operant chains under various reinforcement schedules, that literature is both too voluminous, and, as yet, too poorly documented with humans to warrant detailed analysis here. In general, operant chains can be considered as response units. Reinforcement effects will be similar to the effects noted with any other response unit. Major consideration, however, must be given to the length of a chain. Early responses in longer chains will be less reinforced than later responses, and long chains require a worker to perform more behavior than short chains under the same schedule of reinforcement.

Chain Performance During Extinction

Perhaps the most thoroughly researched aspect of chain performance is the effect that extinction has on the rate of probability of chain completion. Extinction refers to a period during which the terminal reinforcer is withheld from the subject. The effects have several possible vocational applications. Early in extinction the chain is hardly affected; in fact, initially it may be produced at an even higher than usual rate. But as extinction continues, there are long pauses that begin to occur at the very beginning of the chain. For example, a long pause may precede the first component in the chain and then again the second, but once these first steps are performed the chain may be completed as usual. As more and more extinction trials are completed (i.e., more trials are unreinforced), pausing becomes more pronounced throughout the chain and errors begin to occur until, finally, the chain collapses completely.

Again, it is important to remember that, prior to extinction, animals are reinforced for chain performance with food pellets, whereas a human employee receives a paycheck, which is exchanged for coins and paper money, which, in turn, are exchanged for an extremely wide range of reinforcing events. This difference may negate much of what is regarded as true in the light of the animal research.

In general, an operant chain that is not reinforced will eventually break down. This phenomenon is of particular importance for retarded workers, given that identification of reinforcers is one of the most difficult tasks of staff working with a retarded person. Reinforcers can often be identified, but for various reasons (i.e., satiation, fatigue) they may cease to function as reinforcers over time. In these situations vocational chains that were performed accurately and rapidly break down and pausing, errors, or inappropriate responding is likely. The importance of identifying and consistently delivering reinforcers for chain performance cannot be overemphasized.

Chain Performance and Competing Behaviors

Operant chains define a specific sequence of responses. Responses that are not a part of that sequence usually are either irrelevant or incorrect, both of which may be time-consuming and costly. The integrity of a chain is dependent upon strong stimulus control. Two factors affect the performance of inappropriate responding in the chain: 1) the control of non-task-related stimuli over inappropriate responding compared to the control task-related stimuli exert over correct responding, and 2) task-related stimuli that control inappropriate responses.

A worker performing a task is continually exposed to stimuli provided by the task as well as to stimuli provided by the training and production setting. To the extent that task-relevant stimuli control on-task behavior, the worker will progress through the chain. To the extent that extraneous stimuli (loud noises, supervisors walking around, activity visible through the windows) control inappropriate responses, the chain will be broken by pausing and irrelevant or incorrect behavior. Therefore, if a chain is to be performed accurately over time, procedures must exist to maintain stimulus control. These procedures will usually focus on manipulation of reinforcement variables.

Inappropriate responding within a chain also occurs if task-relevant stimuli come to control inappropriate behavior. It is all too easy for an irrelevant response to occur within the chain and be reinforced by the terminal reinforcer. It will be recalled that a reinforcer delivered at the end of a chain reinforces all responses in the chain (relevant and irrelevant). If this cycle is repeated over several trials, the irrelevant response can become controlled by task-relevant stimuli. Skinner (1948) has noted this process develop in the behavior of pigeons, and Horner (1978) has documented task-controlled irrelevant responding with a severely retarded adult. Once again the focus of attention rests on stimulus control. In a vocational context this focus will be on ensuring that task-relevant stimuli only control task-appropriate responses. Clearly, an environment designed to maintain the performance of specific operant chains will need to carefully attend to worker, setting, and task variables that affect stimulus control within those operant chains.

VARIATION IN CHAIN ELEMENTS

As will be detailed in ensuing chapters, we feel an analysis of vocational habilitation from an operant chaining perspective leads to useful implications for training and supervising severely retarded workers. At the same time we recognize that the viability of a worker's vocational skills will rest on more than his or her ability to perform one rigid chain of responses. A worker will need to know several tasks; s/he will need to maintain high, accurate rates of performance; and s/he will need to adapt to stimulus and response variation within a chain. This latter requirement is of particular interest. It focuses on the need to shift analysis of operant chains from highly controlled laboratory settings to applied settings that are continually changing.

Vocational tasks in workshop or industrial settings generally involve the repetition of a particular chain of responses. It is not uncommon, however, for a worker to be faced with variation over time in the stimuli or responses within the chain. Discriminative stimuli may vary as incoming parts are arranged or rotated differently, or when functionally equivalent but visually different components are substituted for familiar parts. Responses may differ from one time to the next as different movements are required to achieve a specific result (i.e., placement of a part). These variations in stimulus and response components often have direct relevance for habilitation procedures.

Figure 2.4. A cam switch bearing before and after placement on a cam switch axle.

Stimulus Variation

Each response in an operant chain is controlled by stimuli generated by the previous response. In many contexts these response-produced stimuli vary from one time to the next, so the discriminative stimuli for succeeding responses vary over time. For example, in a task reported by Bellamy, Peterson, and Close (1975) a worker was trained to place the plastic bearing shown in Figure 2.4A over the stemmed end of a cam switch axle (see Figure 2.4B). To place the bearing with the correct side up, one or more small slots into which hex nuts could be inserted were to face away from the cam axle. Placement of the bearing was one response (R_{11}) in the operant chain defining this task. The response was under control of the plastic bearing (S_{11}). Using chaining notation, the eleventh step in this chain could be represented by:

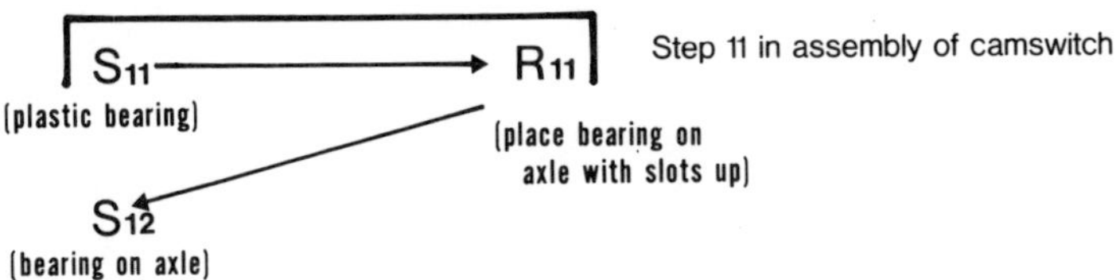

The worker who was trained to perform this task, however, was faced with considerable stimulus variation when he was actually assembling the task in production. Industry demands required that the bearing used in assembly be changed from time to time. Figure 2.5 presents four different bearings used in assembling the cam switch. When a bearing was switched, the stimuli present at step eleven of the chain changed. While S_{11} could have been the bearing in Figure 2.5A for two weeks, industrial demands might require that S_{11} be changed to the bearing in Figure 2.5B or 2.5C or 2.5D. Following these slight changes the worker was expected to perform R_{11} in the presence of the new stimulus.

This same phenomenon occurs in tasks where a response is controlled by a stimulus that is continually varying in some way. Sorting of coupons for instance, frequently requires that a response [(R)=place coupon in box number 9] be performed to any 5¢ coupon regardless of size, shape, color, decoration, or degree of wear. This is of particular importance because seldom will all the different kinds of stimuli for a step be available during training.

Similar stimulus variation occurs in most work situations. This means that the responses in an operant chain quite often are not really under stimulus control of a specific event, but rather of a *class* of events. Members or instances of such a class are similar to each other in some critical respects and different in other respects. Further, members of the class are different from non-members, in that non-members do not have all of those critical characteristics. To use the terminology introduced earlier, each member of the class displays the positive level of the relevant stimulus dimension, while each non-member does not display this characteristic. Both members and non-members may vary along many irrelevant dimensions. For example, the different bearings pictured in Figure 2.5 have a 1.12-cm hole in the center and have one or more small hex nut slots on one side. These features represent the positive level of the relevant shape dimension, and in their presence the response, put bearing on axle, is appropriate, regardless of the bearing's color, thickness, or type of material. However, a different response (turn the part over, or reject the part) would be appropriate if these critical shape features were absent.

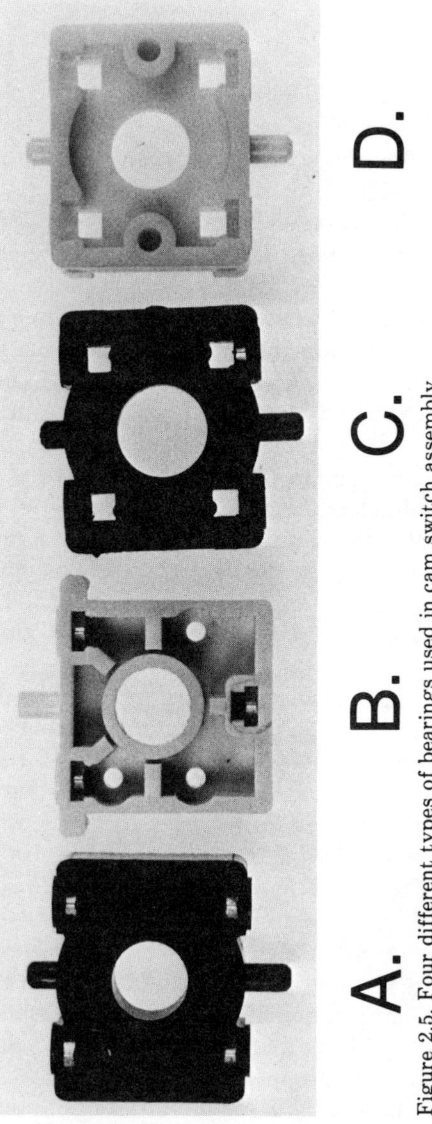

Figure 2.5. Four different types of bearings used in cam switch assembly.

Response Variation

Response variation is equally common in performance of vocationally relevant chains. For example, in a chain that involves connecting two parts with a screw, the exact placing, or tightening response, could well be changed from one assembly to the next. Response variation usually occurs because of minor differences in the parts themselves, and because the rotation and position of the parts require different movements in order to achieve the same effect time after time. This variation becomes vocationally significant when quite different responses are required to produce the same effect (the next S^D in the chain). In these cases it is useful to define as a *response class* those responses that produce a common functional effect (Becker, Engelmann, and Thomas, 1975). Horner and Bellamy (1978b) illustrated one such response class required in cam switch assembly. Figure 2.6 shows two types of retaining rings and ring tools used to affix cam bearings to cam axles. Assembly of the two switches requires the use of different tools and involves quite different movements. In each case, however, the functional effect of the ring snapping onto the axle is achieved. Shifting from one bearing to another involves shifting to a new retaining ring, thereby presenting response variation within the task.

Importance of Stimulus and Response Variation

Variations in stimulus and response components of operant chains have several implications for the vocational habilitation procedures described in later chapters. The first relates to task analysis and training procedures. In analyzing the demands of a work task it is usually important to evaluate more than one sample of a task in order to identify possible sources of variation both within and between tasks. When a significant variation is noted among stimuli that should control similar responses or among responses that should produce similar effects, training efficiency can often be enhanced by defining and teaching stimulus and response classes. Procedures for teaching responding to stimulus classes and for developing response classes are discussed in detail by Becker, Engelmann, and Thomas (1975) and Horner and Bellamy (1978b).

The second implication of stimulus and response variation reflects production supervision concerns when unplanned task variations are imposed by modification of component parts, quality criteria, or tools. In such instances it will be important for supervisors to evaluate the potential impact of these changes and the retraining needs that could result from them. The effect of stimulus changes will be greater when

Placement with plier tool

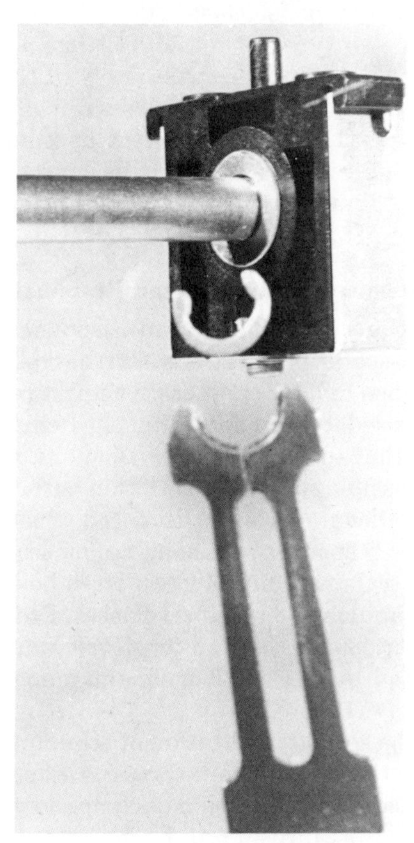

Placement with push tool

Figure 2.6. Two ways in which retaining rings are used to affix bearings to cam axles.

parts share few relevant dimensions with previously used parts and when new parts are very unlike the familiar one. Variation in the response requirements of a task are typically associated with a parallel variation in stimuli. As such, response variation most often requires retraining to ensure that the new steps of the operant chain are under appropriate stimulus control. The amount of retraining required will frequently depend on 1) the similarity of the two responses, 2) the degree to which the new response produces the same outcome as the original responses, and 3) the extent to which training focused on teaching a generalized skill.

Response and stimulus variation occurs in most vocationally relevant chains that are performed over extended time periods. Identifying these variations can facilitate task analysis and training, if classes of stimuli or responses can be taught as a group rather than individually (Becker, Engelmann, and Thomas, 1975). Sensitivity to these variations in production can help the supervisor predict work errors and retraining needs.

SUMMARY

The behavioral model from which we approach vocational habilitation of severely retarded individuals has several implications for the way habilitation issues are conceptualized and procedures are defined. The first is an emphasis on response analysis. Objectives are defined in terms of measurable behaviors that are performed in defined situations, not in terms of individual traits or personality characteristics. A second impact of the behavioral model is that it provides an experimental basis for intervention procedures. Widely replicated research is available to support a few basic principles of behavior from which habilitation procedures can be derived. Finally, the measurement of behavioral outcomes that has characterized behavioral research provides the basis for a technology of habilitation. As such, scientific methods can be used in applied habilitation efforts, so that advances in technique need to await progress in basic research.

We have made a concerted effort to demonstrate that most vocational tasks can be viewed as operant chains. From this chaining perspective a wealth of experimental and applied literature becomes applicable to the problems of task planning, training, and production supervision with severely retarded adults. The utility of operant chaining for vocational habilitation specialists, however, rests in the effect such a perspective has for improving the ability of trainers and supervisors to increase the vocational competency of severely retarded people.

The present chapter suggests that this goal can be reached by focusing on the specific stimulus-response relationships that define a chain of behavior. The technology of vocational habilitation will use as its dependent measures: 1) the probability that accurate responses will follow the S^Ds within a chain, 2) the performance of irrelevant responses within the chain, 3) the training time required for chain acquisition, 4) the durability of chain performance to stimulus and response variation, and, ultimately, 5) the speed and accuracy with which the entire chain is performed. The techniques that form vocational habilitation technology must demonstrate functional impact on these dependent variables.

Acquisition of an operant chain involves two objectives. The particular responses required by the task must be learned, and these responses must be brought under control of task-relevant stimuli. A worker can only be said to have learned a task when s/he performs each of the responses required by the task, and those responses are under appropriate stimulus control. The development of chains can occur through backward chaining or forward chaining. The comparative efficacy of these two training approaches is much debated, but as yet unequivocal data are not available.

Once an operant chain has been learned, many variables affect maintenance of performance accuracy and rate. Uppermost among these is maintenance of stimulus control. Data from experimental studies with infra-human subjects indicate variables affecting stimulus control include the type, kind, amount, and schedule of reinforcement. Given the difficulties involved in transferring infra-human results to program implications for humans, a current need exists for experimental analysis of operant chain performance with humans.

The performance of vocational chains in natural settings will frequently involve variation in the stimuli and/or responses of a chain. Maintenance of performance across stimuli and response variation will be affected by 1) shared stimulus dimensions, 2) dissimilar stimuli dimensions, 3) similarity of response topographies, and 4) similarity in response outcomes.

PART II

TASK PLANNING

chapter 3
TASK DESIGN

After a workshop has secured a production or assembly agreement with a customer, it is often the responsibility of the direct-service staff to determine exactly what production method will be used. Most jobs can be performed in a variety of different ways, and the way the contracting industry organizes production may or may not be entirely appropriate. The purpose of task design is to identify the *one* production method that is best suited to the shop's particular human and material resources, objectives, and economic condition. Choosing a production method involves determining how work situations will be defined and clarifying for each station the assembly sequence, or the specific operant chain, that the workers will perform.

Professional literature on production management identifies several possible production goals on which task design decisions can be based. Jobs can be organized, for example, to increase individual production efficiency, to increase effective utilization of available resources, to minimize training needs, or to increase worker satisfaction (Donnelly, Gibson, and Ivancovich, 1975; Gruneberg, 1976; Schneider, 1976). While all of these approaches provide useful considerations, they relate to two general task design strategies that are central in production management. The first strategy is to minimize *production* time and cost by maximizing assembly efficiency. The second strategy involves minimizing *training* time and costs by reducing the difficulty of the assembly sequence.

Careful attention to these two strategies is particularly important in sheltered workshops, which typically must deal with longer and more expensive training than industries employing non-handicapped workers. As is illustrated in Figure 3.1, the two strategies may or may not be compatible in any given situation. Training costs will be related closely to task difficulty, and production costs will be tied to efficient task design. If it is possible both to reduce task difficulty and to increase production efficiency by using a particular production method (Part I in Figure 3.1), that method generally would be preferable to all other alternatives. For example, arranging a circuit board stuffing

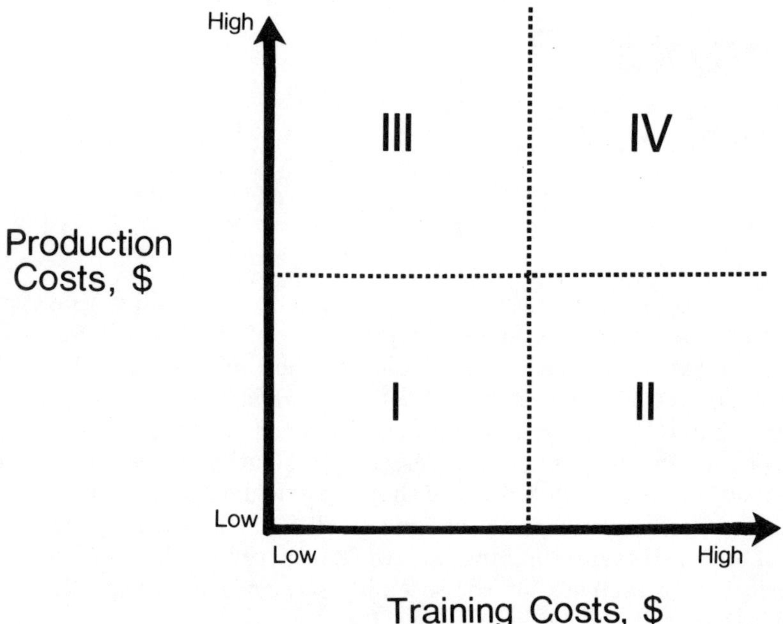

Figure 3.1. The relationships between two task design strategies that attempt to minimize either production costs or training costs.

task so that components are introduced in the order of use often reduces both the time required for training and for later unit production. Production methods that are less efficient can almost always be rejected in favor of one that implements both design strategies simultaneously. It is also possible to design production methods that are inefficient for both training and production (Part IV in the figure). For example, teaching a single worker to assemble an entire television would probably require expensive training and also result in production costs that were higher than alternative methods. A task design that falls into Part IV thus can be easily rejected in favor of other options that are more efficient in terms of cost per unit produced.

However, most tasks in sheltered workshops fall into one of the other two parts of the figure (II and III), and thus require a choice between these two general design strategies. Specifically, a shop must usually choose whether to accept high training costs that facilitate efficient production or to allow high production costs in order to lessen the time needed to train the task. In these situations, pragmatic task design decisions can be made by evaluating various strategies in light of benefits associated with each and limitations imposed by the task or setting. The remainder of this chapter focuses on selection of task design strategies when a compromise must be made between minimizing training costs and minimizing production costs.

TASK DESIGN TACTICS

Either of the two task design strategies can be implemented using a variety of possible tactics. As with selection among strategies, choice of a specific design tactic will require the direct-service staff person to evaluate the costs and benefits of each possible production method in light of the constraints imposed by the job, setting, and program goals. Figure 3.2 provides an overview of task design tactics that implement each of the two strategies.

Tactics for Minimizing Production Costs

Two primary design tactics can be used effectively to minimize production costs in workshops that employ severely retarded adults. The first involves teaching the most efficient assembly sequence possible, regardless of the complexity of skills that the worker must master. This *teaching* tactic should result in production behavior that requires minimal supervisor assistance and eliminates all unnecessary movement on behalf of the worker. As such, this tactic is similar to most industrial engineering suggestions that promote production efficiency, e.g., simultaneous use of both hands should be required whenever possible, and materials handling time should be minimized (Antes, Honeycutt, and Koch, 1973). This tactic is based on the reasoning that although added training expense may be required to teach the task, the investment is justified because of either the resulting increase in production efficiency or the long-range value of the skills learned.

Production costs can also be minimized by a second tactic, namely *automation.* Tools, equipment, or fixtures can substantially reduce production labor costs by shortening the chain of behaviors that the worker must emit to produce each unit of work. Such automation may range from a simple homemade device to expensive equipment. The logic of this automation tactic is that the savings that accrue through production efficiency can more than offset the initial investment.

Tactics to Minimize Training Costs

Three tactics can be used to minimize task difficulty and thus reduce training costs. The first is the use of *assembly lines,* or the completion of a job through numerous job stations, each of which requires only a few assembly steps. The scope of each worker's assignment is thus reduced. The rationale behind this tactic is that teaching several

Strategy	Minimize Production Costs		Minimize Training Costs		
Tactics	Teach worker all skills for the most efficient production method	Automation	Assembly Lines	Fixtures	Partial Supervisor performance
Advantages	Increases production efficiency	Increases production efficiency May reduce training time	Reduces training time	Reduces training time	Reduces training time
Disadvantages	Increases training time and cost	Increased cost to shop for machinery	Often increases production costs due to difficulty in line balancing and developing piece-rate pay scale	Often increases production time and costs	Increases reliance on supervisors during production Increases cost to shop per unit completed

Figure 3.2. Overview of task design strategies and tactics, with the major advantages and disadvantages associated with each.

workers to perform short chains seems easier than teaching longer chains to a few workers. On the surface, it appears this might be especially true with severely retarded adults.

However, several drawbacks of the assembly line approach also deserve attention: 1) Assembly lines usually require more materials handling than alternate production methods that utilize fewer workers. Moving parts from station to station may involve either additional time on the part of workers, investment in parts-moving equipment, or movement of parts by a supervisor, each of which can increase production costs. 2) Line balancing, the coordination of work stations so that the product moves through the production line without parts build-up or waiting at any station, is always troublesome. It presents especially difficult problems for severely retarded workers, whose rate can be quite variable over time (Bellamy, Inman, and Yeates, 1978). It takes considerable staff skill and organization to make sure that each worker does the proper amount of work in the proper amount of time. This is necessary to keep the line moving smoothly and to prevent workers from waiting at their stations for work stalled up the line. For effective line balancing it is necessary to plan not only for current production rates but also for future production rates. If one worker becomes much more efficient after a couple of months, the entire line must be shifted to take advantage of the worker's increased rate, or that worker will be under-utilized. Such balancing is a practical impossibility if each worker's production rate is highly variable over time. When assembly lines become unbalanced, some workers are necessarily required to wait on others. Our experience indicates that deviant behavior is more likely to occur during such periods of waiting or inactivity. 3) Assembly lines are less flexible to changes in production methods or to changes in the task being performed. This is a particularly important consideration in production procedures subject to rapid technological improvements, such as many electronics assemblies. Assembly line production is also less flexible to changes in the individual workers or their particular production methods. Even minor changes require either a rebalancing of the line or a loss in the line's overall efficiency. 4) Since assembly lines require several workers to perform small portions of a job, the task of computing piece rates for each portion and paying each worker according to his or her productivity is complicated considerably. This increases the time required of professional workshop staff and therefore adds to total production costs. 5) Individual workers must learn to perform quality checks on partially assembled products received from previous job stations, in order to respond differentially to correct and incorrect components. Therefore, each worker must learn not only his or her part of the overall chain, but at least a part of the chain (the final criterion discrimination) performed by the previous worker. The net result is an increase in the total number of responses that must be taught when assembly lines are used. 6) Finally, assembly lines often have been criticized, albeit usually without data, for their dehumanizing effects. It is possible that performance of longer response chains (i.e., enlargement of each individual's job) may increase the intrinsic reinforcement associated with the task completion.

The second tactic for minimizing training costs is the use of *fixtures* or equipment. Difficult discriminations or manipulations often can be eliminated by providing the worker with prosthetic aids. While it may be possible to identify some fixtures that facilitate both training and production, it is not uncommon for aids that reduce task difficulty to have a deleterious effect on later production efficiency. For example, when precise measurement skills are required by a task, it frequently is possible to design equipment or fixtures to eliminate difficult counting or comparison steps. The use of such equipment in production, however, often increases the number of production steps and the unit production time. Specific fixtures may be necessary to overcome or compensate for a physical disability or to reduce training difficulty; however, because they often increase production time, fixtures that reduce task difficulty at the expense of later production efficiency are recommended only in very special circumstances.

The third strategy for minimizing training costs is to plan assembly so that difficult steps are always performed by supervisors. While this *partial supervisor performance* may well decrease training time, it also results in continuing reliance on supervisors in production. Since supervisory time is usually more costly than worker time, the net income from the contract may well be reduced when this tactic is employed. Nevertheless, it may be appropriate in some production situations. For example, a 20-minute assembly task might involve one assembly step or quality check that requires considerably more training than all the other steps. To allow a worker to begin producing the assembly quickly, a supervisor may perform the difficult step until needed training time is available.

CONSIDERATIONS FOR SELECTING AMONG DESIGN TACTICS

To determine the most appropriate tactic for designing a task, the supervisor should consider five characteristics of the job, work setting, and workers. These five considerations are:

1. *Expected gross revenue* The expected revenue from a contract refers to the product of the price per unit, and the total anticipated volume. If expected revenue is high, the comparatively greater costs associated with training and automation tactics are usually more feasible. That is, the initial expense may be justified by the income generated later through increased production efficiency. Tactics that reduce training costs are more likely to be appropriate when expected revenue is low or when contract duration is short, so that costs of extensive training or automation cannot be recouped. Even when expected revenue is low, however, other considerations, such as skill value and lead time, may argue for tactics that improve production efficiency.
2. *Value of new skills required by the task* The anticipated future value of skills learned by a worker provide an important consideration for evaluating the appropriateness of designs that require extensive training. Worker skills may be valuable because of the expectation that other work will be available in the future that will require similar abilities. A skill may also be valued by a worker or program for therapeutic reasons, as when adaptation to important life situations is enhanced. For example, counting skills required by one task might be taught because of other possible vocational and non-vocational applications. An obscure minimal difference discrimination with no probable utility beyond the task would be a less likely focus for training, unless it contributed significantly to net income on the specific task under consideration. Therefore, the individual worker's habilitation plan should be a consideration in task design.
3. *Task difficulty* Task difficulty refers here to definable characteristics of tasks that result in increased training time or cost. Of course, task characteristics are not the only factors that affect training time; existing worker and trainer skills are also important. From a task design perspective, therefore, the skill requirements of the task should be assessed in light of currently available personnel resources.

   Task characteristics that affect difficulty can be best understood if it is recalled that, in training, the worker learns to perform an operant chain. A chain is composed of a series of responses, each of which is under control of a task-related stimulus produced by the previous response. Difficulty in learning a chain can result from characteristics of the responses themselves, the nature of discriminations that must be made, or characteristics of the entire chain.

Responses in a chain usually are difficult for one of two reasons. The first is the necessity to perform several response components simultaneously (as when both hands are used in coordinated movement), or when several response characteristics, such as holding, pushing, and turning, must be coordinated. This difficulty is particularly acute when such simultaneous movements do not begin and end at the same time (Engelmann, 1977). For example, many parents experience some difficulty teaching young children to tie shoe laces. The difficulty usually is encountered on those steps that require the child to continue holding one lace while releasing or manipulating the other. The second important response characteristic that increases task difficulty is the precision with which movements must be performed: tiny parts, lack of room for movement, and strict quality control standards can all increase the demand for movement precision and thus increase training time for many workers.

Several characteristics of discriminations also can increase difficulty of a task. For example, the worker may be required to discriminate between stimuli that differ only slightly. Teaching differential responding to such minimal differences typically requires more time than other discriminations. It is especially difficult when the worker must discriminate positive from negative stimulus instances when the stimulus dimension is continuous. For example, without a torque wrench, most individuals would have difficulty learning to tighten bolts to a specified level. The relevant stimulus dimension, amount of force in turning, is composed of a series of continuous values, or levels, rather than discrete differences that can be distinguished easily. Training such a discrimination often requires more time because the individual must learn both to respond differentially to "tight" and "not tight" and to make the difficult discrimination of the stimulus boundary between the two concepts. Similar problems are presented by clean versus not clean and smooth versus not smooth distinctions. Other important characteristics of the discrimination process that can increase task difficulty for a given worker are the sensory modality used to make the discrimination and the extent to which the worker must apply "if-then" rules in order to respond appropriately. These are discussed in Chapter 7.

Task difficulty can also be increased by aspects of the total chain. Principal among these are the overall cycle time, that is, the time required to complete one chain, and the repetitiveness within the chain, i.e., the number of different discriminations and manipulations required.

In selecting a design tactic, task difficulty should be considered in relation to current employee skills, inasmuch as current skills determine whether or not the necessary training is possible in the available time. Furthermore, the importance of task difficulty in choosing a design tactic will be affected by anticipated revenue and value of required skills, either of which could support use of the training tactic even with very difficult tasks.

4. *Lead time* One of the most important determinants of available training time is the time period between when parts are available for training and when delivery of completed products is expected. Longer lead times facilitate the use of strategies that require more training. If lead time is short, tactics that reduce training time and costs should be considered.
5. *Anticipated contract duration* The expected duration of the contract often affects task design decisions, inasmuch as the available time for producing a given number of units affects the number of workers who must be assigned to the task. Clearly, if a short duration and a high volume require assignment of several workers, usually a tactic is chosen that avoids lengthy training. On the other hand, if the expected duration is long, thereby increasing total revenue generated by the contract, lengthy training or automation is feasible.

DESIGN SELECTION

One of the most frequent mistakes made while selecting among task design possibilities is focusing on only one or two of the above considerations, rather than attending to possible interactions among all of them. For example, study the assembly illustrated in Figure 3.3. This task requires placing a different quantity of each of 14 wire terminals into the correct compartment in a plastic tray. Assume that available workers are severely retarded and do not have reliable counting skills. Several task design options are available, including:

1. *Minimize production costs (and increase training time) by teaching the most efficient production method.* Workers could be taught the required counting skills, so that a numeral printed on each parts bin provided the only necessary cue.
2. *Minimize production costs (and increase equipment costs) by automation.* Counting scales or mechanical loading devices that significantly decrease labor costs could be located and purchased.
3. *Minimize training costs (and complicate production management) by employing assembly lines.* The task could be designed so that

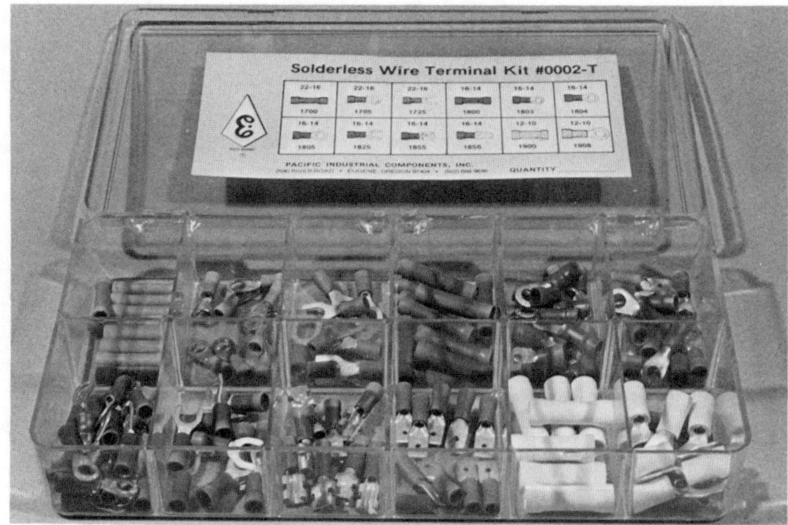

Figure 3.3. A task requiring placing different quantities of 14 wire terminals into correct compartments.

each worker filled only one bin. Since any given worker would only have to discriminate a single quantity, a less sophisticated counting skill would be required of each.

4. *Minimize training costs (and increase production time) by using fixtures.* This is the familiar approach of putting one wire terminal on each spot on a prepared card, then placing the contents of a filled card in the tray. Similar strategies include use of an abacus, a hand counter, or other prosthetic counting device that simplifies the required quantity discriminations.
5. *Minimize training costs (and increase supervisor time and cost) by partial performance.* For example, the supervisor could prepare quantities of each terminal, which the workers could then package.

If expected revenue from the task is high, if a high value is placed on counting skills, and if lead time and contract duration are long, the first strategy would be appropriate in many programs. A shorter duration or lead time would lead to serious consideration of the second option. If revenue is expected to be low, or if low value is placed on counting skills by the worker or program, one of the remaining three strategies would be more appropriate.

As the example illustrates, selection of a task design tactic involves evaluation of possible interactions among many design considerations. Each of the considerations we have emphasized — total expected revenue, value of new skills, task difficulty, lead time, and anticipated contract duration — affects the potential importance of others. In general, if a choice must be made between reducing production or training costs, we recommend the use of tactics that reduce production costs rather than those that reduce training costs. Exceptions are those tasks in which combinations of low expected revenue, task difficulty, and low skill value argue for reducing training costs through fixtures, partial supervisor performance, or assembly lines. For most other tasks, selection of training or automation tactics is usually profitable for the workshop and beneficial to the worker. Of course, these decisions will vary from one shop to another, depending on staff and worker skills, program goals, and community expectations.

DEFINING THE OPERANT CHAIN

Implementation of a design tactic results in defining a general production system, including identification of tools, materials, and work station arrangement. The next step is to define the behavior chain that will be required of production workers. Defining the chain provides additional opportunities to reduce task difficulty and to increase production efficiency. There are six general guidelines for defining and sequencing the production behaviors into an operant chain:

1. *Minimize the number of different discriminations to be taught by defining stimulus classes to which similar responses are required.* It is often possible to define a sequence of assembly behaviors so that the number of different discriminations required of a worker is relatively small. When this is possible, it results in a reduction in training time. Procedurally, this involves attempting to group required discriminations into categories so that similar discriminations are made in a number of task situations. Several examples of this approach are available. Among the most versatile is the use of a series of bins to sequence the *order* in which parts are picked up (see Figure 3.4). Without a bin set-up the worker must attend to unique task-cues at each step to determine which part is needed next. With bins the worker simply follows the sequence of parts in the bins. Gold's (1972) use of a sequential array of parts changed a series of sequence discriminations (What part comes next?) into a single class (Get one part from the next bin in a left-to-right sequence). Permanent match-to-sample cues can accomplish a similar result by changing a series of position or placement discriminations into a single requirement: that the position of the sample be matched (Bellamy, Oliver, and Oliver, 1977; Merwin, 1974).

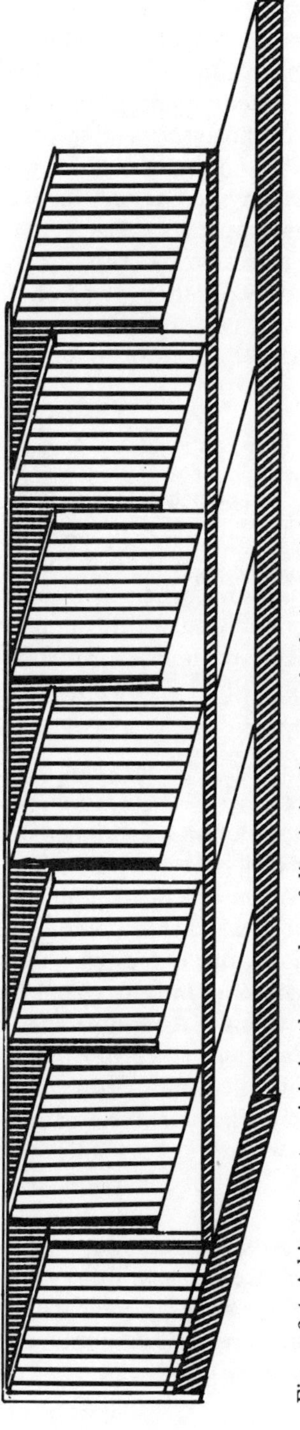

Figure 3.4. A bin set-up to minimize the number of discriminations taught during training.

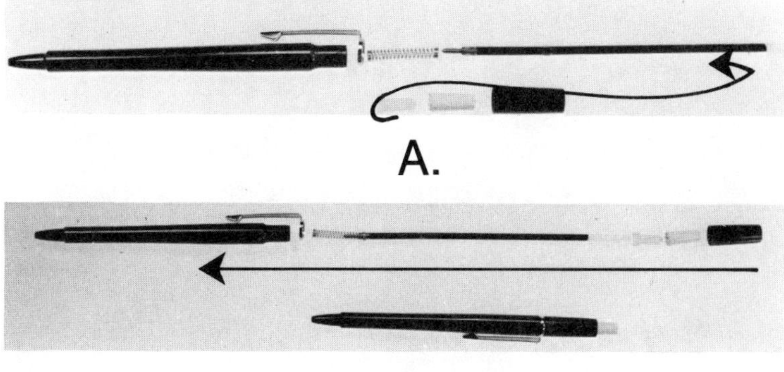

Figure 3.5. Two methods of assembling a ballpoint pen.

2. *Minimize the number of different manipulations that is required by defining appropriate response classes.* Teaching efficiency can be improved by reducing the number of different manipulations or response topographies to be taught. This involves identifying all possible common response characteristics that are occasioned by similar cues. For example, much of the assembly of a bicycle brake (Gold, 1972) involves repetition of the response class, "pick up and place on the axle." Other response classes frequently encountered in vocational tasks include placement of retaining rings and other fasteners (Horner and Bellamy, 1978b) and a variety of tool use skills (Prill, 1977). A task frequently performed in workshops is assembly of ballpoint pens. The pen shown in Figure 3.5 can be assembled in a variety of ways. One task design strategy involves assembling all the pieces that fit in the base of the pen, then assembling the pieces that fit in the top, and finally attaching the top and base. This is the approach depicted in Figure 3.5A. An alternative strategy, which minimizes the number of different manipulations required, involves placing the base with the point down and then picking up each piece, orienting it, and placing it in or on the base. This strategy (shown in Figure 3.5B) uses the same "pick up and put on" response with each piece. It would be expected that the strategy would be both easier (faster) to teach and that it would promote faster production than the alternative shown in Figure 3.5A.
3. *If stimulus and response classes are identified, and if exceptions to the general rule exist, sequence the task so that the general case can be taught first and exceptions later.* Learning the general rule before exceptions are presented usually increases overall efficiency of learning a variety of skills (Becker, Engelmann, and Thomas,

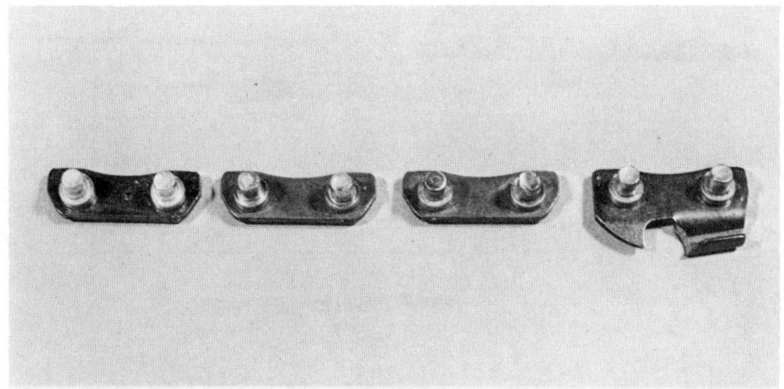

Figure 3.6. A saw chain assembly with a repeating sequence of steps.

1975). Thus, when such exceptions exist, an attempt should be made to sequence assembly responses so that these exceptions occur after instances of the general response. The assembly shown in Figure 3.6 illustrates how this guideline was applied by O'Neill and Bellamy (1978). The components pictured in the figure are part of a repeating sequence of steps involved in assembly of a chain-saw chain. Assembly requires the worker to position these and other parts in the correct rotation on both horizontal and vertical dimensions. The vertical rotation was taught by the general concept that the rivet goes up (see guideline 1 above); the horizontal rotation involved the general rule of placing the slightly concave side away from the worker. On every fourth component additional cues for rotations were provided by the cutting blade, which faced the worker in a correct assembly. The addition of the cutting blade created an exception to the general case. Since the concave side defined the general case, the three spacers having only this cue were taught first in the assembly sequence; the cutter placement with its additional cues was taught later.

4. *When possible, maximize the distinctiveness of cues that are provided by the task for each assembly step.* If the task itself provides clear discriminative stimuli for each assembly step, acquisition is more efficient and errors in production can be reduced. The sequence in which the task is completed often can affect the distinctiveness of these cues. For example, the order in which electronic components are placed on circuit boards may affect the difficulty of placement discriminations. At each step, components already on the board, together with the board itself (overall shapes, presence of holes, and circuit tracks), provide natural cues about

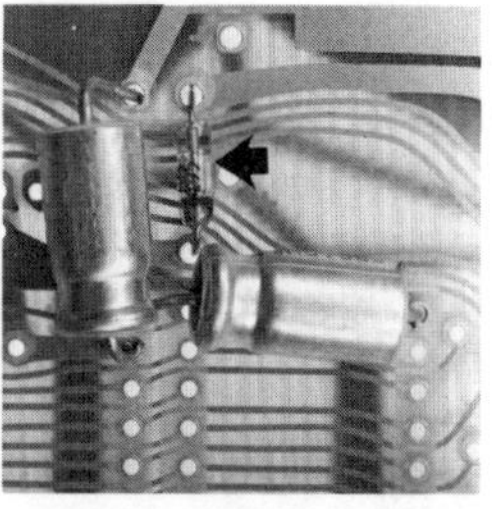

Figure 3.7. A circuit board requiring placement of a small resistor between two others (actual size).

where to place the next component. When cues provided by the board itself make correct placement of a component difficult to learn, these natural cues often can be enhanced by the sequence in which components are inserted.

5. *Avoid precise manipulations when possible by changing the response sequence.* Efficiency of both training and production can be affected by the kind of movements required by different response sequences. Design of sub-assemblies that are completed before the final product is assembled often increases working room and facilitates use of both hands in hard-to-reach areas. The circuit board shown in Figure 3.7 requires that a small resistor be placed between two large resistors. Figure 3.7A shows the room available for placement of the small resistor if it is placed before the large resistor. Figure 3.7B provides an alternative design in which placement of the small resistor is much more difficult because of the limited space remaining after the larger resistors were positioned. By simply attending to the order of placement, the task design depicted in Figure 3.7A likely would facilitate more rapid training and production.
6. *When designing a task for a particular worker, maximize the use of skills that the worker already can perform.* If a part of a task can be done equally efficiently by two different approaches (i.e., tighten a bolt with a crescent wrench or a socket wrench) and the worker is trained and skilled on one approach but not on the other, design the task so that his or her current skills are used.

SUMMARY

Task design is a process of determining how a job will be performed in training and in subsequent production. The importance of task design in vocational programs for severely retarded individuals lies in the fact that different design strategies may be more efficient for different tasks, different workers, and different production conditions.

There are two general strategies for designing tasks in workshops: minimizing training costs and minimizing production costs. Design tactics that minimize production costs involve providing the necessary training, so that workers can perform independently and efficiently, and investing in automated production. Tactics that are usually used to minimize training costs are use of fixtures, assembly lines, and partial supervisor performance of the task.

Selecting among these various design approaches requires careful attention to characteristics of the job, the workers, and the program's goals and economic condition. Five particularly important considerations in selecting task design tactics are the total expected revenue, the value of skills required by the task, the difficulty of the task in relation to current worker skills, the lead time, and the anticipated duration of the contract.

After a tactic is chosen and used to define a production method, the operant chain required to complete the task should be delineated. This involves defining and sequencing the production behaviors required for accurate performance. Six guidelines were presented to aid in defining an efficient assembly chain: 1) minimize the number of different discriminations, 2) minimize the number of different manipulations, 3) teach the general case first, 4) maximize the distinctiveness of task cues, 5) avoid precise manipulations, and 6) maximize use of the workers' current skills.

Task design provides a foundation on which both habilitation and business efforts can be based. The skills that a worker learns in vocational training are related directly to the way in which available work is designed. Task design affects the revenue generated by the shop, the wages earned by workers, and the fixed costs of program operation. Therefore, the planning time required for careful task design is a good investment for both habilitation and business outcomes.

chapter 4
TASK ANALYSIS

The label "task analysis" has been used extensively by professionals in the fields of business, psychology, and rehabilitation. Unfortunately this wide use has also been accompanied by a wide variety of definitions. From a business perspective, task analysis refers to a process through which production tasks are divided into components in order to facilitate simplification of jobs and specialization of staff (Schneider, 1976). In psychology and education, the focus of task analysis has been on identifying and sequencing a set of tasks to be learned in some instructional program (Mager, 1962; Davies, 1973). Both uses appear in the rehabilitation literature, and still another use has emerged recently with Gold's (1975) use of task analysis to describe actual procedural steps in teaching a task.

For the purposes of this text, task analysis is defined as the process of: 1) breaking a task down into its component responses, 2) listing these responses and the stimuli that should ultimately come to control them, and 3) identifying a criterion for each response. The overall purpose of task analysis is to facilitate training. This is done in two ways: first, by focusing trainer attention on the specific demands of a task, and second, by providing a simple, inexpensive method of collecting acquisition data during training.

By focusing attention on task demands, task analysis prepares a trainer in three important ways: 1) The trainer performs the task several times and thus becomes familiar with the task demands before training begins. 2) The trainer defines a specific response chain, which remains constant from training trial to training trial. Consequently, the worker is not presented with slightly varying response sequences from day to day. This chain constancy reduces the unplanned complexity of the task and facilitates a rapid rate of acquisition during training. 3) Task analysis requires the trainer to define operationally each response the worker will be expected to perform. By specifying the exact instructional objective of each step in the task analysis, ambiguity about whether or not a response is performed correctly during training is minimized. Thus, the trainer will be better able to provide consistent feedback to a worker on the accuracy of his or her performance.

A second characteristic of task analysis is that it affords a trainer access to a simple method of collecting data on worker behavior. In many cases these data provide information needed for making accountable training decisions. To teach a complex task to a worker who has great difficulty learning requires that the trainer be constantly responding to the performance of the worker. Within a training session the trainer will be monitoring his or her own behavior and the behavior of the worker. Decisions such as when to provide assistance, how much assistance to provide, when to reinforce, how much to reinforce, what kind of reinforcement to use, etc., must be made rapidly and in many cases simultaneously.

To respond most effectively to these training demands, a trainer needs a set of decision rules related to the task that will facilitate quick, fluid, consistent behavior on behalf of the trainer. While such preparation is valuable in any instructional setting, it is especially important for trainers of severely and profoundly retarded individuals because many of the procedural luxuries (e.g., techniques that require sophisticated language imitation or reading skills of the learner) that are available to trainers of higher functioning people are not appropriate in the training of severely and profoundly retarded persons. When teaching a vocational task to a severely retarded adult, for instance, it is not acceptable to have the worker stop and wait a third of the way through the task while the trainer tries to recall exactly how the next step is to be performed, or whether the worker's last response was "just barely acceptable" or "not quite acceptable." Task analysis is an effective way for a skilled trainer to prepare himself or herself to make these decisions quickly in a consistent, data-based manner.

Task analysis is not, however, a method of training, nor is it the skill that discriminates good trainers from poor trainers. Task analysis is a process that people who are already competent trainers use in preparing themselves most effectively to train a specific worker in a specific task. Task analysis is done after a task has been designed. Decisions related to use of fixtures and order of operations already should have been made. The objective of task analysis is to define the specific sequence of behavior that a worker will need to perform when he or she is producing the task. By identifying this sequence the trainer should become aware of the particular demands of the task, the potential errors, and the task-relevant stimuli to which a worker will need to attend if s/he is to perform the task independently.

CONSTRUCTING A TASK ANALYSIS

Constructing a task analysis involves deciding what steps will be used to complete the task and recording these sequentially so that data on learner progress can be collected during training. Six guidelines should be used in the construction process:

1. *The person who will be doing the training should construct the task analysis.* The initial benefit of performing a task analysis is its effect on trainer behavior. By having a clear idea of what skills are to be taught, the sequence in which they will be taught, and the relevant stimuli to which a trainer will need to attend, the trainer will be in a much better position to assist the trainee effectively and systematically as s/he learns the task. Because the initial effect of performing a task analysis is directed at trainer behavior, it follows logically that the trainer is the person who should construct the task analysis.
2. *The trainer should perform the task several times exactly the way the worker will be expected to perform it.* Attention should be paid to the topographical demands of each step, with the easiest, most efficient topographies being identified. By performing the task several times, the trainer gains familiarity with the specific response demands at each step in the chain. Normal workers often make small changes in the way they perform a task after only a few repetitions. These changes may pertain to something as simple as holding a part with one's palm up rather than down. In general, such changes facilitate performance but are not readily apparent to someone who has not actually performed the task over a period of time. Severely and profoundly retarded workers also make small changes in the way they perform work. Sometimes these variations facilitate performance, frequently they do not. It is important, therefore, that very efficient assembly methods be identified in the task analysis. When preparing a task analysis, perform the task many times. Find the most convenient way to meet the specifications identified in the initial task design. Do not depend on the trainee to find the best ways of completing a task.
3. *Break the task down into its functional response units. List these in the order they will be performed.* When performing the task, the trainer should list the response units (operants) that must be performed to complete the chain. These response units comprise the steps of the task analysis. However, defining the specific steps in the chain is a difficult and arbitrary process because it is unclear exactly how large or how small each step should be. As is stated in Chapter 2, any behavior chain can be conceptualized as a single response or as a practically infinite number of tiny responses. Neither approach, of course, would be particularly helpful in teaching most tasks to most individuals. Optimum step size in any given situation will depend on the difficulty of the task and the

current skill level of the learner. In much vocational training with severely retarded adults, however, a more uniform approach to defining step size is possible. We recommend that *functional response units* be identified. Functional response units are those sequences of behavior that result in distinct observable changes in the item being assembled. For example, in a task analysis the step of placing components in circuit boards would be listed as, "place capacitor in board in correct location," rather than smaller units of behavior like, "grasp capacitor with thumb and forefinger." Defining these functional units of behavior facilitates data collection, in that each results in a change in the task that can be readily recorded by the trainer or an observer.

Functional response units are *observable behaviors* that the worker will be expected to perform. These behavioral units should be defined and listed in a concise, clear manner. General decision rules for identifying functional response units have been provided by Davies (1973). He suggests task analysis steps be written so that each step: 1) is at the same level of generality as all other steps; 2) is written in the form of a simple, declarative (kernel) sentence; 3) avoids negatives, qualifications, and conjunctions; 4) possesses only *one* active verb; and 5) is critical and essential to the task.

Frequently the response demands of a task do not fit the model of a simple linear chain. The worker may, for example, perform a step in the task and then be faced with an "if-then" decision. In other words, the chain may branch into two or more subchains at critical steps in the overall chain. The task analysis should indicate such branching. A step may read "If the part is tight go to step 7; if the part is not tight go to step 4." Most tasks involving soldering would fit this model. For example, after the worker actually touches the solder to the iron, s/he must stop and assess if enough solder flowed to the right places. In effect the worker is faced with an "if-then" situation. If the solder joint is complete, the worker should proceed through the chain. If the solder joint is not complete, s/he should reheat and add more solder. Given that the solder will flow slightly differently on each trial, the worker must deal with the branching chain on each soldering trial. The task analysis should reflect this branching. Figure 4.1 provides a partial task analysis of a task that requires placement and soldering of resistors and capacitors in a circuit board.

The above guidelines and examples for identifying functional response units should produce a sequence of task analysis steps

6. Place iron on terminal
5. Place solder at iron tip
4. Apply 1 inch of solder
3. Remove solder and iron
2. Branch a) If solder fills terminal hole go to step 1
   b) If solder does not fill terminal hole go to step 6
1. Place terminal in box

Figure 4.1. Partial task analysis indicating the branching necessary to index the task demands of a soldering sequence.

that accurately identify the response demands of the task. The steps should be large enough (contain enough behavior) to be a meaningful representation of what a worker may need to learn and yet small enough to adequately index progress during training.

For any one worker, however, a task analysis of functional response units may not provide an adequate breakdown of the response demands. Clearly, setting variables and worker competencies can interact with task demands in ways that would make a fine-grained breakdown of certain steps more appropriate. Generally, however, breaking a step into finer components occurs after training has begun. As such, these additional problems are considered in Chapter 7 within the context of training procedures for difficult steps.

4. *For each step in the chain identify and list the stimulus that should function as the S^D for the step.* Training involves more than just teaching a worker *how* to perform certain responses. It also involves teaching him or her *when* it is appropriate to emit each behavior. A person who knows how to use needle-nose pliers to insert a spring in a small component does not necessarily possess a functional skill unless s/he also knows precisely when that skill should be performed. Teaching this involves training the worker to discriminate task-related stimuli that serve as S^Ds for task-relevant skills in the worker's repertoire. The presence of a spring on the work table and an empty space in the component may be the S^Ds for putting the spring where it belongs. A task analysis should index both the responses to be learned and the stimuli that will "control" each response when training is completed. By specifying the S^D for each response the trainer will also

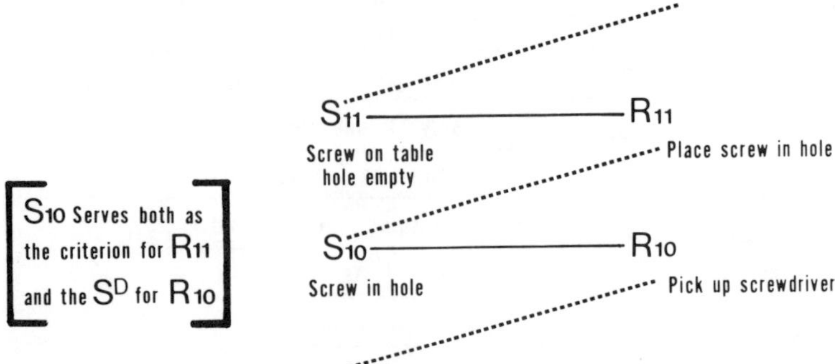

Figure 4.2. Part of a response chain indicating the dual role of task stimuli.

be specifying the criterion for the preceding response. The criterion for a response (or step) is the outcome that should result from the worker performing the response correctly. The criterion for one step, however, is usually the S^D for the next. For example, if a step involves placing a screw in the hole with the threads down, the criterion will be met only when the screw is in the hole with the threads down. As indicated in Figure 4.2, however, the screw sitting in the hole also functions as the S^D for the next step, reaching for a screwdriver.

5. *Review the steps of the task analysis to ensure that similar S^Ds do not cue different responses.* If two very similar stimuli control different responses, it is likely the worker will have difficulty determining which response to emit when either stimulus is presented. The aluminum heat sink shown in Figure 2.2 illustrates this point. As can be seen, one part is placed in the fixture with the curved side up. The next piece is also placed in the fixture, but with the curved side down. The task is complete when the two pieces are then screwed together. In teaching this task two different responses (i.e., place part one in the fixture with the curved side up, and place part two in the fixture with the curved side down) are essentially controlled by very similar stimuli (i.e., the curved side of parts that look alike). In training the task to one profoundly retarded worker at the Specialized Training Program we observed repeated errors on placement of the parts. The curved side was placed up or down in a near random pattern. After extensive observation, it seemed that because the S^Ds for the two responses were so similar, the worker was having great difficulty determining which response was appropriate. To overcome this confusing situation the task design was changed so that the worker picked up part one and matched it to a sample part glued in front of bin one with its curved side up. A similar process was done with part two, ex-

cept that the sample in front of the second bin had the curved side down. In this way the worker had very distinct cues (S^Ds) to use in determining how the part should be placed. When this task was redesigned so that the two responses were occasioned by more easily discriminable S^Ds, the worker learned the sequence very quickly. Soon after he had reached criterion on this task, his trainer noted that the match-to-sample steps were no longer being followed. The worker positioned the parts accurately without aligning each part with the sample. To avoid confusion and unnecessary time in training, always review a task analysis to ensure that different responses are cued by clearly different S^Ds.

6. *Use the sequence in the task analysis to construct a training data sheet.* Good trainers allow a great deal of their behavior to be controlled by worker performance. Assistance is delivered as a function of worker errors, and reinforcers are delivered as a function of worker success. The trainer is, in effect, constantly making decisions based on the worker's behavior. This requires that the trainer continually gather information (data) on worker performance. To the maximum extent possible, trainer behavior should be based on data obtained by monitoring observable responses of the worker. Of critical importance is the ability of the trainer to respond to day-to-day patterns of performance. As such, it is important that a trainer have a method of indexing progress across training trials or days. These data will serve many functions, not the least of which is providing the trainer with information that can be used in making training decisions, such as when to change the task design, when to conduct massed practice on difficult steps, or when to alter the method of assistance. The use of a task analysis data sheet developed by Saunders and Koplik (1975) is an efficient and effective method of collecting such data.

   A data sheet is constructed by listing the S^Ds and responses that make up the steps of the chain. As the data sheet in Figure 4.3 indicates, these steps are listed with the step the worker will perform last at the bottom of the page, the next to last step above that, and so forth. Rows of numbers to the right of each step are then added. When the data sheet is complete, it provides a concise listing of the S^Ds and responses (response units) that define each step in the chain and several columns of numbers immediately to the right of the steps, for use in data collection.

   To be practical, a data sheet should provide relevant training information, and at the same time not interfere with ongoing training. The present system meets both criteria. Generally, training should be conducted for 10 to 30 minutes (or a set number of trials)

S^D	Response				
		8	8	8	8
		7	7	7	7
screw on table hole empty	place screw in hole	6	6	6	6
screw in hole	pick up screwdriver	5	5	5	5
screwdriver in hand	place nose in screw head	4	4	4	4
screwdriver in screw	rotate clockwise	3	3	3	3
screw tight	place screwdriver on table	2	2	2	2
screwdriver on table	raise hand	1	1	1	1

Figure 4.3. A task analysis data sheet indicating the task S^Ds, responses, and numbering system used for data collection.

without collecting any data. The exact interval should be determined by the length and difficulty of the task and the skills of the worker. Longer intervals would be used when training is expected to require more time because of task or worker characteristics. Following whatever interval is chosen, a probe should be conducted in which the worker is given the opportunity to perform *each* step in the chain independently (i.e., without prior assistance from the trainer). At this time, the trainer uses the data sheet to indicate if a step were performed correctly and independently. This can be scored by making a slash over the number corresponding to the step performed. If an error occurs, the number corresponding to that step is left blank. Then, to enable the worker to continue through the task, the trainer provides whatever assistance is necessary to create the S^D for the following step. Figure 4.4 indicates

S^D	Response			
		10	10	10
		9	9	9
		8	8	8
		7	7	7
screw on table hole empty	place screw in hole	~~6~~	6	6
screw in hole	pick up screwdriver	5	5	5
screwdriver in hand	place nose in screw head	~~4~~	4	4
screwdriver in screw	rotate clockwise	~~3~~	3	3
screw tight	place screwdriver on table	2	2	2
screwdriver on table	raise hand	~~1~~	1	1

Figure 4.4. A task analysis data sheet with data from one probe trial.

a probe trial in which steps 1, 3, 4, and 6 were the only steps performed correctly and independently. It should be noted that this method of determining a correct step requires that the worker know how to perform the requisite response, and that s/he do so in the presence of the task-relevant S^D that cues that response. The trainer provides assistance only after a response has been scored as incorrect and only to give the worker access to the S^D for the next functional response unit in the chain.

After each probe trial the total number of correctly completed steps are added up and that number is circled in the same column. In the above example, the number 4 is circled since a total of four steps (1, 3, 4, and 6) were performed correctly. The next probe trial would occur after another 20 to 30 minutes (or a set number of trials) of training. This probe would be scored in the next column to the right, and would again produce information about *which* steps were being performed completely independently and the total number of correct steps. When the total number of correct steps for the second probe is circled, a line should be drawn from that number to the total correct for the first probe (i.e., 4). This would be the beginning of a graph that indexes worker progress and patterns of errors.

Figure 4.5 presents data from a task trained at the Specialized Training Program. The figure depicts five probe trials in which a worker performed four steps correctly on the first probe, six correctly on the second probe, five correctly on the third probe, and eight correctly on the fourth and fifth probes. Figure 4.6 shows the same task analysis data sheet after twenty probes. Note how the data provide information on the total number of steps being performed correctly, exactly which steps these are, and the error patterns over time on each step.

There are a number of advantages to collecting training data with this type of data sheet: 1) It allows a trainer to both collect and graph raw data on the same page. This eliminates a great deal of time usually required for collection and collation of data. 2) Data do not need to be collected on each training trial, hence the trainer can focus his or her full attention on the worker during training. 3) The ease of data collection increases the probability that trainers will be willing to use the data sheet, thereby increasing the probability that the data will be available for making training decisions and evaluating worker performance. 4) The data sheet allows for easily interpretable, visual inspection of the data, hence the information it provides is instantly obtainable and more likely to be used. 5) Since the data sheet indexes small gains in worker com-

	S^D	Response					
25			25	25	25	25	25
24			24	24	24	24	24
23			23	23	23	23	23
22			22	22	22	22	22
21			21	21	21	21	21
20			20	20	20	20	20
19			19	19	19	19	19
18			18	18	18	18	18
17			17	17	17	17	17
16			16	16	16	16	16
15			15	15	15	15	15
14			14	14	14	14	14
13	Parts in bin	Pick up bearing and place on table	13	13	13	13	13
12	Bearing on table	Place hex nut in one bearing corner	12	12	12	12	12
11	Nut in one corner	Place hex nut in second corner	11	11	11	11	11
10	Nuts in two corners	Place hex nut in third corner	10	10	10	10	10
9	Nuts in three corners	Place cam base in bearing	9	9	9	9	9
8	Cam in bearing	Place roller in bearing	8	8	8	8	8
7	Roller in bearing	Place red spring in bearing	7	7	7	7	7
6	Red spring placed	Rotate bearing and cam 180°	6	6	6	6	6
5	Bearing rotated	Place roller in bearing	5	5	5	5	5
4	Roller in bearing	Place green spring in bearing	4	4	4	4	4
3	Green spring placed	Wipe bearing with cloth	3	3	3	3	3
2	Bearing cleaned	Place camed bearing in bag	2	2	2	2	2
1	Cam in bag	Place bag in box	1	1	1	1	1

Figure 4.5. A task analysis data sheet with data from five probe trials.

petence, it may serve as a reinforcer to trainers. Several of our frustrated trainers have persevered and ultimately succeeded with workers who were exhibiting great difficulty because they could *see* that gains (small though they might be) were occurring over time. 6) Finally, the data sheet can be extremely useful when a trainer is trying to obtain consultation from other trainers or supervisors. Difficult steps can be readily identified, and descriptions of a worker's progress (or lack thereof) can be quickly translated into quantifiable terms.

The above advantages have convinced us that the task analysis data sheet is an eminently useful tool. A trainer should use

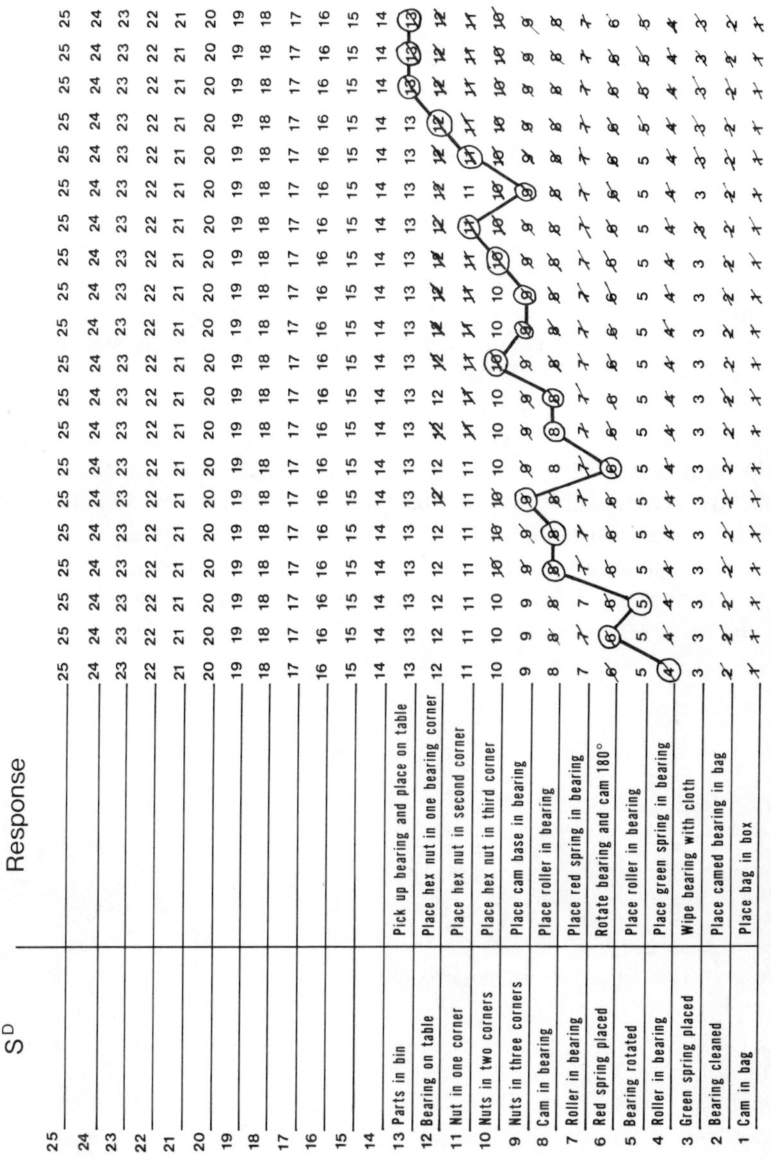

	S^D	Response																				
25			25	25	25	25	25	25	25	25	25	25	25	25	25	25	25	25	25	25	25	25
24			24	24	24	24	24	24	24	24	24	24	24	24	24	24	24	24	24	24	24	24
23			23	23	23	23	23	23	23	23	23	23	23	23	23	23	23	23	23	23	23	23
22			22	22	22	22	22	22	22	22	22	22	22	22	22	22	22	22	22	22	22	22
21			21	21	21	21	21	21	21	21	21	21	21	21	21	21	21	21	21	21	21	21
20			20	20	20	20	20	20	20	20	20	20	20	20	20	20	20	20	20	20	20	20
19			19	19	19	19	19	19	19	19	19	19	19	19	19	19	19	19	19	19	19	19
18			18	18	18	18	18	18	18	18	18	18	18	18	18	18	18	18	18	18	18	18
17			17	17	17	17	17	17	17	17	17	17	17	17	17	17	17	17	17	17	17	17
16			16	16	16	16	16	16	16	16	16	16	16	16	16	16	16	16	16	16	16	16
15			15	15	15	15	15	15	15	15	15	15	15	15	15	15	15	15	15	15	15	15
14			14	14	14	14	14	14	14	14	14	14	14	14	14	14	14	14	14	14	14	14
13	Parts in bin	Pick up bearing and place on table	13	13	13	13	13	13	13	13	13	13	13	13	13	13	13	13	13	13	13	13
12	Bearing on table	Place hex nut in one bearing corner	12	12	12	12	12	12	12	12	12	12	12	12	12	12	12	12	12	12	12	12
11	Nut in one corner	Place hex nut in second corner	11	11	11	11	11	11	11	11	11	11	11	11	11	11	11	11	11	11	11	11
10	Nuts in two corners	Place hex nut in third corner	10	10	10	10	10	10	10	10	10	10	10	10	10	10	10	10	10	10	10	10
9	Nuts in three corners	Place cam base in bearing	9	9	9	9	9	9	9	9	9	9	9	9	9	9	9	9	9	9	9	9
8	Cam in bearing	Place roller in bearing	8	8	8	8	8	8	8	8	8	8	8	8	8	8	8	8	8	8	8	8
7	Roller in bearing	Place red spring in bearing	7	7	7	7	7	7	7	7	7	7	7	7	7	7	7	7	7	7	7	7
6	Red spring placed	Rotate bearing and cam 180°	6	6	6	6	6	6	6	6	6	6	6	6	6	6	6	6	6	6	6	6
5	Bearing rotated	Place roller in bearing	5	5	5	5	5	5	5	5	5	5	5	5	5	5	5	5	5	5	5	5
4	Roller in bearing	Place green spring in bearing	4	4	4	4	4	4	4	4	4	4	4	4	4	4	4	4	4	4	4	4
3	Green spring placed	Wipe bearing with cloth	3	3	3	3	3	3	3	3	3	3	3	3	3	3	3	3	3	3	3	3
2	Bearing cleaned	Place camed bearing in bag	2	2	2	2	2	2	2	2	2	2	2	2	2	2	2	2	2	2	2	2
1	Cam in bag	Place bag in box	1	1	1	1	1	1	1	1	1	1	1	1	1	1	1	1	1	1	1	1

Figure 4.6. A task analysis data sheet indicating task acquisition across 20 training probes.

use this or an equivalent method of collecting training data. Only from these data will the trainer have the information needed to respond effectively to worker behavior.

SUMMARY

Task analysis refers in this text to the process of breaking down the task into functional response units, listing these responses together with the S^D for each, and identifying the operational criterion for each. Task analysis facilitates training by ensuring that the trainer has detailed knowledge of task demands and by providing a simple method of collecting data on learner progress during training.

There are six guidelines that facilitate construction of a useful task analysis: 1) the person who will be doing training should construct the task analysis; 2) the trainer should perform the task several times exactly the way the worker will be expected to perform it; 3) the task should be broken down into functional response units, and these should be listed in the order they should be performed; 4) the trainer should identify and list the stimuli that should function as the S^D for each functional response unit; 5) the steps of the task analysis should be reviewed to ensure that similar S^Ds do not cue different responses; and 6) the task analysis should then be used to construct a training data sheet.

PART III

VOCATIONAL TRAINING

chapter 5
INTRODUCTION TO TRAINING

Competent adults are clearly different from incompetent adults, in that the former have learned, or have been taught, a broad repertoire of behaviors that facilitate independence. The teaching process behind this skill acquisition has been characterized in various ways depending on what aspect of the teaching environment is emphasized (Skinner, 1968). For example, if learning is thought to be the result of practice, then one might characterize skill acquisition as *learning by doing,* that is, performing without regard to the setting in which a behavior is practiced or to the consequences of the new behavior. On the other hand, if learning is thought to result from experience, then skill acquisition might be characterized as *learning by exposure.* This view emphasizes things like the instructional setting and ignores the benefits of practice and, again, the effects of the consequences of the behavior to be learned. A third way skill acquisition has been characterized is the well-known *learning by trial and error* philosophy. This position emphasizes the effects of reward and punishment, i.e., the consequences of behavior, but it ignores important aspects of the instructional setting and the possible role of practice. Following Skinner's (1968) suggestion, we contend that any characterization of the teaching process is incomplete unless it incorporates all three of these positions.

For our purposes, training is defined as a process resulting from an interaction between the setting, trainer, and worker that is designed to: 1) develop new response topographies in a worker's repertoire, or 2) bring existing response topographies under control of new stimuli. Vocational training is successful only if the worker's behavior changes as a function of this instructional interaction. From this perspective the sole criterion for *adequate* training is a worker's acquisition of vocationally significant skills. Moreover, from our viewpoint the purpose of vocational training is to enable a worker to perform accurately and without assistance an operant chain specified in a task analysis.

As is stated in Chapter 2, an operant chain is a sequence of responses, each of which is controlled by stimuli produced by the preceding response. Vocational training thus is designed specifically to: 1) teach the component responses of the chain; 2) establish stimulus control within the chain, so that particular task characteristics set the occasion for particular responses; and 3) enhance the conditioned reinforcing function of task-related stimuli correlated with performance of the task.

Although successful training is defined in terms of changes in worker behavior, the training process involves changing setting, task, and trainer variables by adding stimuli that precede or follow a worker's responses. Much of training involves determining how and when to add these stimuli and which stimuli to use as antecedents and consequences of worker responses. When this is done correctly, the worker adapts to the stimulus changes by exhibiting closer approximations to the desired response. When it is done incorrectly, the worker learns to depend on trainer assistance or to exhibit behaviors during training that are incompatible with learning.

Characteristics of the task, the training setting, the training procedures, and the worker all may affect the extent to which training is successful and efficient. Our suggestions in the following chapters emphasize the interaction among these sets of variables. Given that task variables often are determined by available contracts, and given that worker variables (e.g., physical status, current skills) are assessed but not manipulated, our major emphasis is on the effects of setting and procedural variables. The central concerns in our discussion of training procedures are those variables involving *trainer* behaviors and the utility of these behaviors in accommodating specific task and worker characteristics.

TRAINING FORMAT

Training formats refer to the general arrangement and sequence of activities in a training session. Several formats are possible for vocational training, and choice among them is still largely a matter of personal preference in the absence of clear comparative research. In Chapters 6 through 9 we describe procedures for a training format that involves individual training with a forward chaining approach.

Our emphasis on individual training, i.e., on teaching interactions in which a trainer provides instruction to a single worker, is consistent with most published demonstrations of vocational skill acquisition (Gold, 1972; Hunter and Bellamy, 1977). Nevertheless, we recognize that individual training may not be the only efficient way to teach vocational skills. The small group instruction techniques used in educational research with severely retarded students (Brown, Bellamy, and Sontag, 1971) may also prove useful, as may self-instruction systems using teaching machines. Some training can also be done efficiently by supervisors in workshop production settings. No doubt future research will identify the relative utility of these various formats in vocational training. In lieu of such research, we will emphasize an individual training format, reflecting our own experiences in teaching vocational skills.

There is a similar paucity of research comparing the efficacy of forward chaining with alternative approaches. As stated in Chapter 2, operant chains can be taught either in the order of performance or in reverse order. Furthermore, in either forward or backward chaining, each step can be taught to a criterion before introducing the next step, or several steps (or the whole task) can be taught simultaneously. Most demonstrations in which severely retarded adults learned vocational skills involved use of forward chaining with assistance, and simultaneous training on several task steps (Bellamy, Peterson, and Close, 1975; Crosson, 1966; Gold, 1972). This method requires the trainer to spend less time in partial assembly or disassembly to prepare the task for training. The training procedures outlined here are formulated with this general training method in mind.

In this forward chaining procedure, instruction typically consists of training trials in which the worker begins at the start of the task and completes all of it. Each repetition of the entire task is considered another trial. In some training situations, however, it will be useful to repeat smaller segments of the task, often single difficult steps. The term "trial" is also used to refer to repetitions of these smaller response units. The data collection system recommended in Chapter 4, in which correct responses to all steps in the task are recorded during scheduled probes, complements the flexibility of this individual, forward chaining format for training.

TRAINING STRATEGIES

Training strategies are sets of guidelines that a trainer uses in planning and managing the instructional interaction in vocational training. During the training process, a trainer is deciding continually how and when s/he should react to the worker's behavior. At any point in training the trainer must select from among several possible strategies in order to: 1) provide the worker with enough information about the demands of a task to ensure that the worker performs a part of the task correctly, 2) provide consequences for worker behavior that both inform the worker of the accuracy of his or her behavior and differentially reinforce correct responding, and then 3) fade out all trainer intervention so the worker performs the task without trainer assistance. Our suggestions are designed to help trainers meet these objectives by describing the kinds of trainer behaviors that may be useful and by presenting a process for selecting among alternate possibilities.

The specific trainer behaviors that are necessary to provide information and consequences while fading out trainer intervention will change dramatically as a worker develops proficiency on individual steps of the task. Because of this change we have defined four different training strategies to assist the trainer in identifying useful instructional behaviors for different teaching contexts. Specifically, the ensuing chapters define training strategies for: 1) Step Training (Chapter 6), 2) Teaching Difficult Steps (Chapter 7), 3) Chain Training (Chapter 8), and 4) Setting Training (Chapter 9). Each strategy is appropriate for learners with particular skill levels in relation to the requirements of individual steps of a task. The Step Training strategy is designed for task steps that the worker does not perform correctly; its purpose is to develop the required response topographies and bring these under control of task-related stimuli. The Difficult Steps strategy should be used when a worker does not progress in Step Training. When the worker begins to respond correctly on most occasions, the Chain Training strategy should be used. The purpose of Chain Training is to develop stimulus control over larger units of behavior, until a criterion for accurate performance is met. The Setting Training strategy is then appropriate. It is designed to increase the probability that skills acquired in training will be performed in the natural work environment.

The worker's performance on each step of the task analysis dictates which training strategy should be used for that step. As the worker gains proficiency on the step, the trainer shifts sequentially from the Step Training or Difficult Steps strategy to Chain Training and finally to Setting Training. It should be emphasized, however, that in most vocational training situations, many or all of the strategies will be used simultaneously on different steps of the same task. That is, most workers will enter training with skills required by some steps of the task, and Chain Training procedures should be used from the outset with these steps. More difficult or less familiar steps usually will require the Step Training or Difficult Steps strategy. Then, as training progresses, the strategy used on each step will change as the worker learns individual steps, integrates these into larger response units, and finally performs them under varied stimulus conditions. A smooth transition from one strategy to another is accomplished as the trainer's behavior gradually changes in response to the worker's performance on each step of the task.

Our distinction among the four training strategies facilitates detailed description of the interaction between trainer and worker at each level of skill development. Although each strategy involves unique guidelines for trainer behavior, it should be clear that the identification of distinct strategies represents only a convenient division of ongoing changes in trainer behavior as the worker's skills improve. In effect, the strategies reflect the template through which we have chosen to view and organize issues in training. Training always involves gradual changes in the way a trainer responds to the learner's behavior as the learner develops competence. The trainer criteria that we define for progression from one strategy to the next reflect the boundaries of our definitions of each training strategy more than an empirically established basis for abrupt changes in trainer behaviors. It is hoped that the detailed procedural description, which is made possible by separate treatment of the four strategies, will facilitate the development of needed trainer behaviors without necessarily segmenting the training process.

SELECTING TRAINING STRATEGIES

To determine which strategy to use for each step of a task, the trainer should conduct two or three training trials using the procedures for Step Training outlined in Chapter 6. Complete data on each of these trials should be maintained on the task analysis data sheet described in Chapter 4. The purpose of these initial trials is to gain information about the independence, accuracy, and reliability of performance in each step. Then deciding what training strategy to use essentially involves predicting, on the basis of these assessment trials, what the learner's future response accuracy will be on each step. As is illustrated in Figure 5.1, if the trainer *predicts* that the step will be performed accurately without assistance in less than 80% of the opportunities, Step Training procedures should be used. When Step Training procedures do not result in improved performance, the Difficult Steps strategy should be implemented. Chain Training procedures are appropriate for those steps that the trainer expects to be performed accurately more than 80% of the time. Finally, the Setting Training strategy is designed for those steps on which the worker is expected to perform correctly on all occasions in the training setting.

SKILLS FOR TRAINING

The purpose of this section is to provide an overview of trainer skills that are important in vocational instruction. The definition of training

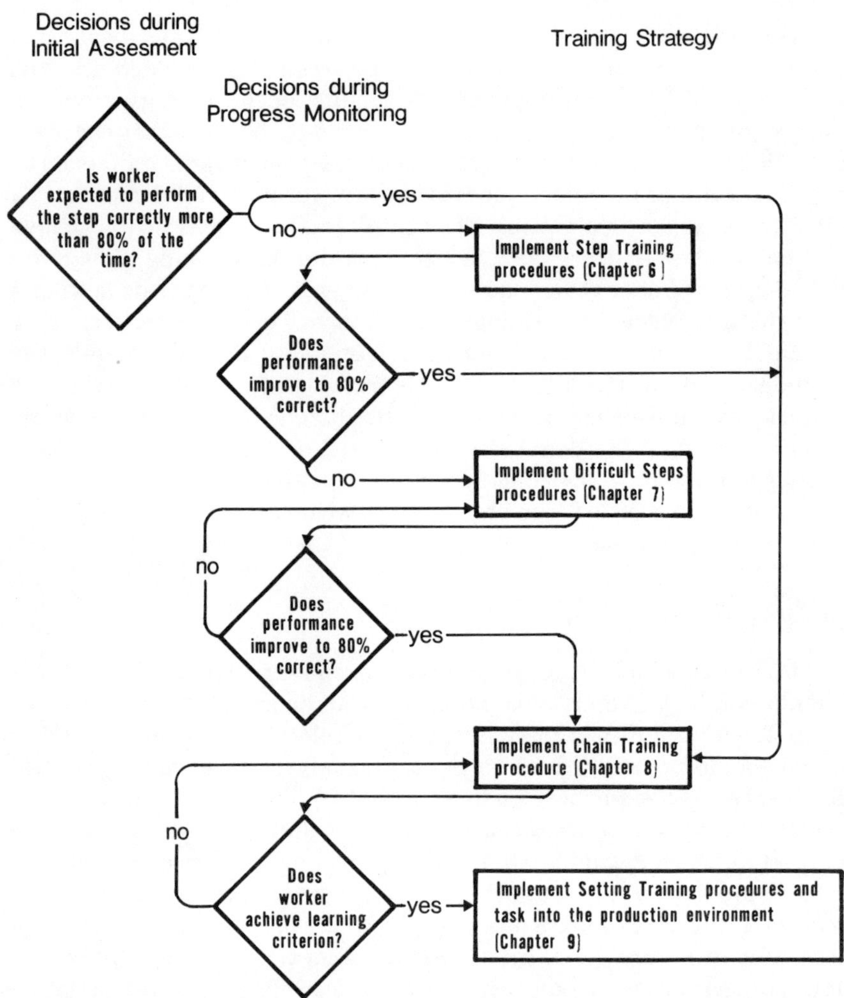

Figure 5.1. A flow chart of the decision rules used by trainers to determine the appropriate training strategy.

strategies in later chapters clarifies specific application of these skills in different training contexts. Trainer behaviors that facilitate acquisition of vocational tasks fall into three broad classes: *assisting, reinforcing,* and *assessing.* The trainer provides *assistance* by augmenting available discriminative stimuli so that correct responding is promoted; the trainer differentially *reinforces* correct or improved responding; and the trainer continually *assesses* trainee performance to determine when, how, and how much to assist and reinforce.

Assistance Skills

Assistance is the process by which the trainer adds specific cues to which the worker responds. The purpose of these cues is to help the worker respond appropriately by ensuring that effective discriminative stimuli for accurate responding are paired with naturally occurring task changes. A trainer's assistance skills should be versatile, so that s/he can provide assistance that is appropriate to the individual worker and his or her skill level. This involves the ability to provide assistance in various amounts, kinds, and methods.

Amount of Assistance In giving assistance it is important that the trainer provide no more help than is absolutely necessary for the trainee to respond correctly. Otherwise the worker simply may learn to rely on the trainer in any new situation. Providing more assistance than is needed may also prevent the worker from improving performance over previous efforts and thus reduce the opportunity for the trainer to reinforce more independent responding. To avoid these difficulties, the trainer should be able to provide assistance in varying amounts. For example, the verbal direction "Put the end through the loop" might be used initially to assist a worker learning to tie a knot. After the worker's skills have improved, the less specific instructions, "Try again" or "Try another way" might be more appropriate, in that they require a more independent response from the worker.

Kinds of Assistance There are three kinds of assistance that the trainer can provide. First, s/he can make a relevant (task-provided) S^D more salient, to increase the chance that the worker will attend and respond to correct characteristics of the task. For example, as the worker finishes one step in the chain, the trainer might gesture to the next part in order to ensure that the worker will attend to the relevant characteristics of the task and materials array. The second kind of assistance relates to providing information about response topographies. The desired behavior can be described, illustrated, or otherwise emphasized. The verbal direction "Turn it over" or a model of a required placement response could provide this type of assistance. Finally, assistance can emphasize the functional effect, or criterion, to which the behavior is to be performed. This is conceptually similar to the first assistance type, in that the criterion situation for one functional response unit is the discriminative stimulus for the next. The difference is essentially one of timing. Emphasizing the criterion situation for one step is done earlier in the response chain than is emphasizing the S^D for the next. The verbal direction used by Gold and Barclay (1973a), "The flat side goes up," illustrates this third type of assistance. With the ability to tailor assistance to the specific kind of error that is anticipated, the trainer avoids situations in which assistance is provided for aspects of a response that the worker could have performed independently.

Methods of Assistance Many industrial workers who receive training on how to perform a new job obtain information and assistance through diagrams, part specifications, and written instructions. Most severely retarded workers have not had the opportunity to learn how to use information presented in these ways. Fortunately, several other assistance methods are available to trainers, including physical guidance, physical cues, verbal cues, modeling, and matching-to-sample cues. As the following descriptions indicate, each of these methods is useful in providing particular amounts and kinds of assistance. To be maximally effective with different workers and different tasks, a trainer should have considerable facility with each assistance method:

1. *Physical guidance* is a technique in which the trainer physically manipulates the worker's body through a sequence of movements. Physical guidance of hand movements typically required in vocational tasks can be accomplished by placing the trainer's hand over the worker's. The worker's hand and fingers are then placed in the desired relationship to the task, and moved through the required manipulations. The amount of assistance provided through physical guidance can be varied by providing only partial assistance. This can be accomplished either by maintaining a superior hand position and gradually reducing pressure and assistance ("shadowing") or by providing assistance from positioning further and further up the worker's arm. The kind of assistance that can be provided efficiently by physical guidance usually is limited to information about response topographies. The technique is less useful for accentuating the relevant aspects of the task to which a worker should attend or the criterion to which a response should be performed.
2. *Physical prompts* include such trainer behaviors as pointing, gesturing, and touching the worker or task. These prompts can be used both to accentuate relevant stimuli to which trainees should respond and to accentuate the criterion for completion of a step, and may be useful at times in illustrating desired responses (e.g., pointing to where a part is to be placed). Specificity of physical cues can vary considerably, thus allowing the trainer to provide different amounts of assistance in response to worker competencies.

3. *Verbal cues* are probably the most widely used and misused assistance method. All too often one sees a worker swamped with trainer verbiage while attempting to perform a task. Useful verbal cues usually are short explicit statements that describe performance or call attention to specific stimulus characteristics. If a worker has requisite language skills, verbal cues can provide an extremely versatile and useful assistance method (Gold and Barclay, 1973b). The amount of information can be varied according to worker ability, the timing can be varied, and the cues can be given by a trainer who is some distance from the worker.
4. *Modeling* can be a quite efficient way of assisting workers who have generalized imitation skills. The trainer simply performs the response after which the trainee, to the extent that imitation skills are present, may immediately imitate the behavior. The amount of assistance provided can be reduced by varying the amount of the response that is modeled (i.e., the trainer does only the first part of the response, after which the worker is expected to do it all). Modeling usually is used to provide information about response requirements. It is less useful in accentuating stimulus characteristics that should function as the S^D or criterion for a response.
5. *Matching-to-sample* can be a particularly useful way of providing information about the stimulus situation that defines the criterion to which a behavior is to be performed. If the worker can respond by manipulating parts until they match a standardized sample, an efficient method of providing assistance is readily available (Merwin, 1974).

The utility of each of these assistance methods in any given training context will depend on whether the method can be used to provide the required amount and kind of help and whether the worker has the generalized skills needed to utilize the information provided. Determining which assistance methods are appropriate for an individual worker is an assessment issue that is discussed later in this chapter.

Reinforcement Skills

Reinforcement during training involves systematic delivery of events as consequences for the worker's behavior in order to increase the occurrence of particular behaviors in the presence of specific task stimuli and the extent to which those task stimuli function as conditioned reinforcers for the worker. Whether or not an event functions as a reinforcer for a given behavior of a worker at a particular time can only be determined after the fact by noting whether the consequated behavior was more likely to occur in the presence of the task stimuli. Therefore, the trainer must be able to: 1) make good guesses about events that might function as reinforcers for a worker; 2) deliver these events in a systematic fashion, so that their effect can be evaluated; and 3) continually assess the effectiveness of chosen reinforcers, so that needed changes can be made. In this section, trainer skills relevant to reinforcement delivery are described. The assessment skills required to identify and evaluate potential reinforcers are discussed in the next section.

Delivering Reinforcers The trainer skills required to use reinforcement effectively in instruction include the ability to define behaviors that will be reinforced and to specify and follow contingency rules for reinforcement delivery. Defining a behavior to be increased in frequency through reinforcement procedures involves 1) specifying the response itself, 2) identifying the situation in which the behavior is expected to occur, and 3) specifying the criterion to which the behavior should be performed. For most vocational behaviors this is accomplished in the task analysis. However, other behaviors in the training setting often are targets for change. For example, the trainer may choose to increase the probability that a worker will begin working without having to be told to start. To accomplish this, a target behavior could be defined as the worker, when seated in front of a completely disassembled unit (situation), begins to work by picking up the appropriate part (behavior) within 2 seconds after sitting down to work (criterion). Defining behaviors in this way is a trainer skill used extensively during training. In fact, much of training involves gradually, but systematically, redefining the behaviors that will be reinforced.

In addition to defining the behavior to be increased, the trainer should be able to specify contingency rules for delivery of reinforcers. This typically involves determining the frequency with which reinforcement will be provided. Except for early training trials (Step Training and Difficult Steps procedures), it seldom will be useful to provide reinforcement after every occurrence of a target behavior. Rather, the desired response should be reinforced intermittently, in order to avoid satiation, increase resistance to extinction, and increase response rate. Experience has taught us that a considerable degree of trainer skill is required to change gradually and systematically from continuous reinforcement early in training to the intermittant reinforcement schedules found in typical production settings.

Another skill in reinforcer delivery is timing. Reinforcers should be delivered immediately after the behavior criterion is met. Immediate delivery avoids inadvertent reinforcement of inappropriate behaviors that might intervene between correct performance and the reinforcer. Immediate delivery also ensures that the reinforcer will be paired with the natural (task-related) consequences of the response.

Adventitious Reinforcement The trainer should be able to identify unintended reinforcers in the training setting. Often some of the most powerful reinforcers operating in a training situation are not those planned by the trainer. When this type of adventitious reinforcement occurs, behaviors irrelevant to, or incompatible with, appropriate task performance often are increased in frequency. For example, eye contact with the trainer may function as an effective reinforcer for some workers. For them, each time the trainer establishes eye contact, the worker's behavior of looking at the trainer instead of the task will be strengthened. For other workers, a correction procedure in which the worker is shown how to do a step that was missed might reinforce making errors. Because there are such wide individual differences in stimulus function, the trainer must be alert to all stimuli in the training setting that might function as reinforcers for a worker, so that these can be made contingent on desired work behavior. If this is not possible, these events often can be removed from the training situation.

Assessment Skills

Assessment is a process of obtaining information about a worker's skills and performance in order to make appropriate training decisions. Assisting and reinforcing behaviors employed by a trainer usually cannot be used in cookbook fashion with trainee after trainee. This is because an assistance method selected for one individual sometimes provides no useful information for another. Events that reinforce some trainees may be totally ineffective with others, and may even punish the responses they follow. Even for the same individual across training trials, assistance and reinforcement techniques often must be modified. Good assessment skills allow a trainer to tailor his or her assistance and reinforcement methods to the specific worker, task, and situation. The trainer's repertoire of assistance and reinforcement skills then can be used as needed in each training situation.

The assessment skills described here result in information that the trainer needs for day-to-day or even moment-to-moment decision-making during training. It seems unlikely that the needed information could ever be supplied by someone other than the trainer who performed a prior evaluation of the worker. The expense of such an evaluation in relation to benefits seems extreme. Therefore, we are suggesting that the trainer himself or herself be responsible for ongoing assessment activities that result in training decisions.

Assessment begins before training and continues throughout the training process. Before training, information is collected to determine potentially useful assistance methods, to identify potential reinforcers, and to determine which training strategy to use with each step. During training, assessment activities are designed to monitor the effectiveness of assistance and reinforcement decisions in light of worker performance on the task, and to determine when to progress from one training strategy to the next.

Selection of Assistance Methods Selecting methods for providing assistance involves estimating whether verbal cues, modeling, physical guidance, match-to-sample, or physical cues will provide effective discriminative stimuli for the worker's task-related behaviors. To choose among assistance methods, the trainer should observe how the worker responds to a variety of verbal, physical, imitative, or other cues. This can be accomplished with the two to three assessment trials recommended earlier in this chapter, in which the worker is given the opportunity to perform each step of the task. In general, the effectiveness of any assistance method will depend on the extent to which the trainee has learned the generalized skill of following that method of assistance with an appropriate matching response. For example, verbal cues will be useful if the worker has receptive language skills, follows directions from the trainer, and knows the vocabulary required by the task. Modeling cues will be useful if the worker has a generalized imitation skill, so that s/he can match any modeled response involving movements required by the task.

For all but the most severely handicapped workers, several effective assistance methods usually are available. In these situations, modeling, physical cues, and verbal instructions can be used effectively in combination. For a few workers who do not have the required generalized skills, physical guidance is the only option. The selection of assistance methods prior to training represents only the formulation of a working hypothesis, the utility of which is evaluated throughout training.

Selection of Reinforcers Several strategies can be useful in developing an initial list of events that might function as reinforcers. Observation of apparent "likes" and "dislikes" of the worker can provide some information. Simply asking a worker with language skills what s/he likes, or asking him or her to choose among alternative events also can be useful. Another helpful technique is to identify behaviors that occur at high rates in unstructured settings. The opportunity to perform these high rate behaviors may be useful reinforcers. For example, if a worker frequently chooses to listen to music, it is possible that contingent access to a radio will function to reinforce a targeted response.

If difficulty is experienced in identifying likes or high rate behaviors, a technique that can be useful is to expose the worker briefly to a variety of stimuli while the trainer records the response to each. For example, present a variety of tastes, scents, textures, and sounds, and select as potentially useful reinforcers those to which the worker appears to respond favorably.

Whenever possible, select as potential reinforcers stimuli that can be delivered in very brief time periods. Avoid lengthy reinforcers that take the worker off the task. When more lengthy reinforcers are particularly effective with a worker, plan to use these at the completion of a very successful training trial or session, rather than during training itself.

When several potential reinforcers have been identified for a worker, select those that are age- and situation-appropriate. In general, however, do not sacrifice reinforcer effectiveness to achieve this appropriateness during training. Individual training is usually an expensive undertaking for vocational facilities. To the extent that powerful reinforcers (such as edibles, for some workers) reduce training time, they seem preferable, even if they are less situation-appropriate. After a skill has been learned and is being performed in a production setting, renewed efforts should be made to provide reinforcement in more normal ways (see Chapter 10). For additional suggestions on procedures for identifying reinforcers for severely retarded individuals, the reader should consult Striefel (1974).

Monitoring Progress in Training The ability to monitor the worker's progress in training is essential to good instruction. The trainer will use information from this monitoring to adapt his or her training behaviors to the changing skill level of the worker. To do this effectively, the trainer must make decisions throughout training. The trainer will be making ongoing decisions as to the effectiveness of events chosen for use in assistance and reinforcement procedures and when to change from one teaching strategy to another. The trainer should be able to collect information related to these decisions in two ways: by use of the task analysis data sheet to measure acquisition of the task, and by close observation of fine details of the worker's performance that are not recorded on the data sheet.

The task analysis data sheet allows the trainer to maintain a continuous record of the worker's general progress over time, as well as to monitor the exact steps that are consistently performed correctly, and those that are consistently missed. Several trainer decisions follow directly from this information on variability in step accuracy. For example, Figure 5.2 presents hypothetical performance data on acquisition of the heat sink assembly task described in Chapter 2 by a vocationally unskilled worker. The first three trials represent assessment probes prior to training and the remaining 10 trials are records of performance during probes that occurred after every 15 minutes of training.

As is apparent in Figure 5.2, Step 2 (the next to last step in the assembly) was missed on every probe trial. In such a case, the trainer should evaluate his or her assistance procedures. Specifically, the method, type, and amount of assistance should be studied to determine a more effective way of acquainting the worker with the correct response topography and the conditions under which the response is to occur. In general, when there is little change in the variability of incorrect performance, assistance procedures rather than reinforcement should be questioned first. The opposite is usually true when performance is extremely variable. For example, Steps 3, 4, and 5 in Figure 5.2 are sporadically correct and incorrect with no apparent trend one way or another. Clearly it is not that the worker does not know how to perform the response. It is more likely to be either a discrimination problem, i.e., the worker may not know exactly *when* to perform an already acceptable response topography, or it may be that the event used as a reinforcer following the step is ineffective. In the first case, the trainer might decide to enhance the salience of the S^D that immediately precedes the desired response so as to increase the worker's chances of exhibiting the response at just the right moment. (See Chapter 7.) If, on the other hand, the trainer suspects the consequences of the step are non-functional, then an attempt should be made to strengthen the reinforcement. In any case the outcome of the trainer's decision should be that a trend develops in the data that shows the step being performed correctly more and more often. Steps that consistently are performed correctly, such as Step 1 in Figure 5.2, usually signal the trainer that the amount of reinforcement should be reduced by either increasing the amount of work required to earn reinforcement or reducing the magnitude of reinforcement delivered after these steps.

The task analysis data sheet also provides a means through which the trainer can determine when to change the teaching strategy for a step or group of steps. Each of the criteria for changing from one strategy to another, which are outlined in Figure 5.1, involve predicting how well the worker will perform on subsequent training trials. For example, after only two or three probes on Step 2 in the heat sink training illustrated in Figure 5.2, the trainer might well have predicted continued poor performance, and chosen to use the Difficult Steps strategy. Similarly, it should be apparent after only a few probes that Step 1 would be performed correctly more than 80% of the time, so that Chain Training techniques could be used. After continued correct performance on Step 1 during these probes, it would be appropriate to pre-

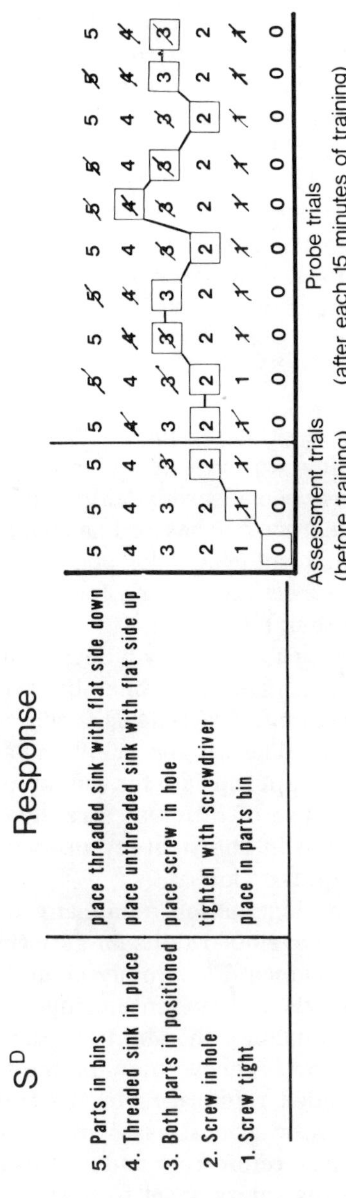

Figure 5.2. A task analysis of a heat sink indicating worker performance on both assessment and training (probe) trials.

dict reliable accuracy and begin using Setting Training procedures. In each case the decision to change from one strategy to another is based partly on the recorded data and partly on trainer observation of performance during unrecorded training trials. Both kinds of information assist the trainer in predicting future response accuracy.

Several kinds of information are available to the trainer that are not recorded on the task analysis data sheet. The trainer should be alert to changes in variability or level of task-attending behaviors, to behaviors incompatible with working, and to consistently inappropriate responding to the trainer's assists, reinforcers, or corrections. On the basis of these observations the trainer often determines an overall level of reinforcement for the worker's performance and terminates inadvertent reinforcement of unwanted behavior.

SUMMARY

Vocational training is a process that is designed to develop new response topographies in a worker's behavioral repertoire. Training involves an interaction between a learner, trainer, and setting and is successful only when the learner's behavior has changed in a measurable way. The training format suggested for vocational training involves providing individual instruction, using a forward chaining procedure with instruction on all task steps.

Four separate training strategies will be described in the following chapters to provide guidelines for trainer behaviors in the instructional setting: Step Training, Teaching Difficult Steps, Chain Training, and Setting Training. The worker's skill on each step of the task dictates which strategy is appropriate for that step. Most training situations will involve the use of different strategies on different task steps and gradual change in the strategy used for each step as the worker develops the required skills.

To provide efficient instruction using any of the strategies, a trainer should have well-developed skills for assisting, reinforcing, and assessing worker performance. The trainer should be able to provide assistance in varying kinds and amounts using a variety of methods. The reinforcement skills include the ability to define responses to be reinforced, to identify contingency rules for reinforcement delivery, and to identify unintended reinforcers in the training setting. The trainer should also possess several assessment skills, including the ability to identify potential reinforcers and useful assistance methods, and to use the task analysis data sheet to monitor task acquisition.

chapter 6
STEP TRAINING PROCEDURES: *Development of Response Topographies and Stimulus Control of Individual Steps*

Training involves using the skills described in Chapter 5 in response to the behaviors of the worker and the changing characteristics of the task. Developing good training techniques, therefore, is largely a matter of learning both what training skills to use and when to apply them. This involves bringing a trainer's skills under the control of worker behaviors.

Training procedures described in this chapter are useful for steps of a task that the worker does not perform independently in response to cues provided by the task. The purpose of Step Training is to establish the response topographies required by each step in the task analysis and to bring these under the control of task-relevant stimuli correlated with the response. That is, in Step Training the worker learns how to perform each step without trainer assistance.

Step Training typically involves progression through an entire task, although tasks requiring 20 to 30 minutes to complete may be taught in smaller segments. In either case, Step Training procedures are designed to result in independent performance of single steps in response to task-provided cues. As soon as the trainer expects performance to be correct about 80% of the time, procedures for Chain Training, which are described in Chapter 8, should be used to fade out trainer involvement and establish the entire chain as a cohesive response unit.

OVERVIEW OF STEP TRAINING

As in all training, procedures during Step Training involve application of a trainer's assistance, reinforcement, and assessment skills. The focus of *assistance* efforts is on the prevention of errors by providing necessary help prior to each step. Similar assistance skills are involved in correction procedures that involve help from the trainer, which is provided after incorrect responses. Reinforcement procedures are used to develop and maintain the behaviors of task attending and independent initiation of work as well as the behavior outcomes of correctly completed steps and completed tasks. *Assessment* efforts during Step Training focus on determining the appropriate assistance method, kind, and amount for each step and evaluation of events chosen as possible reinforcers.

Figure 6.1 provides a schematic illustration of the interaction between the worker, task, and trainer in completing a task step during Step Training. The task analysis step is indicated on the far left side of the figure. The next column represents the continuous stimulus changes in the task that accompany correct responding, with shaded areas denoting the specific stimuli defined as S^Ds and criterion stimuli for each step in the task analysis. The central area of the figure illustrates trainer activities, with assistance behavior represented by squares, reinforcement behaviors by circles, and assessment decisions by diamonds. The task-related responding of the worker is indicated in the righthand column in parallel time dimension with changes in task-produced stimuli. As the figure illustrates, the trainer decides prior to each step whether or not assistance will be given and what events will be used to reinforce task attending and completion of previous steps. The worker then responds to the task-relevant stimuli for the step, which are augmented by trainer assistance. The trainer assesses and records the accuracy of the worker's response and, if the response is correct, provides a reinforcer and assists the worker in performing the next step. If the response is incorrect, the trainer repeats the entire step with additional assistance designed to prevent repetition of the error. Periodically, the trainer may provide reinforcers for the task-attending behaviors of the worker during these early training trials.

LOGISTICAL CONSIDERATIONS

Before beginning training, it is useful to organize the training setting for efficient instruction. Four guidelines are presented in this section that will assist in preparing the training setting to maximize the effectiveness of Step Training. Preparing the training setting normally

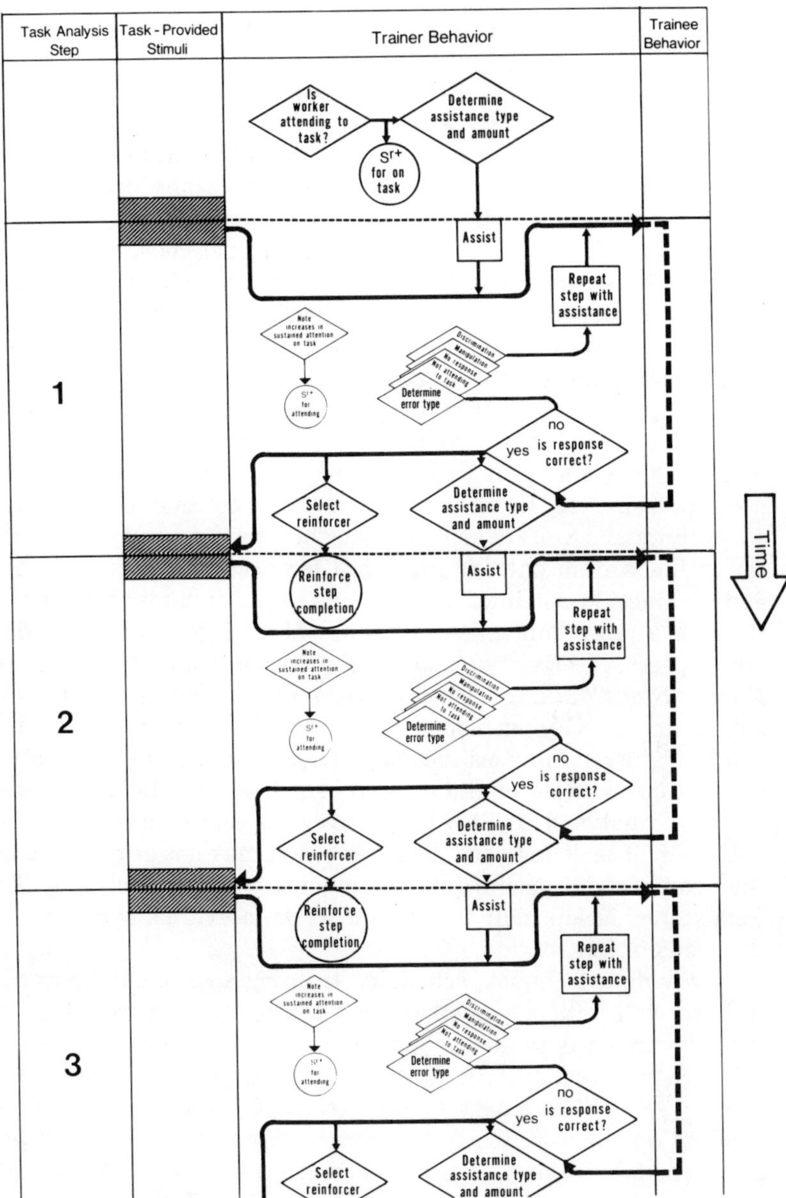

Figure 6.1. A schematic illustration of the interaction between the worker, task, and trainer during Step Training.

should occur after an assembly method has been selected, the task analysis has been completed, and assessment trials have been conducted to identify potentially effective reinforcers and assistance methods.

1. *Establish a specific area where Step Training will be conducted.* Using the same area in each training session will help bring the trainee's behaviors under stimulus control. Some behaviors are always required in the training setting; others are always inappropriate. Attending to the task, following trainer cues, and manipulating the task are behaviors for which the training setting should set the occasion. (A comparable suggestion is frequently made to high school and college students who are advised to establish a specific time and place for study.)

   The training area should approximate as closely as possible the environment where production will occur. This approximation might include the same task arrangement, same noise level, same peers present, etc. In fact, it often is useful to conduct training at an individual's workbench, so that the presence and behavior of the trainer are the only significant differences between the training and production settings. For some trainees it may be helpful to train in a more controlled environment and gradually introduce noise, peers, interruptions, etc., only in later training strategies.
2. *During Step Training, schedule frequent training sessions with a single trainer.* Giving responsibility for training one worker to a single trainer minimizes inconsistencies in the smaller details of how a task is performed (i.e., steps smaller than those defined in the task analysis). It also takes advantage of continuous observation of on-task and other behaviors that may not be recorded but that can provide useful information for training decisions. This consistency is especially important while individual responses are the focus of instruction.

   Providing frequent, scheduled training sessions ensures that training will not be dependent on a trainer finding free time. Although current data do not support rigid rules, it has been our experience that training sessions should occur at least three or four times weekly. The length of each training session may vary, depending on the experience and competency of the worker. In general, schedule frequent short sessions in the early stages of training. Then gradually increase the duration of sessions as the worker's competence improves. It has been our experience that most severely retarded adults easily can learn to sustain attention and effort for training sessions in excess of an hour.

3. *Prior to each training session ensure that there are sufficient parts and materials at the training station.* Before the worker enters the training station, take time to arrange tools, parts, chairs, data sheets, etc. Make sure that consumable supplies are sufficient for the entire session. The training station should not become an S^D for off-task or waiting behaviors. Yet, if the trainer must locate supplies or parts, such waiting is often the only available response.
4. *Have several potentially reinforcing events available at the training station.* Do not rely on a single event to function as a reinforcer throughout the training session or for all responses. If possible, have several options readily available so that presentation can be varied or the worker allowed to choose among alternatives. These could include various edibles, social contact, or access to potentially reinforcing events set up near, but not at, the immediate training setting.

WORKER ATTENTION

One of the trainer's first and most persistent activities in Step Training is to assess whether or not the worker's attention is focused on the task. Training on each step begins only when the worker is attending to the task materials. Some workers enter training with high rates of attending to stimuli relevant to a task. Others attend instead to themselves, the trainer, or other aspects of the training environment and need to be taught to perform sustained task-attending behaviors.

1. *Shape attending behavior by contingently delivering trainer attention and the opportunity to perform the task.* Especially during the early stages of training, it is useful to assume that all contact from the trainer will reinforce, or increase the frequency of, the worker response that it follows. Thus, the trainer must be very particular when, where, and in response to what worker behavior the trainer's attention is delivered.

   If the trainee periodically sustains attention to the task for one or two seconds, it is usually unnecessary to work exclusively on attending behavior. Rather, attention is taught at the same time as work skills by requiring the worker to attend before each interaction with the task and before delivery of each assist or reinforcer from the trainer (see Figure 6.1).
2. *Do not ask the worker to attend. Wait for him or her to orient to the task, then provide a reinforcer and begin training.* If trainer attention is assumed to be reinforcing, asking the worker to come on-task could be expected to increase off-task behavior. Although im-

mediate compliance might result each time (i.e., the worker may always attend when asked), s/he also may learn that being off-task is a reliable method of obtaining trainer attention. The short-range benefits of asking the worker to attend are usually outweighed by the long-range negative effects. It is usually more effective to ignore off-task behavior.

3. *Delay delivery of reinforcement for attending so that the worker is reinforced for being on-task rather than coming on-task.* Delivering a reinforcer as soon as a worker orients to the task can increase the frequency of an off-task→on-task response chain rather than simply increasing the duration of on-task behavior. Kazdin (1977b) demonstrated that reinforcement for task-attending responses that were preceded by task attending was a more effective strategy than reinforcement for task-attending responses that were immediately preceded by off-task behaviors. Of course, for some workers it may be necessary initially to reinforce very brief periods of attending. When this is done it will be important to increase as soon as possible the amount of on-task behavior required before delivery of reinforcement.
4. *Periodically provide reinforcement for sustained attending during early training trials.* It is often useful to provide reinforcers for increasing periods of task attending throughout early training. If a worker completes one or more steps without going off-task, a simple comment like, "You're really trying hard" can often increase sustained attending in the future.
5. *Provide reinforcement for worker initiation of task behaviors.* Since attending is required for initiation of work behaviors, reinforcement of initiation should increase the frequency of initiating work independently: R_1=attend to task→R_2=begin work. Reinforcement for initiation is thus a useful way of increasing the criterion for reinforcement. It also allows the trainer to illustrate to the worker that independent work is expected.
6. *Eliminate reinforcers for attending to a step or group of steps as soon as the worker begins to perform correctly and receives reinforcement for correct responding.* The natural reinforcer for attending is the opportunity to perform another behavior and be reinforced for it. In his analysis, Skinner (1968) discussed attending as a "precurrent" behavior, the strength of which is determined by the reinforcement for the behavior that the attending response enables. It is not surprising, for example, for individuals considered to have short attention spans to maintain attention for sustained periods to television sets, food and utensils at mealtime, and other stimuli in the environment that provide reinforcement

for the individual's behavior. To the extent that effective reinforcers follow work completion, attending to work tasks should follow a similar pattern.

7. *If a worker is off-task (and being ignored), do not allow him or her to manipulate task materials or tools.* The task should serve as an S^D for task-appropriate work behavior and nothing else. Our own awareness of this potential problem resulted from working with two trainees who frequently flicked a screwdriver or task component in front of their eyes, a similar topography to the self-stimulating behaviors that occurred at other times. To prevent this behavior, trainers simply held the worker's hands on the table in front of the task and looked away from the worker until s/he oriented to the task.

ASSISTANCE

Assistance procedures are designed to give the worker just enough help so that s/he can respond appropriately to task-provided stimuli. With skillful assistance, the worker can experience a great deal of success early in training. This helps establish the work setting as a positive situation, it minimizes the chance that a worker will learn inadvertently to perform steps in the wrong way, and it increases the trainer's opportunities to reinforce correct step completion instead of simple task attending.

1. *Use the worker's previous performance on a step as a guide in determining assistance method, kind, and amount.* Determining the *amount* of assistance to give on each trial is an important decision to be made in training. Too little help can result in performance of incorrect or unskilled behaviors that then require a correction procedure. The attention involved in correcting a response often functions as a reinforcer, increasing the probability of a similar error in the future. Other workers whom we have trained have responded emotionally to the implied failure of their efforts when several corrections were necessary on early training trials. Although these possibilities are clearly not problematic with every worker, they can be avoided by enough assistance early in training.

   Providing too much assistance, on the other hand, is equally detrimental to worker progress. More help than is absolutely necessary prevents the worker from performing independent or improved responses that the trainer can reinforce. Furthermore, it often teaches the worker to depend on and attend to the trainer instead of the task at difficult steps in the chain. The general rule on assistance amount is to provide the least help possible that still results in correct performance.

As was discussed in Chapter 5, decisions concerning assistance *method* frequently can be made prior to actual training. Often these original plans should be revised as training progresses. While the initial choice of kind, type, and method of assistance will be based on the trainer's judgment, modification of these decisions during training should be based on worker performance.

The *kind* of assistance provided on any particular step depends on the kind of error or difficulty experienced by the trainee on that step during previous trials. It will be recalled that assistance can be given to 1) accentuate the relevant discriminative stimulus that should set the occasion for a response, 2) illustrate or describe the behavior, or 3) accentuate the criterion stimulus situation to which the behavior should be performed. After the first few trials on many task steps, most workers will require assistance of only one or two kinds.

2. *Provide assistance only when the worker is attending to the task.* Assistance procedures are designed to augment the naturally occurring discriminative stimuli for work performance. As assistance is faded over trials, the worker is expected to continue attending and responding to cues provided by the *task* not the trainer. To increase the probability that trainer-provided cues *augment* those provided by the task rather than *replace* them, give assistance only when the worker appears to be visually attending to relevant aspects of the task.

   Additional difficulties are encountered with many workers when assistance is provided while the worker is off-task. Trainer assistance often functions as a powerful reinforcer. If it is delivered immediately following off-task, incompetent, or dependent behaviors, these behaviors are likely to increase in frequency. A characteristic example is the worker who has learned to look up at the trainer as soon as any difficult step is encountered. The trainer should be skilled at anticipating such situations and providing assistance before they occur. Otherwise, the possibility exists that these off-task behaviors will be reinforced, or even if they are ignored until the worker again attends to the task, the off-task→on-task chain might be reinforced.

3. *Preclude worker pausing by delivering assistance immediately before steps where pausing frequently occurs.* The pace of worker performance during training should be constant and fluid. Trainer assistance can facilitate an even training pace by precluding

worker pausing. When the worker exhibits pauses between certain steps, the trainer may choose on the next trial to provide assistance (in any of a variety of forms) immediately prior to those steps. In this way assistance would occur before the worker has the opportunity to pause. Providing assistance while the worker is still on-task increases the pace of training and avoids building pauses into the operant chain.

4. *As the worker develops proficiency on a step, fade out trainer-provided assistance.* Fading involves gradually reducing the amount or specificity of information provided by the trainer prior to each response. It is a technique designed to transfer stimulus control of correct responding from cues provided by the trainer and task to cues provided by the task alone (Horner, 1977; Bellamy, Inman, and Schwarz, 1978; Sidman and Stoddard, 1967; Terrace, 1963; Touchette, 1971).

   Begin fading assistance as soon as the worker begins responding correctly to a step. Be sensitive to opportunities to fade in each step. If a worker is performing correctly on one step but not others, fade assistance only for the correct step(s). As assistance is faded, pay particular attention to the worker's responses to avoid fading too quickly or too slowly. Problems resulting from providing too much or too little assistance on a step were discussed above.

   Fading can be accomplished in several ways. The first involves gradually reducing the amount or specificity of information provided to the trainee. It will be recalled that this can be accomplished with verbal directions by making them less specific (e.g., fading from "Look for the curved edge" to "Try again"), with modeling by demonstrating only the initial movements of a step, with physical guidance by providing assistance from points more and more distant from the workers' hands, and with physical cues by making gestures less and less explicit (Bellamy, Inman, and Schwarz, 1978).

   Fading can also be accomplished by providing assistance progressively earlier in the chain. For example, the verbal direction, "Remember, the flat side goes up," can be given initially as the worker begins responding on the step, but on a later trial the same instruction might be given as the worker is performing earlier steps in the chain. This timing requires the worker to respond to the task stimulus in the absence of immediate assistance.

   A third fading approach is often useful with workers for whom several assistance methods are effective. Lent (1974) describes a progression of trainer assistance in which physical guidance is used during early training trials, modeling cues used as the worker gains proficiency, then verbal directions, and finally no assistance at all. Although these fading procedures are useful with many sheltered workshop employees, they may be less efficient with workers who do not have skill in following instructions and imitating trainer movements.

ASSESSING RESPONSE ACCURACY

The trainer's behavior after each response in the chain depends on the accuracy of the worker's performance. A critical assessment activity thus involves monitoring the worker's behavior on each step in relation to the criterion specified in the task analysis and in relation to previous performance on the step. The trainer's observations provide the basis for immediate selection between correction and reinforcement procedures as well as decisions on subsequent trials as to the amount of assistance and reinforcement to provide on that step.

1. *Maintain continuous attention to the worker while s/he is performing each step.* The immediacy that is important in both correction and reinforcement procedures is possible only if the trainer is alert to exactly when a response is completed or exactly when an error is made. A correct response is followed *immediately* by a reinforcer. When an error is committed, the worker is interrupted immediately and a correction procedure implemented. Timing of these trainer responses is possible only when the trainer maintains continuous attention to the worker.
2. *Maintain a clear, consistent criterion for what constitutes correct or improved performance on each step.* Letting the worker "get by" with lesser approximations by scoring them as correct or not following them with corrections defeats the purpose of training. Training involves systematically *increasing* the skill required of the worker; instances in which incorrect responses are apparently accepted usually lengthen the training process. In other words, the worker should be taught to discriminate acceptable from unacceptable responses by the trainer's differential consequation of each (corrections for unacceptable responses and reinforcement plus the opportunity to continue through the chain for acceptable responses). Unless the trainer maintains a clear definition of what distinguishes the two kinds of responses, it is unlikely that the worker will learn to discriminate between them. The written task analysis helps the trainer maintain a consistent definition of correct responses, since the effect of each functional response unit is specified.

Frequently a worker will not respond at all when presented with the S^D for a step or an assist from the trainer. It is useful to treat a delay of three to four seconds as an incorrect response, record it as an error, and follow it with a correction procedure. This simplifies the recording process and results in use of training procedures very similar to those advocated by Touchette (1975).

3. *Maintain a record of response accuracy on scheduled probes.* Determining assistance and reinforcement levels on later trials involves study of accuracy and variability of the worker's previous responses on each step. This information can be maintained easily on the task analysis data sheet described in Chapters 4 and 5 (see Figure 4.3). An important aspect of this sheet is that it allows general monitoring of overall progress as well as the specific study of performance over time on each step.

   There are several characteristics of performance that could be recorded, including amount and kind of assistance received, response accuracy, pauses, etc. It has been our experience that most trainers can learn to observe and utilize considerably more information than would be feasible to record. In our own training, we limit data to notations of step accuracy, i.e., correct performance without assistance, and the duration of each probe trial. Data are not recorded on the type of errors made on a step, the type of assistance a trainer provides, or a worker's gradual improvement within a step.

   Although the task analysis data sheet could be used to record performance on every training trial, we have found it useful to record data only at regular intervals during training. Typically, this involves collecting data on one complete assembly cycle after 10 to 30 minutes of training, or after a defined number of training trials. Although this increases reliance on the trainer's ability to observe and remember important information about performance, it decreases the time required to record data, and it increases the overall flexibility of the training process. As is emphasized in the next chapter, it is often useful to repeat one step several times during training. Such repetition disrupts trial-by-trial data collection efforts, but is easily accommodated when measures are taken only at set intervals.

REINFORCEMENT FOR CORRECT PERFORMANCE

Each correct or improved step is reinforced in Step Training to increase the probability that in the future the task-provided S^D for a step will be followed by the correct response. A second purpose of the reinforcer is to increase the conditioned reinforcement function of the next stimulus in the chain. The reinforcement skills described in Chapter 5 apply directly to reinforcement of accurate step completion: clear definition of the behavior to be reinforced is necessary, as are planned contingency rules for reinforcement.

In general the task completion behavior to be reinforced in Step Training is correct or improved performance on a step. A continuous schedule of reinforcement usually is appropriate until performance is consistently independent and correct. Since improved performance in Step Training usually results from the trainer's removal of some assistance, the trainer's reinforcement and assistance activities are closely related. The worker usually can meet the criterion for reinforcement if the trainer has reduced assistance in some ways from previous trials. Fading of assistance discussed earlier is thus a critical element in reinforcing improved performance on a step.

Several aspects of reinforcer delivery are particularly important during Step Training:

1. *Select a reinforcing event on the basis of initial evaluation of the worker and apparent function of events used on previous training trials.* Selecting a specific event to use as a reinforcer for a correct or improved step always involves a guess by the trainer as to what will effectively reinforce any particular behavior at any given time. The functioning of an event as a reinforcer for work behaviors in the past provides some help to the trainer in selecting among options. However, do not assume that events will maintain their reinforcing function in different situations, at different times, or when used as consequences for different behaviors.

   A fairly good rule of thumb is to vary the specific event used as a presumed reinforcer as the worker completes the various steps of a task. It is also useful during early training trials to pair possible social reinforcers with each other and with other potential reinforcers. For example, a compliment, a pat on the back, and another selected event might be given together during the first few training trials and then alternated during later trials.
2. *Pair all reinforcers for step completion with the naturally occurring consequences for correct performance.* The naturally occurring consequence for step completion in most vocational response chains is a change in the task, which serves as the S^D for the next response, and the opportunity to perform the next response. It will be recalled from Chapter 2 that sustained performance of chains depends at least in part on the conditioned reinforcement function

of these natural consequences. Pairing these task-related consequences with other presumed reinforcers is one important strategy for increasing their conditioned reinforcement value. Several conditions are necessary for reinforcers delivered by the trainer to be paired with those provided by the task:

(a) The reinforcer should be delivered immediately upon completion of the step. The changes in the task produced by the response usually occur as soon as the response is exhibited. Any delay in delivery of the reinforcer creates the possibility that the reinforcer will be paired with some stimulus other than the criterion situation for the step. As was discussed in Chapter 5, such a delay also increases the chance that an inappropriate behavior will intervene between task completion and reinforcement delivery and thus be reinforced.

(b) The reinforcer should be delivered only when the worker is attending to the task. Pairing a reinforcer with the appearance of relevant task cues is useful only if the worker attends to those cues. If the worker consistently attends to the trainer or any other aspect of the setting when reinforcement is delivered, one would expect those stimuli, rather than task changes, to become conditioned reinforcers. Of course, little is gained by delivering a reinforcer for on-task behavior at the end of an off-task→on-task chain. The trainer should be able to provide the chosen reinforcer quickly enough that the worker's attention does not leave the task.

(c) The reinforcer should be delivered at the same time as assistance on the next step so that the worker continues through the task without interruption. This requires that the trainer be able to deliver reinforcers without bringing the worker off-task. The importance of this rule is apparent when it is noted that the reinforcer is being paired not only with the effect on the task produced by the functional response unit but also with the task characteristics that are to serve as the S^D for the following response. Thus, lengthy reinforcers that require the worker to attend to the event or the trainer should be avoided, and delivery of any reinforcer should be terminated as soon as the worker looks away from the task. Social reinforcers should be short and sweet. Brief compliments, pats on the back, or placement of items in a cup for later consumption (e.g., between trials) often are useful reinforcers for this reason. There should be no break between the reinforcer and assistance on the next step. In fact, for many workers, this assistance functions as an effective reinforcer by itself.

3. *Do not establish any cues other than the task and setting that signal an increased probability of reinforcement.* If the worker learns to expect reinforcement for work behaviors in some situations but not others (i.e., trainer present vs. no trainer present) progress during training generally will be impeded and generalization of work skills to other settings will be less likely. Typical of such cues is the promise of reinforcement by the trainer ("If you finish this step correctly, I'll give you a   "), the obvious presence of specific items, and consistent facial expressions or gestures of the trainer. To prevent such trainer behaviors from signaling availability of reinforcement, ensure that any behavior performed by the trainer that is not intended to assist or reinforce the worker occurs without regard to performance accuracy or likely consequence.

CORRECTION PROCEDURES

If after receiving the trainer's assistance, the worker performs a step incorrectly or fails to respond, a correction procedure is used in which the missed step is repeated with just enough additional assistance so that it can be performed correctly. The correction serves three purposes in training: 1) It allows the worker to perform the step correctly and be reinforced for correct responding. 2) It prevents natural reinforcement for the incorrect response that can be provided by progression through the chain. 3) The correction gives the worker more practice on difficult responses. In general, correction procedures are used less frequently during Step Training than in later phases of training, since most errors will be precluded by assistance prior to the response. Often, however, the worker's performance is variable, or assistance is faded too quickly, and correction procedures are needed. To implement a correction, stop the worker's performance as soon as the error occurs and:

1. *Determine from the worker's response what kind and amount of assistance will likely result in correct performance on the step.* Observing the specific kind of error made by the worker should allow the trainer to select the kind of assistance needed. It will be recalled from previous discussions that assistance procedures can be used to accentuate the relevant aspect of the task to which the worker should respond, to illustrate the desired response, or to accentuate the criterion to which the response should be performed. Similarly, the optimum amount of assistance within any of these kinds can be hypothesized on the basis of the worker's previous performance on the step. As with all assistance procedures, the

trainer should provide corrections with the least help possible that results in subsequent correct performance.

2. *Return the task to the stimulus situation that serves as the S^D for the response that was performed incorrectly, and allow the worker to repeat the step with appropriate assistance.* This allows the worker to perform the step again with just enough additional assistance so that it can be completed correctly. Remember that the purpose of the correction is not to punish the worker's response. Avoid punitive intonations and questions. The purpose is simply to prevent reinforcement of incorrect performance and to ensure that each step is performed correctly and reinforced before continuing through the chain. It usually is useful to repeat the step a second time during each correction to provide additional practice and to attempt to fade out some of the additional assistance.

SUMMARY

Step Training procedures are designed to teach the responses required by single steps of a task and to bring these under stimulus control of task-relevant stimuli. Step Training involves particular attention to developing worker attending to the task, providing assistance, assessing response accuracy, reinforcing correct responses, and using correction procedures after incorrect responses.

To increase a worker's attention to task the trainer should utilize his or her attention to the worker and the worker's access to the task as likely reinforcers for task attending. These consequences might initially be provided after brief periods of task attending, but longer periods should quickly be expected. Reinforcement for independent initiation of work behavior and for accurate step completion can replace contingencies for attending to task after a few training trials.

Assistance is used in Step Training to increase a worker's success early in training. Before each response the trainer should assess the least possible assistance that will allow the worker to respond correctly and receive a reinforcement. Assistance should be provided as soon as possible after completion of the previous step, to avoid pausing, and should be faded out as rapidly as possible over training trials.

Assessing response accuracy in Step Training involves continuous monitoring of each response exhibited by the worker. It is important that the distinction between correct and incorrect responses be clear to the trainer so that differential responding can be immediate. The task analysis data sheet should be used during scheduled probes to assess response accuracy.

Each correct response is reinforced in Step Training. In delivering reinforcers, the trainer should be able to choose from several possible events, should pair reinforcers with naturally occurring task stimuli, and should carefully avoid situations in reinforcement delivery that can be predicted on some basis other than task performance. Incorrect responses should also be consequated immediately with correction procedures. This involves interrupting the worker, returning the task to the S^D for the step, and providing additional assistance so that the worker can respond correctly.

Step Training is complete for any step when the trainer predicts that the worker will perform the response independently on 80% of future opportunities. At this time procedures described in Chapter 8 on Chain Training should be used to ensure that steps are linked together in a cohesive behavioral unit. When the worker does not progress during Step Training, the Difficult Steps strategy described in Chapter 7 should be implemented.

chapter 7
TEACHING DIFFICULT STEPS

The training procedures described in Chapter 6 are designed to be effective across a wide range of tasks, workers, and settings. We recognize, however, that these general procedures will not be successful in training all workers on all steps of all tasks. Despite well-conducted training efforts there will be individual steps of some tasks that prove problematic. A worker may perform most of a task accurately yet make consistent errors (or require a consistent level of assistance) on a few remaining steps. With these steps, modifying the kind, type, and amount of assistance and manipulating the kind and amount of reinforcement often will not be effective in improving worker performance. The worker's consistently poor performance on such steps functionally defines them as "difficult steps."

In addressing the problems presented by difficult steps, a trainer has two options. The first is to manipulate task design variables so that the worker does not need to learn the difficult steps. The second is to teach the deficit behavior directly. The first option can be implemented by 1) using an assembly line production method in which the most skilled workers perform the difficult steps, 2) adding fixtures to the task design to eliminate discriminations or manipulations that are difficult for the worker, or 3) having the workshop staff perform the difficult steps. Each of these changes in task design variables make it unnecessary to teach the difficult step.

In a workshop operating as a small business as well as a social service agency, however, these options frequently will be too costly. An alternative is to modify training procedures in an attempt to teach the difficult step(s). The purpose of this chapter is to identify task characteristics that are frequently associated with difficult steps and outline instructional procedures for improving worker performance of these steps. A general instructional format is presented, and teaching strategies that address potential sources of step difficulty are discussed.

A FORMAT FOR TEACHING DIFFICULT STEPS

The basic teaching format provided in Chapter 6 is designed both to teach the response topographies of a sequence of steps and to bring those topographies under control of task-relevant stimuli. Because each step ultimately should function as a link in an operant chain, the sequencing of steps begins on the first training trial. One step is not trained to criterion before the next step is presented. Rather, the worker learns individual steps within the sequential context of the operant chain. This instructional format is an effective and efficient method of building individual steps into a functional chain. However, this approach precludes the opportunity for repeated practice on any one step. For difficult steps, the amount of training required before a worker gains mastery may be substantially greater than the training required for other steps. As such, difficult steps frequently must be taught individually outside the context of the operant chain. The format we suggest for teaching difficult steps consists of five general guidelines:

1. *Provide massed trials.* In teaching difficult steps we suggest using a *massed trials format.* When massed trials on one step are conducted, that step is removed from the operant chain. The worker is presented with the S^D for the step, performs the step (with or without assistance), and receives immediate feedback on the accuracy of his or her performance. The S^D for the same step is then presented again, and the process repeated. The worker does not progress through the chain but performs the same step many times. The use of massed trials provides the worker more practice on a difficult step and maximizes the effect of training and feedback. The S^D for the step is presented immediately after the worker receives feedback on the previous trial. Unlike the training format suggested for Step Training, massed trials prevent time delay and performance of other steps from occurring between feedback on one trial and access to the next trial. As such, the massed trials format is conducive to the shaping of correct performance in that the worker can be reinforced for successive approximations of the correct response over repeated trials.
2. *Manipulate the demands of the step to ensure worker success.* During massed trials, the trainer manipulates task and assistance variables so that step difficulty is reduced to a level where the worker is performing correctly on approximately 75% of the trials. The worker is not allowed to experience repeated failure. In this way the probability that s/he will exhibit resistive or uncoopera-

tive behavior is minimized, and the focus of training is shifted from what the worker can't do to what s/he *can* do. Once correct responding is reliable, the level of difficulty is increased gradually to that normally required by the step. In this way, approximations to correct performance are reinforced systematically, and the worker is shaped into performing competently. The step is, in essence, broken down along an *easy-to-hard continuum.* The worker enters that continuum at a point where success is very likely, and gradually works up to a criterion. This general approach to teaching difficult steps has long been preferred by advocates of programmed instruction (Skinner, 1968) and is supported by an extensive body of literature on the learning patterns of retarded people (Mercer and Snell, 1977).

The exact nature of the easy-to-hard continuum will vary depending on task characteristics and the type of errors the worker is making. In some cases the physical characteristics of the task may be altered. In others the continuum can be created by simply manipulating the kind and amount of assistance delivered by the trainer. In each case the continuum will be defined in an attempt either to facilitate performance of the response topographies required by the difficult step or to maximize the salience of task-relevant S^Ds that should control appropriate responding. Specific strategies for building the easy-to-hard continuum relate to the particular characteristics of the difficult step and the type of error being made. Several strategies we have found useful are presented in following sections of this chapter.

3. *Increase the level of reinforcement a worker receives during massed trials training.* To maintain worker performance during massed trials it may be useful to increase the amount of reinforcement s/he receives to a level above that normally used when training all steps together. When a worker is required to perform a difficult step repeatedly, s/he is being asked to do a step that previously has been paired with failure, and is being prevented from progressing through the rest of the chain after the step is performed (i.e., is not rewarded by access to the next step in the chain). Massed trials on a difficult step potentially could demand more performance from the worker and provide less reinforcement than normal training trials. As such, a trainer should attempt to increase the level of reinforcement during massed trials and should use task changes and assistance so that correct performance can be reinforced frequently. If a worker becomes negative, resistive, or inactive during massed trials training, the trainer should assess the contingencies of the training setting. Task difficulty should be

at a level such that approximately 75% of the worker's responses are correct (i.e., reinforceable), and careful consideration should be given to the type and amount of reinforcement available to the worker. Is the presumed reinforcer actually functioning as a reinforcer? Is the worker "satiating" on a reward that was previously reinforcing? Is reinforcement being delivered contingently and on a schedule that is better than that used during normal Step Training? The type and schedule of reinforcement should be monitored closely during massed trials training to ensure that the worker's performance is maintained.

4. *Conduct massed trials in short time blocks.* While the amount of time a worker can spend productively in any one training trial will vary considerably, we generally have found that massed trials training periods are best kept substantially shorter than a normal training period. Our massed trials training periods often last for only 10 to 15 minutes. These short periods usually are conducted two or three times a day, however. We have also found it useful to incorporate a brief massed trials training session within a normal 30 to 45 minute training session. As with most decisions made by a trainer, the length of any training session should be dictated by the performance of the worker. A session should last long enough to afford ample access to the task, yet end before the worker begins exhibiting off-task or resistive behavior.
5. *Once a difficult step has been mastered it should be built systematically back into the operant chain of the task.* Training a difficult step includes both teaching the skills necessary for accurate performance of the step, and integrating the step into the operant chain. Before assuming that the step has been learned, the trainer should require 20 to 30 consecutive correct responses that are performed during at least two training sessions. Because of the short duration of the response, fewer correct responses often do not provide a reliable indication that future responses will be consistently correct. After this criterion has been met, it still should not be assumed that, because a worker can perform a step accurately during massed trials training, s/he will perform equally well when the step occurs within the context of the entire chain.

   Building the newly learned step into the chain can be done in the massed trials setting by simply demanding that the worker perform not only the newly learned difficult step but the preceding step as well. If performance is stable and accurate with this added step, the trainer can then require that the step immediately following the difficult step in the chain be performed. It is our experience that this mini-chain then can be incorporated easily into the overall chain of the task.

To teach difficult steps successfully a trainer will need to apply many of the training skills discussed in previous chapters. In addition, however, the teaching of difficult steps will require the ability to identify task characteristics that contribute to a worker's consistently poor performance and construct the easy-to-hard continuum used in massed trials training.

The remainder of this chapter outlines characteristics of tasks that have been difficult for our workers to learn and describes teaching strategies for each. Persistent errors on a step usually relate either to step size, to characteristics of required manipulations, or to difficulty of necessary discriminations. Variables related to each of these error sources will be discussed.

STEP SIZE AND DIFFICULTY

When a task analysis is performed according to the guidelines presented in Chapter 4, the size of individual steps in the analysis will vary. Steps identified in the task analysis are *functional response units* that result in noticeable changes in the appearance of the task. More behavior is required to complete some of these steps than others. For example, placement of a washer on a bicycle brake axle (Gold, 1972) requires simply that the worker pick up the part and place it on the partially assembled unit. To achieve a similar noticeable effect on one step in assembly of a cable harness (Hunter and Bellamy, 1977) the worker must use an elastic cord to tie a self-tightening knot around a wire bundle. This involves placing the cord around the bundle, making a loop in the cord with the left hand, inserting the end of the cord through the loop with the right hand, pulling the cord to tighten the knot while moving it to the correct place on the cable, and finally, checking for slack in the tie. The result of this series of behaviors is a noticeable change in the task, i.e., the addition of one tie around the cable.

Task steps that require more behavior often are difficult to learn. In effect, each of these longer steps can be considered a behavior chain that consists of several sub-steps. Many workers who experience difficulty on longer steps perform the sub-steps in different sequences on different trials, thereby preventing repeated exposure to similar task-provided stimuli and similar response requirements on these sub-steps across trials. Therefore, when a worker makes repeated errors on a step, the trainer should determine whether or not the step might be taught more effectively as a series of sub-steps. Procedurally, this involves application of the task analysis and training techniques we have already described to a more fine-grained analysis of the task. To teach a step that is difficult because of step size, these guidelines should be followed:

1. *Prepare a written task analysis branch that identifies and sequences the component sub-steps.* This task analysis branch should have the same general format as the original analysis. It should include precise behavioral descriptions and should list the criterion for each response as the S^D for the succeeding sub-step. To prepare this written analysis, perform the step several times to identify an efficient sequence of movements that will result in accurate step completion. The task analysis procedures described in Chapter 4 apply to this fine-grained analysis, except that responses will specify simple movements rather than functional response units. For example, the functional response unit "place the threaded component with flat side down," the fifth step in assembly of the heat sink described in Chapter 2, could be analyzed into the following sequence of sub-steps:

   5a) parts available→pick up threaded component
   5b) threaded component in hand→rotate until flat side is down
   5c) flat side down→place on table

   Preparing such a written analysis ensures that the trainer has defined a precise sequence of sub-steps and thus assists the trainer in responding consistently to the worker's performance of these sub-steps across trials. This means that the same sub-steps will be expected in the same sequence trial after trial, a condition that generally facilitates learning.
2. *Use Step Training procedures to develop independent responding on sub-steps identified in the task analysis branch.* After the task analysis branch has been prepared, the assistance, reinforcement, and assessment procedures described in Chapter 6 should be used to teach individual sub-steps. Assistance should be provided as needed to occasion correct responses that can be reinforced. As performance improves, this assistance should be removed gradually so that the worker responds independently to task-provided stimuli.
3. *Begin fading reinforcement for completion of a sub-step as soon as accuracy is reliable.* By fading out reinforcement for sub-steps, the trainer facilitates a fluid performance of the entire step. When each

sub-step is completed with consistent accuracy, reduce reinforcement either by requiring more behavior (two or three sub-steps) before reinforcer delivery or by providing progressively smaller amounts of the chosen reinforcer. This process is very similar to the Chain Training procedures discussed in Chapter 8. After reinforcement for sub-steps has been eliminated, the worker should perform the step accurately as a single response unit.

MANIPULATION VARIABLES AND STEP DIFFICULTY

Each step of an operant chain is characterized by a discriminative stimulus and a response. If performed correctly, the response will produce the S^D for the next response in the chain. Step difficulty related to manipulation variables usually exists if the worker correctly performs only part of the response topography required by a step. A worker who bends the fragile wires on a resistor because s/he is holding it too tightly is exhibiting a manipulation error. A worker who applies side pressure on a screwdriver allowing the tool to slip out of the head of a screw is exhibiting a manipulation error. Similarly, a worker who continually fumbles and drops a small screw as s/he tries to fit it into the appropriate hole is exhibiting a manipulation error.

All manipulations are, in effect, a function of muscle contraction and relaxation. Most vocational manipulations require that several skeletal muscles perform in concert. The combination, sequencing, and timing of muscle contraction and relaxation define the topography of the manipulation. Evaluation of difficult manipulations can condense ultimately to an evaluation of the specific muscle movements required for step completion.

In theory, a step that is difficult because of manipulation variables is one in which the worker "knows" what to do and when to do it, but is unable physically to perform the necessary response topography. In practice it is both difficult and dangerous for a trainer to make assumptions about what a worker "knows" or does not "know." A trainer's behavior should be in response to the worker's observable behavior, not what the trainer thinks the worker "knows." As such, it is very difficult to interpret when an incorrect response is a function of a worker's inability to perform the response topography, or when the worker is not accurately discriminating which response to perform. Two major classes of variables are associated with difficult manipulations: precision demands of the step, and simultaneous performance of more than one manipulation.

Precision Demands of Difficult Manipulations

Precision demands depend upon the size of the material being manipulated, the amount of space in which to perform the manipulation, the margin for error, and the effort required. Each can affect the probability that workers will have difficulty performing a step because of the specific motor requirements of the manipulation. Parts that are exceptionally large or small usually require greater skill to manipulate. A cramped space in which to perform the manipulation, small margin for error, and difficult effort requirements also increase the skill level required for competent performance.

Figure 7.1 shows three steps required in the placement of a .15 × .45 cm hex nut into small plastic bearings. Hex nut placement is part of the assembly of a cam switch. A cam switch is an oscilloscope part assembled by workers at the Specialized Training Program (Bellamy, Peterson, and Close, 1975; Horner and Bellamy, 1978a). Placement of hex nuts is done by: (A) picking up one hex nut, (B) rotating the plastic bearing so its hole is facing up, and (C) placing the hex nut into the hole. Placement of the hex nut frequently has been a difficult step for assembly workers. The part is very small, the hole in which it fits is very small, and the hex nut fits tightly into the hole, so that there is little margin for error in placement.

Step difficulty related to precision of manipulations frequently can be avoided in the design of a task. The decision to use needle-nosed pliers in the placement of hex nuts, for instance, has proved helpful with one worker. With another worker the use of a fixture (see Figure 7.2) that guides resistors into a slot so that the leads can be cut to length has been useful. Without the guide the worker exhibited considerable difficulty placing the resistors in the slot. It is not uncommon, however, to find that task design options that decrease the difficulty of a manipulation also require a substantially longer time for task completion. In such cases the economically viable choice may be to teach the manipulation.

To teach a precise manipulation, physical guidance and repeated practice should be used. The objective of teaching a manipulation is to maximize the worker's ability to perform the correct topography of the response. In teaching the topography of a response, physical guidance techniques discussed in Chapter 6 are very useful. Physically guiding a worker through the step ensures that his or her movements exactly follow those required by the task. Repeated trials with physical guidance, and a systematic fading of that assistance, are often sufficient for mastery of a difficult manipulation.

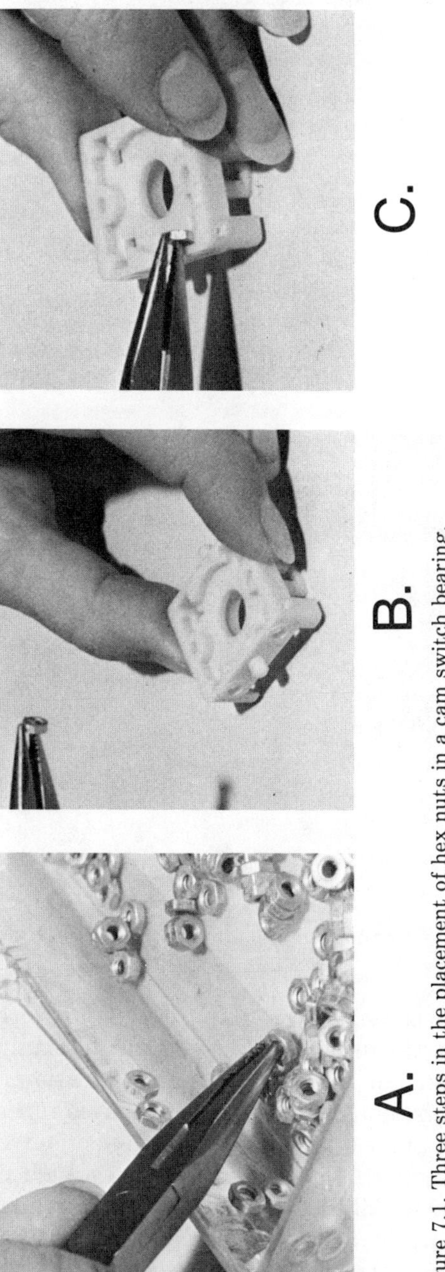

Figure 7.1. Three steps in the placement of hex nuts in a cam switch bearing.

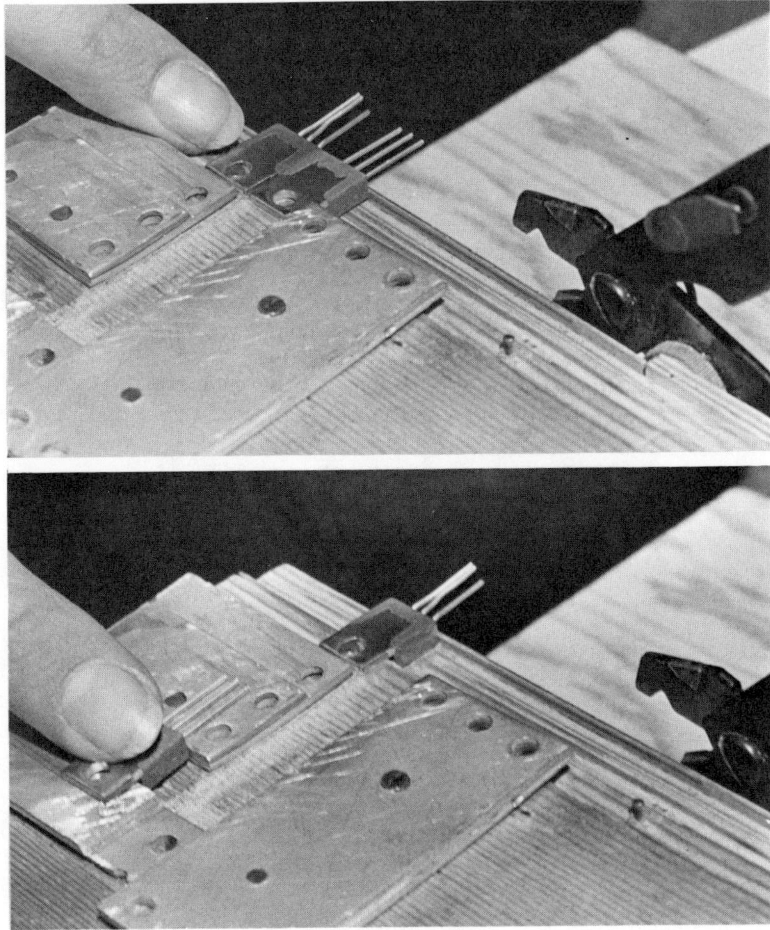

Figure 7.2. A fixture used to facilitate proper placement of resistors prior to cutting leads.

As has been noted across many groups of workers in many contexts, it is also useful to practice a difficult manipulation. Physical skill development in music, athletics, education, and many other aspects of human behavior has been attributed repeatedly to practice. Vocational manipulations such as inserting a hex nut should not be viewed as different from learning to catch a ball, play a cadenza, or write with a pencil. All involve the combining, sequencing, and timing of muscle relaxation and contraction; all involve responses that must be performed in particular ways (i.e., with particular topographies); and all probably will improve with practice. In this context "practice" refers simply to massed trials in which the worker is praised for systematically approximating the desired response. The role of the trainer becomes one of presenting the S^D for the difficult step, observing the worker performing the step, and reinforcing when appropriate. Sufficient reinforcement should be provided to maintain responding, and care should be taken that the worker does not develop irrelevant or inappropriate responses that avoid the difficult step or lead to incorrect performance of the step (Bellamy, Inman, and Horner, 1978; Horner, 1978).

Simultaneous Manipulations

A second manipulation variable contributing to step difficulty is the need for simultaneous performance of more than one manipulation. Many steps in complex vocational tasks require that a worker perform two or more manipulations simultaneously to produce the S^D for the next step. When a worker has difficulty with a step requiring simultaneous manipulations, one of two behavior patterns usually can be identified. The worker may not be performing all the responses that must occur simultaneously for step completion, or else the individual manipulations may not be sequenced correctly.

Simultaneous Response Components A step that requires that two topographically different responses occur at the same time often proves difficult for severely retarded workers to learn. Each response must be performed to its own criterion and still mesh with the other. Inserting the cam switch spring shown in Figure 7.3 involves (A) holding the spring with a pair of needle-nosed pliers, (B) placing the left end in the open bearing slot, and (C) bending and inserting the spring so the right end fits under the bearing lip. It is important to note that at each stage of spring placement the worker is required to maintain enough pressure with the pliers to keep the spring in place. Step *B*, placement of the left end of the spring, actually involves holding the spring with the pliers *while* placing the left end of the spring in the slot. Similarly, placement of the right end involves holding the spring with the pliers *and* maintaining the proper bend in the spring *while* placing the end in the bearing slot.

It is not uncommon on such steps requiring two or more simultaneous manipulations to find that the worker performs one manipulation but not the other. The worker may, for example, move the spring in the correct direction but not hold it tightly with the pliers. As a result, half of the step is performed correctly and half incorrectly with an unsatisfactory result. In teaching the step, "place the left end of the spring in the bearing slot," the trainer should be aware that two dissimilar response topographies must occur simultaneously.

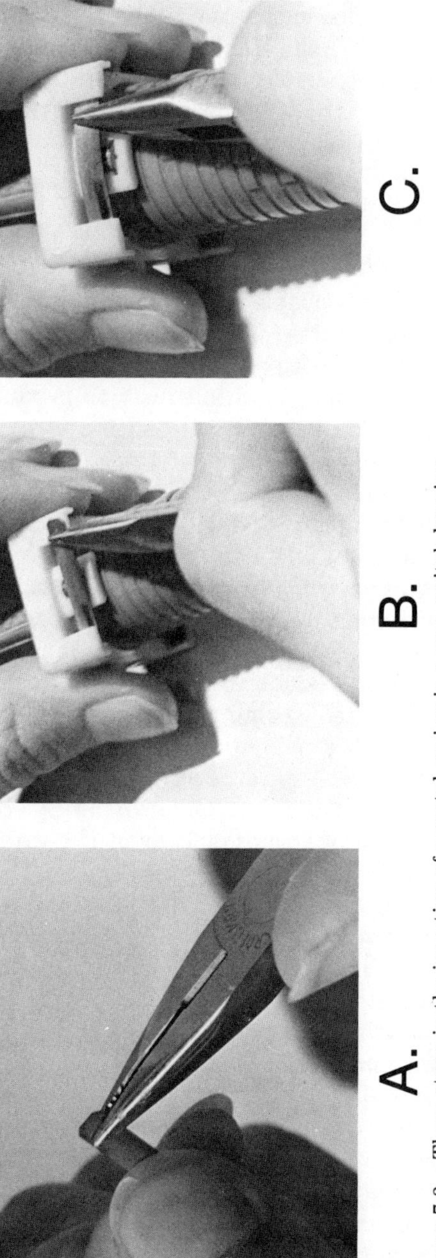

Figure 7-3. Three steps in the insertion of a metal spring in a cam switch bearing.

Another example of simultaneous manipulations leading to step difficulty may be encountered when teaching the use of a screwdriver to tighten a screw. When tightening a screw the worker generally will need to press down on the screwdriver *and* simultaneously rotate it in a clockwise direction. If the worker presses but does not rotate the screwdriver or rotates but does not press down, the screw will not tighten.

When teaching a difficult step that contains simultaneous manipulations, we have found it useful to teach the separate manipulations individually. If a step requires a separate manipulation for each hand, a trainer might conduct training by providing a complete physical guide for one hand while focusing training on the manipulation required by the other. Once the worker performed the first manipulations independently, fading of the physical guidance could begin. Each manipulation would be learned to criterion. This procedure allows the trainer initially to focus all of his or her feedback on the worker's performance of the first manipulation. After this manipulation has been learned to criterion, trainer attention can be focused on developing independent performance of the second.

As noted in the above examples, not all simultaneous manipulations involve manipulations with different hands. In some cases simultaneous manipulations by one hand may be required. In these instances the same general teaching format is applied. The trainer physically guides one manipulation and trains the other.

In teaching the use of a screwdriver to a worker who sometimes pushed without turning and sometimes turned without pushing, a trainer might physically guide downward pressure on the tool but require that the worker perform the rotation independently. As a consistent rotation response became part of the worker's skill repertoire, the trainer would require more and more independence from the worker in determining when and how much pressure should be coordinated with the rotation.

In teaching insertion of the cam switch spring to one worker who exhibited "difficulty" with the required steps, the following sequence of techniques was used:

1. Massed trials on picking up the spring and placing it in the needle-nosed pliers
2. Massed trials with trainer providing physical guidance on both pressure of pliers holding spring, and the placement of left side, bend, and placement of right side manipulations
3. Massed trials with trainer fading assistance of placement and bending manipulations

4. Massed trials with trainer fading assistance in pressure on pliers during placement manipulations

Temporal Sequencing of Simultaneous Manipulations Simultaneous manipulations can also contribute to step difficulty as a function of their temporal ordering. In his work with profoundly deaf children, Engelmann (1977) has noted consistent error patterns associated with those steps that require one of two simultaneous responses to stop while the other continues. Frequently the learner will either continue performing or stop performing both responses. Figure 7.4A depicts the correct response pattern. Figures 7.4B and 7.4C show the most frequently observed error responses under this condition.

In teaching difficult steps in which the temporal ordering of simultaneous manipulations appears to interfere with performance, we advocate teaching the responses independently. The trainer should provide physical assistance to ensure that one response 1) began when it was supposed to, 2) met the topographical requirements of the response, and 3) terminated when it was supposed to. This could be done by physically guiding the worker, or simply by performing the response for the worker. The mode of assistance generally will be dictated by the demands of the step. Trainer feedback then can be focused on teaching the other response. Only when this latter response is being performed accurately should the assistance on the first response be gradually removed. This gradual removal would involve a refocusing of trainer attention to teaching the worker to perform the second response independently in conjunction with the first.

DISCRIMINATION VARIABLES AND STEP DIFFICULTY

To perform complex vocational tasks a worker must make a multitude of discriminations. Some will be obvious, some very subtle, and all will be necessary for accurate (i.e., remunerative) performance. Once a worker has the physical skills required to perform the manipulations required by a task, the focus of training shifts. At this point the trainer should focus on teaching the worker 1) when to perform those manipulations, 2) with what parts or tools to perform those manipulations and 3) to what criterion to perform the manipulations. All of these involve teaching discriminations.

A worker has learned a discrimination when s/he responds one way in the presence of the positive level (S+) of the relevant stimulus dimension and does not respond that way in the presence of the negative level (S–), regardless of irrelevant stimulus variation (see Chapter 2). To discriminate between two objects means that the

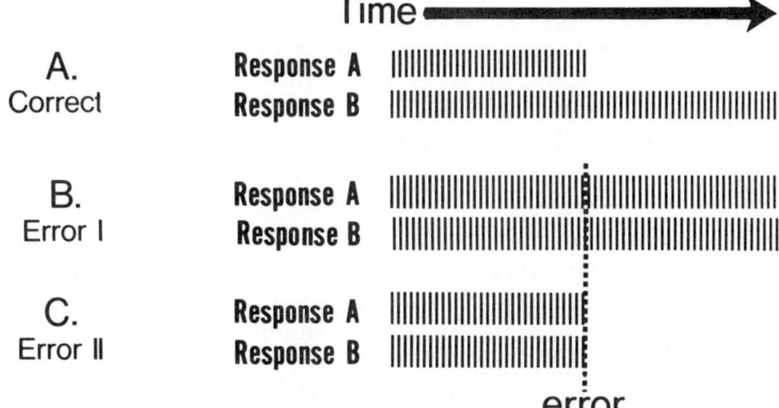

Figure 7.4. Two errors that are likely when one of two simultaneous responses stops while the other continues (from Engelmann, 1977).

worker responds differently as a function of stimulus differences between the objects. Much of training simply involves teaching the worker which differences are relevant. "Discrimination" generally has been used to describe a cognitive behavior. A worker is perceived as looking, feeling, smelling, hearing, or touching several stimuli and "recognizing" differences. Such "recognition" is not observable. Therefore, we define the criterion for determining if a worker is "discriminating" between two or more stimuli as his or her consistent differential responding to those stimuli.

The ability to make discriminations is at the heart of learning vocational tasks. The manipulations (responses) required for task performance must be cued by task-relevant stimuli. The worker must be able to discriminate the S^D for the first step in the operant chain if s/he is to perform that step at the right time. Similarly, s/he must be able to discriminate that the stimulus preceding step six is different from the stimulus preceding step seven. If through training these stimuli come to control task-appropriate responding, then the worker will have learned the task. If a worker exhibits the ability to perform the manipulations required by a step, but performs them at the wrong time, in the wrong place, with the wrong part, or to the wrong criterion s/he is exhibiting difficulty with a step discrimination.

A worker placing electrical components in a circuit board may be adept at picking up the correct parts but may place them in the wrong holes. That is, the effect defined by the functional response unit is not achieved. In this situation, s/he would be failing to discriminate which holes were appropriate. Phrased slightly differently, the component and the correct holes in the circuit board that should control placement responses would not be exerting adequate stimulus control. The responses required for component placement would be clearly in the worker's repertoire, but these responses would not be controlled by the appropriate task-relevant stimuli.

A worker exhibiting the above behavior pattern would be failing to discriminate the correct holes from the incorrect holes. Discrimination difficulty always refers to a situation in which a worker is not responding differentially to different stimuli. All step difficulty related to a worker's discrimination errors ultimately translates to a problem of poor stimulus control. As will be seen below, the teaching strategies used to correct discrimination errors are all aimed at developing or strengthening stimulus control.

Surprisingly, research focusing on the difficulty of retarded individuals to learn discriminations has not focused on stimulus control variables. Focus has been more commonly directed at the cognitive behavior of the person as s/he "discriminates." Nevertheless, the available research provides an extremely useful framework for defining and teaching difficult discriminations. The most thorough analysis is presented by Zeaman and House (1963) and Fisher and Zeaman (1973). These authors suggest that a person discriminating between two or more stimuli actually follows a two-step process. The first step is conceptualized as a discrimination between stimulus dimensions and the second as a discrimination among levels of the relevant dimension. It will be recalled from Chapter 2 that stimulus dimensions refer to any of the attributes of a stimulus. These can include, among others, the height, weight, position, color, shape, size, or function of a particular stimulus. Each object or stimulus a worker deals with in a vocational setting will have many different stimulus dimensions. Some of these dimensions will be relevant to the vocational decision at hand and some will not. The first discrimination task a worker faces is to identify the dimension or dimensions to which s/he must attend (i.e., that are relevant). The second discrimination task in the Zeaman and House (1963) two-step model is to identify to which level within the relevant dimension one should respond. If height were the relevant dimension and twenty centimeters the positive level, the worker would need to: 1) discriminate length from all other dimensions present and 2) discriminate the length twenty centimeters from all other levels of length present.

A major contribution of the two-step discrimination model is its recognition of the immense complexity present in each situation confronted by a learner. As teachers or trainers we must be aware that a stimulus like a wrench has many stimulus dimensions to which a worker could attend.

For example, a particular wrench has weight, size, shape, color, relative position in space, and many other dimensions. Within this perspective it should be noted that a stimulus, any stimulus, is in fact defined by the stimulus dimensions and levels it displays. If someone were to provide information about the dimensions and levels of a particular stimulus, you would eventually know what it was. Figure 7.5 shows a crescent wrench, and a symbolic representation of some of the stimulus dimensions and levels of that crescent wrench. By identifying the dimensions and level of a stimulus, you define what a person presented with that stimulus might respond to.

For a worker who must select an 8-in crescent wrench from wrenches of other sizes and shapes in order to perform a task, length and shape are the relevant dimensions with 8-in and a crescent wrench shape the positive levels of those dimensions. In performing the task, these positive levels of the length and shape dimensions should control a specific response. Only by attending to these attributes of the stimulus will a worker be able to select the correct tool. If color, function, position on the workbench, or any other stimulus dimension is used as the basis for discriminating, the worker will perform inaccurately. Workers who are not responding appropriately to task-relevant stimuli typically are not attending to the relevent dimensions and levels of the stimuli they encounter. Steps of a task on which a worker repeatedly makes discrimination errors are usually steps on which identification of relevant stimulus dimensions and levels are difficult.

We have encountered five major classes of step characteristics that often lead to difficulty in making discriminations: 1) minimal differences between stimuli, 2) dichotomous discriminations along a continuous dimension, 3) the sense modality used to make a discrimination, 4) simultaneous discriminations, and 5) if-then rule learning. Each of these sources of step difficulty is discussed and instructional strategies are suggested.

Minimal Difference Discriminations

An impressive body of research has documented that the more similar two stimuli are the more difficult it is to discriminate between them (Terrace, 1966; Becker, Engelmann, and Thomas, 1975). Similarity can be defined as the sharing of stimulus dimensions and levels by two stimuli. As a general rule, the more stimulus dimensions and levels of those dimensions that two stimuli have in common, the more difficult it is to teach a person to discriminate between two stimuli.

Minimal difference discriminations require a worker to respond differentially to two slightly different levels of the same relevant dimension. To discriminate between 2 in × 4 in and 2 in × 3 in boards of a

= S

Dimensions	Level
a: weight	8 oz.
b: length	200 mm
c: shape	cresent head on handle
d: color	silver

Figure 7.5. Stimulus dimensions and levels of a crescent wrench.

given length a worker would need to perform one way (i.e., put boards in the 2 in × 4 in pile) to stimuli with the following attributes:

S width = 4"
depth = 2"
material = wood

and another way (i.e., put boards in the 2 in × 3 in pile) to stimuli with the attributes:

S width = 3"
depth = 2"
material = wood

The dimension requiring attention is width. The worker would in essence need to learn to discriminate between level 3 in and level 4 in along the dimension width. The research suggests that learning this skill is harder than learning to discriminate between level 3 in and level 8 in (i.e., sorting 2 in × 3 in boards and 2 in × 8 in boards) (Becker, Engelmann, and Thomas, 1975). These research results have important implications for teaching vocational skills. Steps in complex tasks frequently require a worker to discriminate between very similar stimuli. Bolts of slightly different lengths, resistors with slightly different color codes, or electrical components of slightly different shapes could all pose discrimination problems for many severely retarded workers. In each case the worker may have the ability to perform the requisite response (i.e., pick up the bolt, rotate and place the resistor in a circuit board, or select the correctly striped component), but that response may not be under proper stimulus control.

To learn a minimal difference discrimination a worker generally will be faced with distinguishing between two or more levels within a relevant dimension. With workers who have difficulty with a step requiring a minimal difference discrimination we usually provide massed trials in which correct discriminations are reinforced and incorrect discriminations are either ignored or followed simply by "no."

There will be instances, however, in which the worker's performance does not improve even during such massed trials training. In these situations it may be necessary to reduce the difficulty of the task (i.e., manipulate task variables to make the relevant dimension, and positive level(s) of the dimension, more salient).

Many research efforts examining discrimination learning have demonstrated that a person is more likely to learn a minimal difference discrimination task if the discrimination is first presented in an "easy" form, and then made gradually more difficult (House and Seaman, 1960; Sidman and Stoddard, 1967). This easy-to-hard sequence is created by changing stimulus features of the task until the worker responds correctly on most trials. The changes then are removed gradually until responding comes under stimulus control of natural task characteristics. When teaching minimal difference discriminations the changes in task characteristics are generally designed to create a *maximal* difference discrimination that is faded back to the initial *minimal* difference the worker will encounter in production.

At least three methods of stimulus feature change have been used in teaching minimal difference discriminations to severely retarded workers. Irvin and Bellamy (1977) describe these as 1) adding and fading redundant color cues, 2) adding and removing large cue differences, and 3) a combination of the color and large cue difference approaches. The three methods are illustrated in Figure 7.6 as they were used in teaching severely retarded adults to discriminate the flat side of a hex nut from a slightly (.10 cm) raised side.

The task involved placing the flat side of the nut over a bicycle brake axle. The subjects were severely retarded adults who had not learned to discriminate the flat from curved side of the nut during massed trials training in which correct responses were differentially praised.

The three procedures shown in Figure 7.6 were used to establish three easy-to-hard continua. The first involved painting the curved side red. This made it easier to discriminate the curve from the flat side of the bolt. As the paint was faded this discrimination became

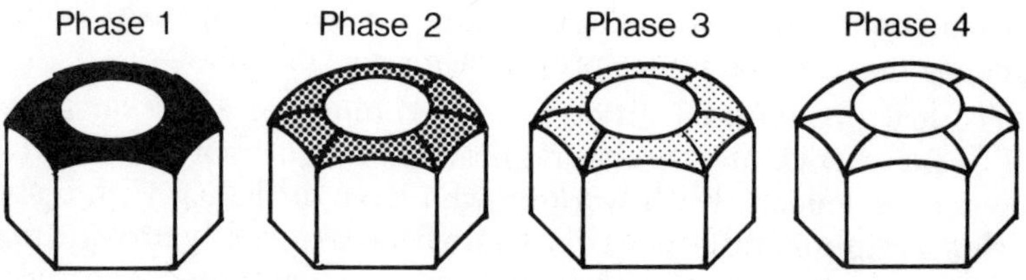

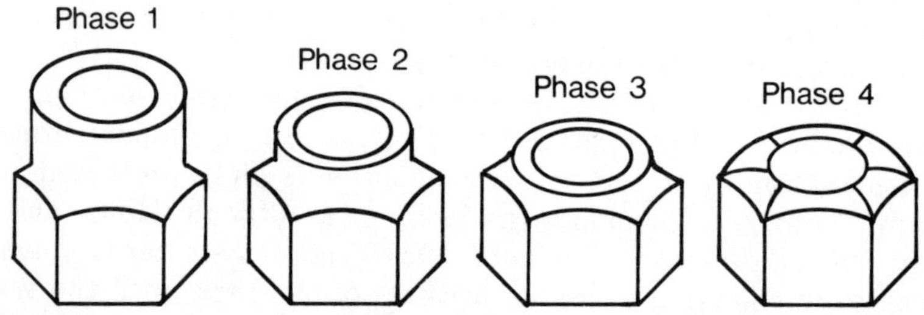

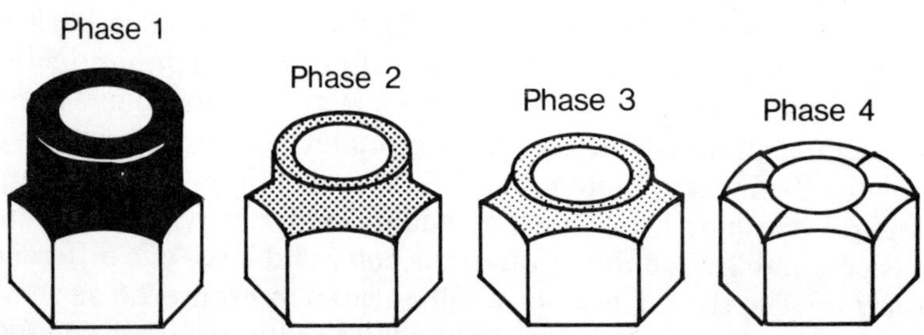

Figure 7.6. Three ways of teaching the minimal difference discrimination required for placement of a hex nut with the curved side up.

more difficult. The second procedure exaggerated the relevant dimension (shape) of the nut. The curved side was made *very* different from the flat side. This difference was then gradually reduced. The third procedure both added color and exaggerated the relevant stimulus dimension.

Irvin and Bellamy (1977) found that for this task the combination fading procedure resulted in the most efficient learning, the color

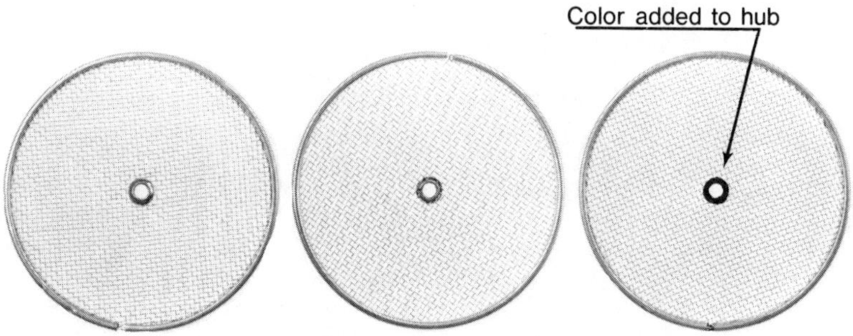

Figure 7.7. Three samples of wire mesh used in assembling sifters. A and B indicate the difficulty in discriminating the rounded side from the broken side. The color added to the rounded side in C makes this discrimination easier.

coding in the next, and the large cue difference approach in the least efficient learning. All three procedures, however, were more effective than simple differential reinforcement of correct responses. The procedures used by Irvin and Bellamy (1977) are applicable across a wide range of tasks requiring minimal difference discriminations. It is likely, however, that different task or worker characteristics might make one procedure more desirable than another. In an attempt to increase the generalizability of the procedures to many different tasks, workers, and settings, we suggest that the following guidelines be used when teaching difficult minimal difference discriminations:

1. *Design stimulus feature changes to accentuate relevant stimulus characteristics.* Stimulus feature changes should call attention to, not detract from, the stimulus differences inherent in natural task material. The precise purpose of adding color or exaggering cue differences is to teach the worker which dimensions of task stimuli are relevant. If the worker is expected to discriminate bolt *length,* it is length that is exaggerated to create stimulus differences, not head size, circumference, or shape (Gold and Barclay, 1973b).

   Similarly, if a task required that the wire mesh shown in Figure 7.7 be placed with the rounded center facing up, a color cue could be added to the rounded center (see Figure 7.7C). The added color cue would be placed on the rounded center (i.e., the stimulus characteristic to which the worker ultimately will need to attend).

   The addition of a color cue provides the opportunity for the worker to discriminate without attending to the relevant stimulus characteristics normally present. As the color is gradually removed, the worker appears to "search" for task characteristics other than color on which the discrimination can be made (Schusterman, 1967; Martin, 1969). The initial location or pattern of the color cue may affect this process.

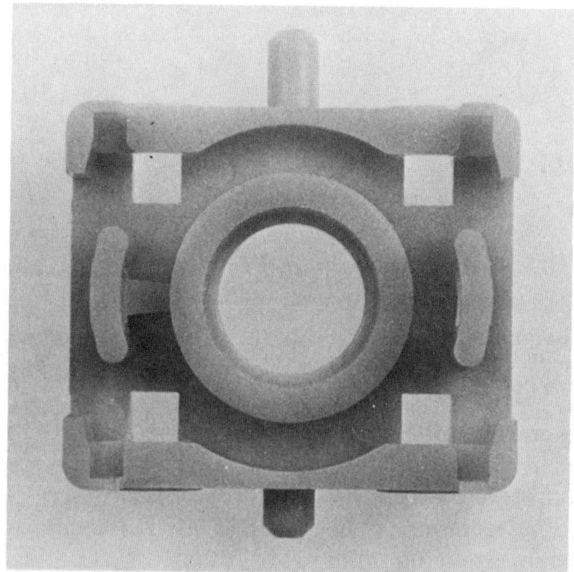

Figure 7.8. Bearing used in the assembly of cam switches.

For example, the bearing shown in Figure 7.8 that is used in assembling a 23-piece cam switch (Bellamy, Peterson, and Close, 1975) should be placed in the cam so the large post faces down. The worker needs to discriminate the slightly longer post from the shorter post when placing the bearing in the cam. One worker who learned this task experienced persistent difficulty learning that the long post faced in a particular direction. Massed trials with differential reinforcement did not improve performance, and the decision was made to add a redundant color cue.

The redundant color cue was added *on* the long post as this was the stimulus characteristic to which the worker eventually should attend. As shown in Figure 7.9 colored dots could have been placed in many different points on the bearing and still provide accurate information about how it should be positioned (i.e., find the dot and make it face in a certain direction). However, since the objective was to accentuate the stimulus dimension or characteristic to which the worker ultimately needed to attend, the only logical position for the redundant color cue was *on* the long post. This would suggest that Figure 7.9A would be a more effective option than 7.9B, 7.9C, or 7.9D. When the color cue is faded out the worker will have learned *where* on the part to look when positioning the bearing and should find that the length of the post provides necessary information.

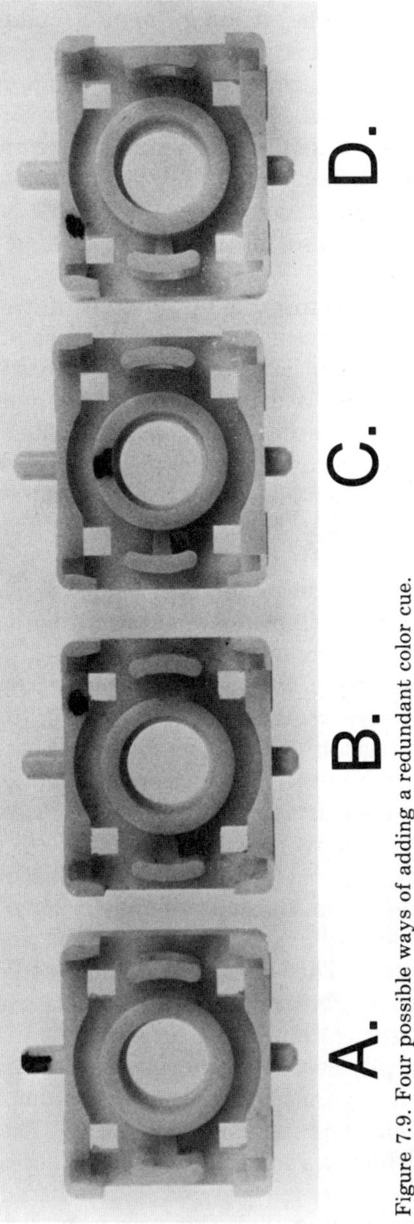

Figure 7.9. Four possible ways of adding a redundant color cue.

2. *Design stimulus feature changes so that relevant stimulus characteristics are substantially different from all other stimulus characteristics.* The trainer should manipulate stimulus characteristics as quickly as possible, as the worker's responses come under stimulus control of the relevant characteristics. By asking the worker to discriminate first between stimuli that differ in obvious, highly salient ways, errors can be minimized and training made more efficient. Bright red has often been a choice of color for adding redundant color cues. Similarly, very large cue differences should be used initially when exaggeration of stimulus features is done.

   The logic for making the initial steps of the easy-to-hard continuum *very* easy stems from results provided by Irvin and Bellamy (1977). When they compared the effectiveness of the three methods of stimulus feature change they found that the differences occurred in the initial (i.e., easiest) phase of training. After the initial phase there were no significant differences in the time required to fade color cues versus exaggerated cues versus color and exaggerated cues. This would suggest that to maximize the cost efficiency of difficult step training the worker should be trained as quickly as possible to attend to relevant stimulus characteristics, even if this means making dramatic changes in those characteristics to increase their salience.
3. *Fade the added stimulus features as soon as the worker responds reliably and correctly.* As noted in our earlier discussion of fading, the gradual reduction of any form of assistance is very difficult to operationalize. The objective is clear: the worker will perform accurately without assistance. The general process is also relatively clear: gradually remove the assistance. In practice, however, fading becomes much less clear. The trainer must be sensitive to day-by-day or trial-by-trial fluctuations in worker performance. Assistance will be reduced gradually or increased gradually, depending on this fluctuation. The worker should not be allowed to experience repeated failure or receive more help than necessary.

   Fading added stimulus features is not different, in theory, from fading a physical or verbal prompt. The stimulus features initially altered to gain stimulus control gradually are presented in closer approximations to their original form. Fading is done as fast as possible without a reduction in worker performance. Two general rules apply: 1) Do not provide so many trials at any one point in the fading continuum that the worker overlearns responding to that stimulus. Overlearning will impede the rate at which fading can occur. 2) Do not fade so fast that the worker's rate of accurate performance falls below 60%–75%. If a worker stops performing correctly, the task-relevant stimuli are no longer controlling responding. The trainer then should back up in the fading continuum and regain stimulus control.

4. *Use differential reinforcement for correct responding throughout.* As noted earlier, reinforcement contingent upon accurate performance is extremely important in all phases of difficult step training. When teaching minimal difference discriminations, reinforcers can function both to provide the worker with clear feedback that a response was correct, and to decrease the probability of negative or resistive behavior. While the importance of reinforcement delivery has been stressed in earlier chapters, it should be emphasized here that all the guidelines presented for teaching minimal difference discriminations assume that contingent reinforcement is being provided. Perhaps the single most important guideline for teaching difficult steps is to present the worker with reinforcers when s/he performs correctly and to deny him or her access to reinforcers when performance is incorrect.

Dichotomous Discriminations Along a Continuous Dimension

One type of minimal difference discrimination that has been repeatedly associated with step difficulty requires the worker to make a dichotomous discrimination along a continuous dimension. A continuous dimension refers to a continuum of stimulus instances. Length, for instance, is a continuum that ranges from infinitesimally short to infinitely long. A worker who is cutting wire to specific lengths must be able to respond correctly to stimuli that occur at any point along the continuum.

Frequently, vocational tasks require that a continuous dimension be divided into two categories (i.e., hot-cold, big-little, tight-loose). When performing the task the worker must determine when a stimulus fits one category, and when it fits another (i.e., less than 12 in versus greater than 12 in). This requires a dichotomous discrimination along the continuous relevant dimension of length.

"Smoothness," for instance, is a continuum that spans a wide range between very rough and very smooth objects. If a worker were asked to sand a piece of rough wood until it was smooth, s/he would progress along the rough-to-smooth continuum as sanding was done. At any point in time the wood would be smoother than it was before, but the worker would still have to determine if it were smooth enough to be considered "smooth." This choice, illustrated in Figure 7.10, involves determining where along the rough-to-smooth continuum the

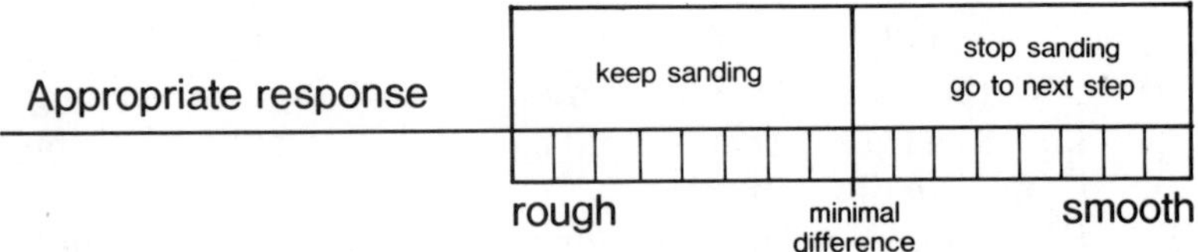

Figure 7.10. Response options along the dichotomized, continuous dimension: rough-smooth.

"rough" wood becomes "smooth" wood. A worker faced with such a task must make the minimal difference discrimination between "almost smooth" and "just barely smooth" and respond differentially to these two stimulus instances. When presented with stimuli that are rough to almost smooth, the correct response is to keep sanding. When presented with stimuli that are just barely smooth to smooth, the correct response is to stop sanding and go to the next step in the chain.

Dichotomous discriminations along a continuous dimension require the same type of two-step process as other discrimination steps. The worker must determine which dimension is relevant and, along the continuous relevant dimension, whether a stimulus instance fits in one category or the other. In the example above, the worker must first learn that "smoothness" is the relevant dimension, and then learn the boundary along this continuum that separates rough objects from smooth objects. The same two steps would be faced by a worker who was washing windows. The worker should ignore size, shape, and other dimensional properties of windows when s/he is deciding if the window is clean. The dimension "cleanliness" is the only relevant one. Along this dimension there can be virtually an infinite number of degrees of cleanliness. For the purpose of window washing, however, there are only two meaningful categories: clean and not clean. In the presence of a window that is not clean, the worker should exhibit washing behavior. In the presence of a clean window, the worker should go to the next window. Within the relevant dimension "cleanliness" the worker must determine if a particular stimulus instance (i.e., a window) fits one side or the other of the dichotomy (i.e., is it clean or not clean). This requires that s/he learn as accurately as possible the boundary that separates clean from not clean.

In teaching retarded adults to make dichotomous discriminations along continuous stimulus dimensions we have used the following sequencing guidelines:

1. *In the early phase of training teach the relevant dimension by using examples from the extreme ends of the continuum.* The logic behind this guideline is similar to that discussed for minimal difference discriminations. The trainer can reduce the difficulty of a

step by decreasing the similarity of the objectives that must be discriminated. If a worker is having difficulty responding appropriately to different instances along a continuum, the trainer should maximize the difference between instances. A worker who is exhibiting difficulty responding one way to clean windows and another way to not clean windows would be presented with windows that are either very clean or very dirty. The worker would not be asked to respond to almost clean or just barely clean windows.

When confronted with maximally different instances, the worker is more likely to begin responding differentially to clean versus not clean windows (i.e., to respond on the basis of "cleanliness"). The objective of restricting examples to instances that are maximally dissimilar is to teach the worker which dimension is relevant. The next training objective is to teach the worker where along the relevant continuum the two categories meet (i.e., where clean becomes not clean, where tight becomes loose, where long becomes short).

2. *Once a worker is responding to the relevant dimension, teach the critical boundary within that dimension by using positive and negative instances that more closely approximate the boundary.* When the worker is responding accurately to maximally different instances, add new instances that more closely approach the boundary point. For many tasks, such as window washing, the boundary should be defined arbitrarily by the trainer to ensure consistency of feedback to the worker. It is usually easier to teach the worker to respond differentially when given a specific boundary than when given a central range of stimuli to which either response is correct. Use instances on both sides of the boundary in teaching. The objective will be to teach the worker where along the continuum s/he should stop responding one way and begin responding in another. This process basically involves fading from easily discriminated instances to instances that are harder to tell apart. The fact that the worker is already attending to the relevant stimulus dimension should facilitate his or her learning the critical boundary. It generally will be important to provide repeated practice with difference instances that converge on the boundary.

   Assume that the discrimination has been learned when the worker responds correctly to stimulus instances on either side of the boundary. A worker who has mastered the step should be able to respond accurately to any instance along the continuum (dimension) being taught.

   Many steps that require a dichotomous discrimination along a continuous dimension involve initiating and continuing a response until the boundary level is reached. In tightening a screw with a screwdriver, a worker continues to tighten the screw as it gets tighter and tighter, until finally it is "tight," and s/he goes on to the next step of the task.

A step of this nature does not lend itself to selecting instances along the continuum for use in training. A trainer is more likely to teach the boundary by providing a verbal or physical cue when the boundary is reached. The verbal or physical cue then is faded rapidly. One of the most frequent training errors we have observed on such steps results from trainers providing too much assistance for too long. Assistance becomes highly predictable and actually hinders acquisition of the step. The worker learns that the relevant stimulus cue for when to stop turning the screwdriver, when to stop washing the window, when to stop sanding the wood, etc., comes from the trainer not the task. The worker will continue performing the response but will look at the trainer for information about when to stop. To avoid this dilemma, trainers should fade assistance cues as soon as possible and provide reinforcers only *after* the step is completed. A worker who receives praise for "getting ready" to stop or emitting an "is this right?" look will not be learning which *task-relevant* stimuli should control responding.

While our experience has stressed the importance of learning a dichotomous discrimination along a continuous dimension, a continuous dimension could easily be divided into more than two categories. When sanding wood, for instance, a worker may need to reach one boundary before changing the type of sandpaper being used, and then continue sanding until a second "smoothness" boundary is reached before stopping. When training multiple discriminations along the same dimension, the procedures described above would still apply, but each boundary would be taught individually.

Non-visual Discriminations

The majority of vocational tasks available to workshops contain steps where the worker visually identifies relevant stimuli. Steps that require differential responding as a function of size, shape, color, and position of parts typically provide visual cues to which the worker attends. An important characteristic of such steps is the equal availability of relevant stimuli to both the trainer and the worker. The trainer has as much information as the worker about which response should be performed next. As such, the trainer can provide immediate feedback to the worker on the accuracy of his or her responding.

Some steps, however, require the worker to respond differentially to non-visual cues. A worker tightening a bolt with a socket wrench must decide when to stop tightening on the basis of tactile cues (the amount of pressure required to turn the wrench). A worker holding a nut under, or inside, a product so it can receive a bolt may not be able to see the nut and would need to rely on non-visual cues to determine where the nut belongs. Steps such as these have frequently been difficult to train. This difficulty is partly due to the trainer's inability to give feedback as consistently as s/he can with steps cued by visible stimuli. Clearly, inconsistent feedback would make it more difficult for a worker to identify exactly what constitutes a correct response. When teaching such steps the trainer should use whatever means are available to monitor the worker's response.

1. *When relevant task stimuli are available to the worker but not to the trainer, maximize trainer information.* The trainer generally can increase his or her access to relevant cues in three ways. The first involves modifying the task design so that relevant information is available equally to both trainer and worker. This approach might be used with a worker tightening bolts with a socket wrench by introducing a torque socket wrench. A torque wrench provides a visual cue about just how many pounds of pressure are being exerted. This information would be available to both the worker and trainer in determining or defining the "tightness" of a bolt.

   A second approach involves the trainer attending to task cues that correlate with the relevant cue. The trainer may not be able to see when a screw is tight but s/he may be able to notice a slight buckling of the part when the screw is appropriately tight, or in some cases the number of turns on a wrench may be a useful way of determining when a bolt is snug. In either case the trainer attends to task cues that may require fine-grained discriminations, but that nevertheless provide enough information to facilitate accurate, consistent feedback to the worker about his or her performance.

   The third approach involves the trainer placing his or her hands over the worker's hands and using feedback based on the worker's muscle tension to glean information about response accuracy. This approach, like the others, is only useful with some tasks, but it is a quick, reliable index of worker performance. As with all trainer intervention, it would be important to remove trainer assistance and the visual and tactile presence of the trainer's hands as soon as possible.

Simultaneous Discriminations

Within the context of difficult discriminations we have discussed vocational steps that require workers to perform differentially to different levels within one stimulus dimension. It must be recognized, however, that many steps in vocational tasks will require a worker to discriminate on the basis of more than one relevant dimension. A worker may not need simply to find a stimulus with level *4* of dimension *a* ($S^{a:4}$), but find a stimulus with level *4* of dimension *a*, *and* level *2* of dimension *b* ($S^{a:4}_{b:2}$). Such a task requires the worker to attend to both dimension *a* and dimension *b* before responding. Even if a stimulus possessed the relevant level of dimension *a*, the worker could not correctly emit the target response unless it also possessed the relevant level of dimension *b*. The response would be controlled by the conjunctive presence of relevant levels of dimensions *a* and *b*.

The sorting of grocery store coupons is a good example of such a task. To sort coupons a worker might need to attend to the number on the coupon and the *name* of the product (see Figure 7.11). Sorting just on the basis of numbers or just on the basis of product names would not produce acceptable performance. The task becomes a difficult one precisely because the worker must attend *conjunctively* to two relevant dimensions of coupons.

Steps involving conjunctive stimulus control require that a worker discriminate along more than one dimension to identify the S^D for a particular response. These steps often are performed incorrectly because the worker only attends to one of the relevant stimulus dimensions. If a step required a worker to select a blue ring terminal from the selection of terminals shown in Figure 7.12, the response, picking up the terminal, should only occur in the presence of a stimulus that had both a *ring head* and a *blue base*. The two stimulus dimensions, color and shape, would be relevant and conjunctive. Only if positive levels (i.e., blue, ring) of these dimensions appear conjunctively should the worker emit the "pick up and place" response.

A worker having difficulty selecting the correct terminal may be attending to only one of the relevant dimensions. If shape were the only dimension being discriminated, the worker likely would select items with ring heads but with variously colored bases. If color were the dimension being discriminated, the worker likely would select blue terminals with variously shaped heads. If error patterns such as these occur, massed trials training should be conducted to teach the relevance of both stimulus dimensions. The following guidelines are suggested for teaching a difficult step that requires conjunctive stimulus control. These guidelines closely follow the direct instruction teaching strategies of Becker, Engelmann, and Thomas (1975).

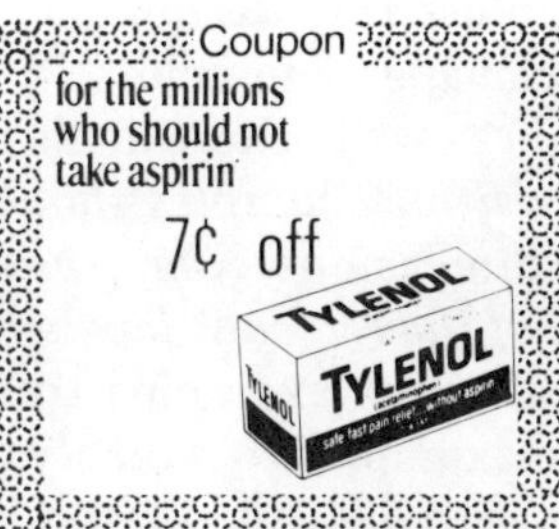

Figure 7.11. Store coupons that vary in value and product.

Figure 7.12. Wire terminals.

1. *Present the worker with examples that s/he should respond to and examples that s/he should not respond to.* Do not limit examples in massed trials training to stimuli that possess the positive levels of all the relevant dimensions. Training with only positive examples will not teach the worker how to respond differentially to positive examples and negative examples. To teach a worker to discriminate blue, ring terminals (i.e., $\substack{S^a:\ \text{shape}=\text{ring} \\ S^b:\ \text{color}=\text{blue}}$) from terminals with other shapes and colors it will be necessary to use blue, ring terminals as well as terminals of different shapes and different colors.
2. *All positive examples should possess the relevant levels of all relevant dimensions. Negative examples should possess either some or none of the relevant levels of the relevant dimensions.* In choosing the stimulus examples to be used during training, be sure that those examples to which you want the worker to respond have all the positive levels of all relevant dimensions.
3. *Vary irrelevant dimensions of positive examples.* Teach the worker which dimensions are relevant by presenting examples with positive levels of relevant dimensions and varying the irrelevant dimensions. To teach selection of blue, ring terminals the worker would "pick up and place" blue, ring terminals that appear in different orientations and appear alone or in groups (see Figure 7.13). The levels of relevant dimensions shape and color remain constant as the levels of irrelevant dimensions vary.

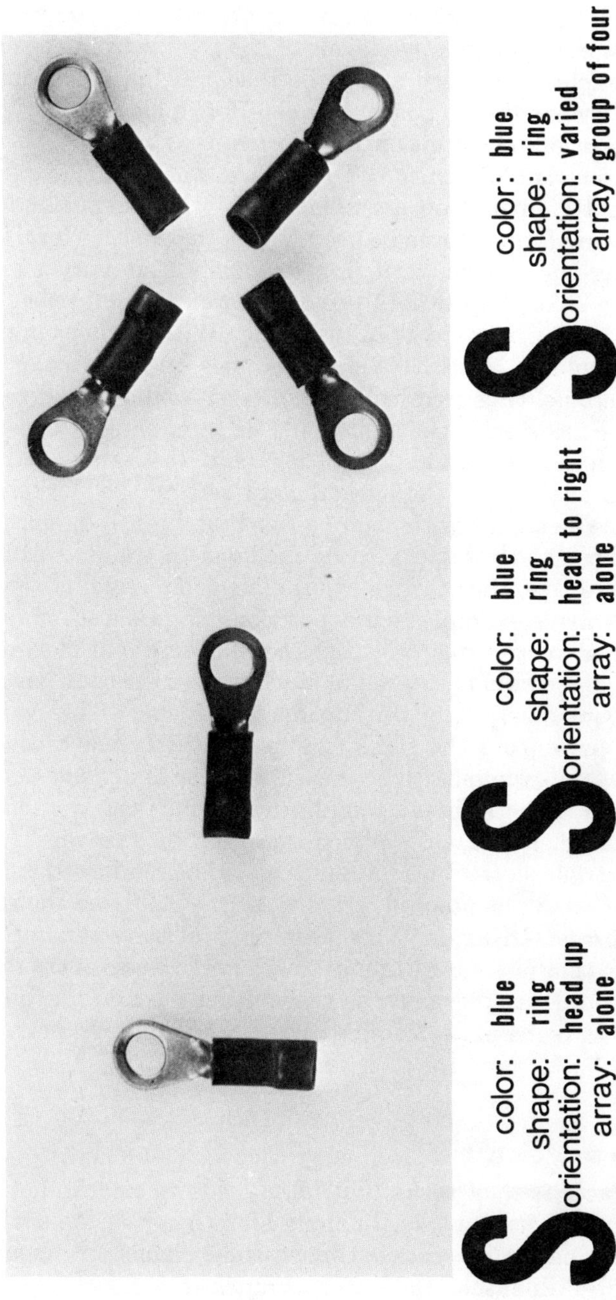

Figure 7.13. Examples of ways in which the irrelevant stimulus dimensions (positions and array) can vary while the relevant dimensions (shape and color) remain constant.

4. *Teach the positive levels of relevant dimensions one at a time by presenting examples that vary along the relevant dimension.* To teach a worker the positive levels of the relevant dimension, present examples that vary along the relevant dimension and only reinforce responding to positive levels. Hold all levels of other relevant dimensions constant until performance is accurate, then vary another relevant dimension. To teach a worker to discriminate blue, ring terminals from terminals with other shapes and colors the following format could be used. Teach the positive level "blue" presenting the worker with ring terminals that vary along the dimension color. Figure 7.14 provides three examples that might be used during massed trials training. With each example the worker would be asked, "Which one goes on the wire?" If s/he chose the blue, ring terminals a reinforcer would be delivered. If s/he chose incorrectly the trial would be terminated, the response either ignored or followed by "no," and the same instruction presented again. If in the normal work setting the worker would experience terminals with colors other than blue, red, and yellow, these other colors would also be included in training examples. Note that shape, the other relevant dimension, remains constant in all the above examples while position and orientation varies.

   Once a worker was selecting the blue terminal consistently, the examples would be altered to teach the worker that "ring" was the relevant level along the dimension "shape." This would be done by presenting the same examples used to teach color, but adding other examples that vary along the dimension "shape." Figure 7.15 depicts three examples with which the worker might be presented, and asks, "Which one goes on the wire?" As in previous trials, correct performance would be reinforced, incorrect responses would be ignored or followed by, "no," and the trial examples presented again. Note that on trial three, examples are presented that possess neither of the relevant levels of the relevant dimensions. Examples such as these usually would not be added until the worker was performing correctly to examples in trials one and two.

If-Then Rules

A final characteristic of tasks that often leads to discrimination difficulty is the need for a worker to apply an if-then rule. As outlined in our earlier discussion of operant chains, some chains are linear while others branch (Millenson, 1967). Any branch in a chain requires the worker to discriminate which branch to follow. If a chain branches

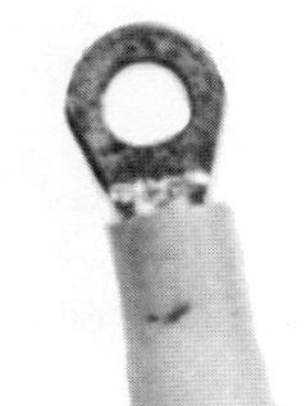

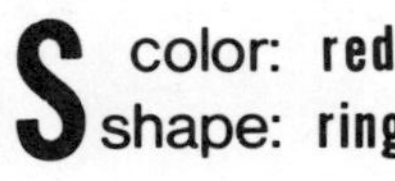
S color: blue
shape: ring
S color: red
shape: ring
S color: yellow
shape: ring
Trial 1

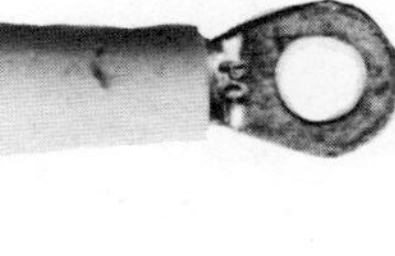

S color: red
shape: ring
S color: yellow
shape: ring
S color: blue
shape: ring
Trial 2

Figure 7.14. Three trials used in teaching the positive level (blue) of the relevant dimension (color).

Trial 1

S color: blue
shape: ring

S color: blue
shape: curl

S color: blue
shape: U

Figure 7-15 continues next page

S color: blue
shape: curl

S color: yellow
shape: ring

S color: blue
shape: U

S color: red
shape: ring

S color: blue
shape: ring

Trial 3

S color: blue shape: square
S color: red shape: ring
S color: blue shape: ring
S color: blue shape: curl
S color: red shape: U
S color: yellow shape: ring
S color: yellow shape: U

Figure 7.15. Three teaching trials used in teaching the positive level (ring) of the relevant dimension (shape).

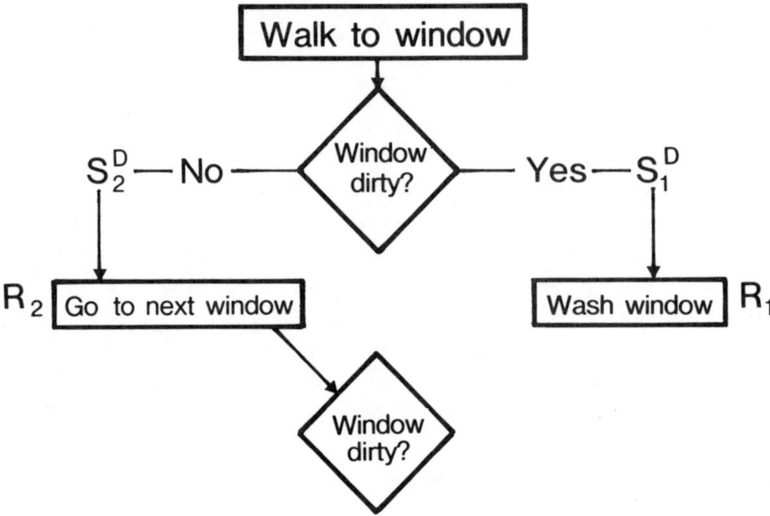

Figure 7.16. A branching chain for window washing.

there will always be a unique S^D associated with each branch. When approaching the branch, the worker must apply the rule: If S_1^D then R_1, if S_2^D then R_2. For instance the operant chain may involve walking up to a window, washing it if it is dirty, or walking to the next window if it is clean. The branch in this chain is depicted in Figure 7.16.

1. *Bring each of the branching responses under appropriate stimulus control.* Using a massed trials format present the S_1^D for one branching response. Prompt correct performance (if necessary), and fade all prompts until the worker performs accurately. Once performance is accurate and stable, begin introducing the S_2^D for another branching response. Use prompts if necessary to ensure correct responding. Continue this approach until the worker is being presented with the S^Ds for all possible branching options. At this point in training all options should occur with equal frequency. That is, S_1^D and S_2^D in a two-choice branch should each be presented 50% of the time during massed trials training. The order of presentation should approximate a random pattern. Take care not to alternate options systematically since this could enable the worker to respond correctly without attending to the task-provided cues.
2. *Once the worker is performing accurately to all S^D options at a step in the chain where branching occurs, vary the probability of those response options to approximate those found naturally in the task.* Many vocational tasks require use of if-then rules, but the S^D

for one option occurs much more frequently than the other. For example, in many assembly tasks workers periodically must reject defective components. That is, at a given step in the task a worker must respond in one way to a defective part (put it aside and reach for a replacement) and in another way to a satisfactory part (attach it to the assembly). Such defective parts are encountered infrequently in normal assembly work. It is important in training, therefore, to ensure that correct differential responding occurs and maintains when one option is encountered more often than the other. Procedurally, this involves gradually reducing the frequency of presentation of the less likely alternative until the natural frequency of occurrence is reached. If incorrect responding is noted at any time during this gradual change, the frequency of the two options should be made more similar until reliable, differential responding is again achieved.

SUMMARY

Difficult steps are steps of a task that consistently are performed poorly during Step Training. In teaching difficult steps it is useful to alter the Step Training format to: 1) provide massed trials in the difficult step, 2) manipulate the demands of the task to ensure worker success, 3) increase the level of reinforcement for correct responding, 4) train during shorter time blocks, and 5) systematically incorporate the step back into the operant chain.

It is useful to distinguish between steps that are difficult because of step size, those that are difficult because of required manipulations, and those that are difficult because of required discriminations. Step size often results in difficulty because the functional response unit identified in the task analysis may contain too much behavior for the worker. For these longer steps it is useful to develop a written task analysis branch that identifies several smaller sub-steps. These substeps then can be taught individually. Manipulations, or the motor movements involved in a step, are usually difficult either because of precision demands or because of simultaneous response components. In either case, physical guidance is used to construct an easy-to-hard continuum in which the worker is gradually expected to perform more of the manipulation without assistance. In the case of simultaneous response components this continuum involves complete priming through one component until the other is learned, and then gradual removal of the priming assistance.

Several discrimination variables affect step difficulty. Discriminations essentially involve differential responding to different stimuli.

The two-step model of Zeaman and House (1963) provides a useful structure for teaching procedures. They suggest that an individual first learns which stimulus dimensions are relevant and then learns which levels of relevant dimensions are positive and negative. This model provides the basis for establishing easy-to-hard continua for teaching difficult discriminations.

For discriminations that are difficult because of minimal differences between positive and negative instances, easy-to-hard continua can be established by three stimulus-feature changes, adding and then gradually removing color cues, accentuating and then gradually reducing relevant stimuli, or a combination of the first two strategies. In each case stimulus feature changes should accentuate the stimulus dimension that is relevant to task performance; the stimulus feature change should result in substantial differences between positive and negative instances; and the changes should be removed as rapidly as possible during massed trials training.

Discriminations that are difficult because they require a dichotomous discrimination along a continuous dimension can be taught with similar training procedures. Differential responding is taught first to maximally different stimulus instances, and then these differences are reduced gradually. The critical boundary between the two stimulus classes then is taught by presenting positive and negative instances that differ only slightly.

Non-visual discriminations are often difficult to teach because the trainer does not have access to critical information about the task. For these steps the trainer should devise techniques to increase his or her knowledge of task changes by noting subtle changes in the task or worker's movements that signal that the worker is performing either correctly or incorrectly.

Simultaneous discriminations are often difficult to learn because they require that the worker's behavior come under stimulus control of more than one stimulus. To develop correct responding, the trainer should present the worker with positive and negative stimulus instances. Teaching correct responding involves gradually changing the variety of the incorrect instances and increasing their similarity to correct ones.

Discriminations that are difficult because if-then rules are involved can be taught by differentially reinforcing correct responding to each of the alternative S^Ds. Typically, this process is more efficient when both S^Ds are presented at equal frequency until differential responding is developed, and then the relative frequence of the natural level is changed.

chapter 8
CHAIN TRAINING: Establishing Stimulus Control Over Larger Response Units

Training procedures discussed in this chapter will be useful for those steps that the trainer predicts will be performed correctly on most occasions. Although no practical empirical basis is available for deciding exactly what "most occasions" means, we suggest that the Chain Training strategy be used with those steps that the trainer predicts will be performed accurately on about 80% of the opportunities. Since the assistance and fading procedures described in Chapters 6 and 7 usually are needed only for exceptionally difficult steps and severely handicapped workers, much vocational training in rehabilitation facilities will involve use of the procedures described in this chapter.

Chain Training procedures are designed to establish the task-provided stimuli as S^Ds and conditioned reinforcers for progressively longer units of work behavior. As was indicated in Chapter 4, step size in the task analysis is largely arbitrary. In fact, steps often are defined as distinct units for the trainee only by the consistent timing of the trainer's assistance and reinforcement. In Chain Training, the trainer's activities should define progressively longer responses as units by providing reinforcement and assistance less often.

Chain Training continues for any group of steps, or for the entire task, until the trainer predicts that the worker will perform accurately on all future opportunities in the training setting. Such a prediction should be made on the basis of the worker's performance on the task. This involves setting a criterion of accuracy that suggests to the trainer that future responses will be correct in the training setting and continuing Chain Training procedures until this criterion is met. In currently available research and demonstration projects, training criteria usually are set arbitrarily. In general, rather stringent criteria have been used, such as Gold's (1972) requirement that subjects complete an entire assembly correctly on six out of eight consecutive trials before it can be assumed that the task has been learned.

We recommend such a difficult criterion of accuracy for Chain Training. The specific number of consecutive correct responses required or the number of correct probes expected will vary, depending on the length of the task. For shorter tasks, more correct responses should be required, and these should be distributed across more than one training session. Whatever criterion of accuracy the trainer chooses to use to predict future response accuracy, when that criterion is met, Chain Training procedures should be replaced by the Setting Training strategy discussed in Chapter 9. A difficult criterion for Chain Training facilitates Setting Training in several ways. First, the purpose of Setting Training is to develop discriminations and responses that facilitate reliable performance of the behavior chain required by the task in the natural work environment. Evidence that the worker discriminates when work is and is not appropriate in the natural environment is provided primarily by his or her performance of the work task at appropriate times. Reliable accuracy in performance is critical to Setting Training, since task errors could preclude reinforcement for correct setting-related discriminations. A second benefit of a difficult criterion for Chain Training is the overlearning that usually results. Overlearning refers to exposure to training trials after a task has been learned; it is associated with superior retention of many tasks by retarded learners (Belmont, 1966). Finally, such a criterion reduces the possibility of errors later in production. In most workshops, there is a distinct possibility that errors will be reinforced inadvertently either by supervisor attention or by the opportunity to continue through the chain. It is thus quite important to reduce the probability that such errors will occur.

OVERVIEW OF CHAIN TRAINING

As with other training strategies, the skills of assistance, reinforcement, and assessment are all important in Chain Training. Assistance skills are used in correction procedures, when a worker has completed a step incorrectly. Assistance is seldom given prior to a worker's response on a step. Reinforcement skills are required to increase gradually the amount of behavior required to obtain reinforcement and to decrease reinforcement magnitude. Reinforcement is delivered for progressively longer units of behavior and for independent imitation but seldom for simply attending to the task. Assessment skills in Chain

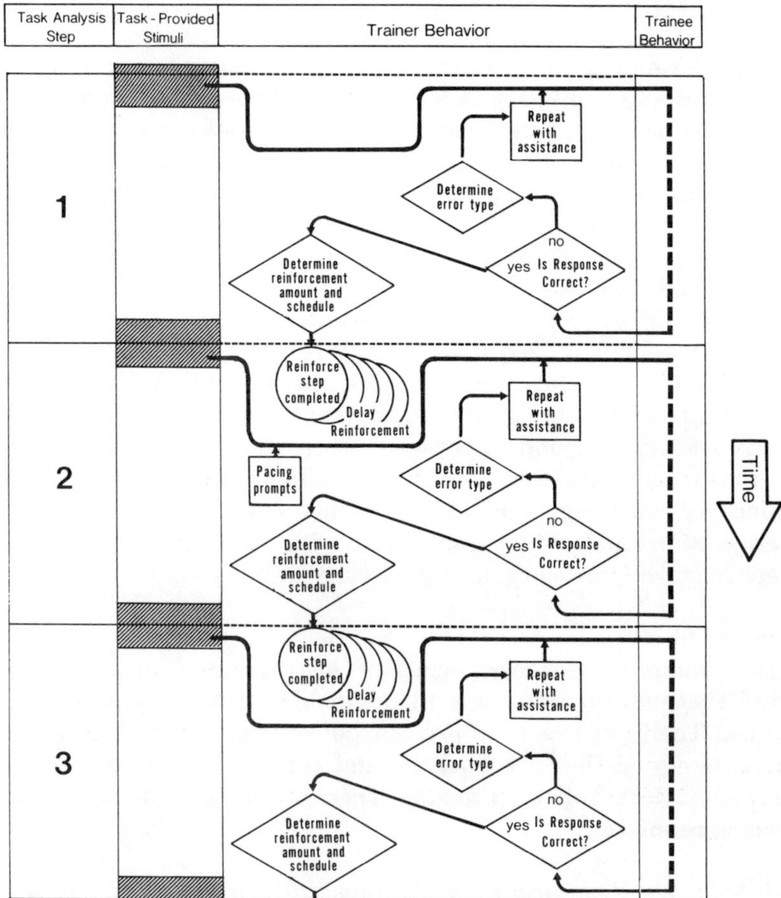

Figure 8.1. A schema of the interaction between the worker, task, and trainer during Chain Training.

Training involve continuous monitoring of the worker's on-task behavior and response accuracy in order to facilitate training decisions related to the effectiveness of fading procedures, as both assistance during corrections and reinforcement level are reduced.

The training interaction in Chain Training is illustrated in Figure 8.1. The worker is expected to respond to the task-provided cues for each step without trainer assistance beyond periodic pacing prompts. The trainer notes the accuracy of each response and acts accordingly. If it is correct, the trainer determines how and when to reinforce the response, and allows the worker to continue through the chain. If the response is incorrect, a correction procedure is used in which the worker repeats the step with some additional assistance.

ASSISTANCE TECHNIQUES

In Chain Training, the trainer provides no assistance prior to the worker's response on a step except for occasional pacing prompts. All other antecedent assistance should have been faded out in Step Training as soon as the worker began some independent responding on a step, or simply should not have been provided at all if the worker entered training with the ability to complete a step correctly on 80% of the opportunities to perform it.

Unintended antecedent assistance often can create difficulties in Chain Training. The trainer should exercise extreme care to avoid allowing any particular expression, posture, hand movement, or other cue to become correlated with a task-provided S^D. Without being aware of it trainers often give such unplanned assistance. Workers frequently learn to respond to these consistent trainers' actions rather than the task. (For an example of this possibility, the reader is referred to Rincover and Koegel, 1975.) When this occurs, difficulty usually is experienced in maintaining response accuracy as the trainer attempts to fade his or her presence during Setting Training.

Pacing Prompts

Pacing prompts are general cues or instructions, such as "Keep going," that indicate that the worker should continue interacting with the task. Their purpose is to prevent pausing and off-task behaviors between steps in the task analysis and thus to ensure smooth continuation of work from step to step. There are three guidelines for use of pacing prompts.

1. *Provide pacing prompts only for those steps on which pauses seem very likely.* Like all assistance procedures, pacing prompts should be used only when the trainer predicts they are needed. Too many prompts, like too much of any kind of assistance, prevents efficient learning by building dependency on the trainer. Pacing prompts should be used for a step when the worker has a high frequency of off-task responses on other steps during this training trial or on this step during earlier training trials. Procedurally, giving a pacing prompt can involve a verbal direction like, "Keep working," a touch on the worker's elbow, or a gesture of the trainer's hand toward the task. The purpose of each is to prevent the worker from pausing before initiating the next step in the chain.
2. *Deliver a pacing prompt just as the worker correctly finishes a step.* It will be useful to assume that pacing prompts, like most other contact from the trainer, often will function as a reinforcer

for whatever behavior the worker exhibits just prior to the contact. Therefore, the importance of delivering pacing prompts just as the worker accurately completes a step should be clear: any delay creates the possibility that pauses, glances at the trainer, or some other inappropriate behavior will be reinforced by the prompt. If the worker does pause before a pacing prompt can be delivered, do not provide the prompt. Rather, wait for the worker to attend to the task, and note that pacing prompts may be useful on that particular step on future training trials.

3. *Use pacing prompts in concert with reinforcement for independent initiation on a step.* Use of a pacing prompt essentially means that the trainer predicted that a pause would occur if the worker were left to work independently. It is important to check this prediction regularly, i.e., to refrain frequently from providing prompts even when pauses are likely. If the worker continues without pausing, reinforcement for independent initiation can be provided, and pacing prompts gradually removed. In general it will be more efficient to reinforce independent initiation, if it occurs, than to prompt continued performance. Therefore, prompts should be replaced by reinforcement for independent initiation as rapidly as possible. As was discussed in the Step Training procedures, reinforcement for independent initiation can also be faded rapidly if the worker is receiving adequate reinforcement for accurate step completion. If very many pacing prompts appear to be needed, the trainer should re-evaluate the reinforcement provided for step completion.

Correction Procedures

As in Step Training, each incorrect response is followed immediately by a correction procedure, in which the worker repeats the step one or two times with some assistance. Corrections play a significant role in Chain Training, since some variability in accuracy is observed as workers develop proficiency on various steps of a task. As was described in procedures for Step Training, correction procedures serve several useful purposes in training, including allowing the worker to practice the correct response and preventing the error response from being reinforced by the opportunity to progress through the chain.

1. *To implement a correction procedure in Chain Training, interrupt the worker as soon as the error occurs, back up at least one step in the task, and provide minimal assistance as the worker repeats the step.* Since the Chain Training strategy is designed for steps that the worker has already performed correctly on several occasions, very little assistance usually is needed beyond the step repetition

itself, which indicates that the response was incorrect. For example, the non-specific verbal directions, "Try again" or "Try another way" (Gold, 1972), usually provide sufficient assistance. Similarly, gestures toward the task or any other consistent signal, such as a touch on the arm, can be an effective correction procedure in Chain Training.

Because the correct response usually follows such minimal assistance in a Chain Training correction, procedures for fading assistance at times can be problematic. That is, when a correct response always follows a correction, but the error persists nevertheless in subsequent trials, the trainer should attempt to minimize the amount of assistance provided during corrections. One useful technique is to interrupt the worker after an error is made and then back up more than one step in the task. This requires the worker to repeat one or two steps preceding the one that was missed, thus increasing the delay between the trainer's intervention and the repetition of the behavior. Of course, the technique is useful only if the preceding steps are performed correctly. Another useful correction technique is to repeat the missed step a second time with no assistance, so that independent performance can be reinforced by the trainer or by the opportunity to continue through the task.

2. *Be aware that correction procedures often may function as reinforcers.* In Chain Training, the attention and reinforcement that the worker receives from a trainer are reduced from that provided in Step Training. The frequency of social interactions is also considerably below normal expectations when two individuals are engaged together in such proximity. Since performing an error response is a reliable method of obtaining trainer attention via a correction procedure, the possibility that these corrections will reinforce the error response should be evaluated continuously. Persistent error patterns, despite careful fading of assistance during corrections, may signal such a situation.

   To guard against this possibility, ensure that the alternate correct response results in more reinforcement for the worker. This has direct implications for fading or reinforcement, which is discussed in the next section: reinforcement for performance on a step should not be reduced until the step is performed correctly and reliably. When correction procedures are necessary on a step, ensure that more reinforcement is provided on subsequent trials for independent performance on that step. It is seldom helpful to make the correction procedure punitive in an attempt to avoid possible reinforcement of errors.

REINFORCEMENT TECHNIQUES

As in Step Training, reinforcement is used in Chain Training to increase the probability that correct responses will be repeated on subsequent trials and to attempt to increase the reinforcement value of changes in the task stimuli as work proceeds. There are several guidelines for using reinforcement in Chain Training:

1. *As the worker develops proficiency on a step, reduce the magnitude of reinforcement for the step and increase the criterion for reinforcement (in terms of the number of steps required).* Reinforcement magnitude should be reduced in two ways. First, the amount of whatever event is used as a reinforcer simply should be decreased, and second, the reinforcer pairing described in Step Training should be eliminated.

   One of the most important concepts in Chain Training relates to reinforcement: once a step can be performed consistently and accurately, the opportunity to perform that step often functions as an effective reinforcer for immediately preceding behaviors. This allows the trainer to increase the amount of work behavior required for each reinforcer, since some responses can be reinforced simply by the opportunity to perform the next (reliably correct and reinforced) response. As the trainee develops proficiency on a group of steps, therefore, the trainer can provide reinforcement for larger and larger units of behavior. When the criterion for reinforcement is increased in this way, it may be helpful initially to provide a pacing prompt instead of the omitted reinforcer for one or two trials.

   There are no clearly established rules for when and how to raise the criterion for reinforcement. The effect that a procedure has on a worker's behavior is the best index of any procedure's appropriateness. If a step has been performed correctly in the past and errors begin to occur as reinforcement is faded, it is likely that the reinforcement magnitude or the performance criterion has been changed too quickly. Conversely, the effects of fading too slowly are excessive worker dependency on the trainer. If the worker's behavior is reinforced only by trainer-provided stimuli, then it is unlikely that work will be performed in the trainer's absence. The worker should learn that reinforcement is associated more strongly with task-related stimuli than with trainer-related stimuli.
2. *In general, do not reinforce the behavior of simply attending to the task.* If the worker displays persistent off-task behaviors on steps

that frequently are performed correctly, assume that there is insufficient reinforcement for task completion. Try to preclude off-task behaviors by using pacing prompts and reinforcing independent initiation. Frequent off-task behavior in Chain Training should lead the trainer to question the effectiveness of presumed reinforcers.

3. *Provide reinforcement at different points in the assembly sequence on each trial.* Reinforcement each time a particular step is completed, which can be critically important in acquisition of individual steps, can be debilitating after the worker begins to perform the step correctly. Our experience suggests that regular delivery of reinforcers can create persistent pauses in operant chains. In Chain Training, therefore, it is important to avoid delivery of reinforcement after the same step on each trial, except when performance on that step is often inaccurate. In fact, it is helpful to provide reinforcement at various points in the assembly sequence not just at the end of steps defined in the task analysis. This assists the trainer gradually to delay reinforcement delivery, so that more and more correct behavior is exhibited prior to the reinforcer.
4. *Consistently provide reinforcement at the end of the entire response chain.* The opportunity to perform each subsequent step in the task analysis will effectively reinforce the worker's behavior only if the series of behaviors ultimately produces reinforcing events. Useful reinforcers in our training have been the opportunity to consume edibles earned during the training trial or to exchange tokens earned. A brief walk with the trainer has also been effectively used. This has the added advantage of removing the worker from the work station while social and consumatory behaviors are exhibited, so that the work setting continues to set the occasion only for work behaviors.

ASSESSMENT TECHNIQUES

Important trainer decisions during Chain Training relate to how and when to correct or reinforce the worker's performance. Assessment procedures are designed to provide information relevant to these decisions.

1. *Continuously monitor performance accuracy on each step of the task.* Although a step may have been performed correctly on many previous occasions, and although reinforcement for completing that step may have been faded, it is still important for the trainer

to monitor closely the accuracy of the response. Without this continuous observation, errors often occur that are reinforced by the opportunity to continue working. Implementing correction procedures in Chain Training requires continuous monitoring of the accuracy of all worker responses.

2. *Use the task analysis data sheet to maintain a record of performance during training.* Trainers should use the data sheet to record the accuracy of each response during periodic probes. The resulting record of correct and incorrect responses provides an indication of change over time in pattern of responding. The data sheet may also provide a basis for defining the criterion for moving from Chain Training to Setting Training procedures on a group of steps, if performance on probe trials provide the basis for the trainer's prediction about future response accuracy.
3. *Monitor carefully the on-task behavior and work rates of the trainee on various task steps.* Although the task analysis data sheet is used to record information only on step accuracy and time required to complete the total task, more detailed information is available to the trainer and can be helpful in evaluating reinforcement fading procedures. Specifically, the repeated occurrence of off-task behaviors at a given step, or performance of a step more slowly than usual can signal that reinforcement for step completion is inadequate, even though performance on the step has remained accurate. When this occurs, the trainer usually will return to an earlier (greater) reinforcement level.

SUMMARY

Chain Training procedures should be used after the learner can perform a step or group of steps accurately on 80% of the occasions, and should continue until the trainer predicts that future performance in the training setting consistently will be correct. The purpose of Chain Training is to establish the task-provided stimuli as S^Ds and conditioned reinforcers for progressively longer units of behavior by gradually removing trainer intervention.

Assistance techniques in Chain Training are used to correct errors and to provide pacing prompts. The direct assistance on each step that is provided in Step Training is not used. Pacing prompts are cues or instructions designed to prevent pausing. They should be provided only for those steps where pausing is highly likely, should always be delivered when the worker is working appropriately, and should be replaced quickly with reinforcers for independent initiation of the step. Correction procedures are similar to those used in Step Training. The worker is interrupted as soon as an error is made, the task returned to the S^D for the incorrect step, and some assistance is given so that the worker will respond correctly. In Chain Training it is important to recognize that corrections can also function as reinforcers for the error response.

The principal goal of reinforcement techniques in Chain Training is to maintain accurate responding while the amount of reinforcement is gradually reduced. The amount of behavior required before reinforcement delivery should be increased and the magnitude of reinforcement should be decreased. Reinforcement for attending to task should be eliminated, reinforcers should be delivered at different points in the chain on different trials, and reinforcement should consistently follow completion of the entire chain.

Assessment techniques in Chain Training are designed to facilitate trainer decisions about how to fade reinforcement and reduce assistance during corrections. The trainer should monitor the accuracy of each response, should maintain a record of responding, and should monitor other aspects of the worker's performance, such as off-task behavior or changes in the rate at which specific steps are performed.

chapter 9
SETTING TRAINING: Generalization of Stimulus Control to The Natural Work Setting

A worker who has learned both how to perform specific vocational responses (cf. Step Training) and the stimulus-response relationships that make those responses a vocational chain (cf. Chain Training) will have learned a viable vocational skill only if this chain can be performed independently in the natural work setting. The purpose of procedures presented in this chapter is to maximize the chance that skills learned during Step Training and Chain Training will be performed in the worker's normal production setting at the appropriate times without trainer intervention. The focus of the chapter is on the broad spectrum of stimuli present in the training and production settings. Setting Training involves assessing the possible impact of these stimuli on work behavior and modifying the training environment to minimize debilitating effects in production.

Setting Training procedures are appropriate for any group of steps when the trainer predicts that accuracy will be reliable, as evidenced by the worker's attainment of a defined training criterion. At this point effective training will involve analysis of those variables affecting transfer of control from the training setting to the production setting. The need for the systematic strategy that we have labeled Setting Training is apparent in the all too common reports of individuals who work well only when a particular supervisor is present, those who are able to perform skills efficiently in a workshop setting but do not perform the same tasks in competitive job placements, and workers who perform well while receiving individual attention from a trainer but do little or nothing in a group production setting.

If the skills a worker has learned in training are to be applied optimally in production, care must be given to both antecedent variables and consequence variables in the training setting. In each case the objective will be to bring appropriate responding under control of work-related stimuli in the natural production setting. With respect to antecedent variables this will necessitate focusing not only on stimuli provided by the task but also on those setting stimuli (such as other workers, supervisor presence, noise level) that will be present when the worker is in production. With respect to consequences this will necessitate focusing on the kind, type, and schedule of reinforcement naturally available in the production setting.

The objectives of Setting Training procedures are to 1) ensure that those stimuli that control correct responding during training are also present in production, 2) minimize the control that irrelevant stimuli (i.e., a specific supervisor, a specific corner of the training room) exert over work and work-related behavior, and 3) ensure that the consequences available in the production setting will be sufficient to maintain high, accurate rates of performance. The first two of these objectives focus on stimuli occurring as antecedents of work responses, the third focuses on stimuli that occur as consequences of responding.

ANTECEDENTS OF WORK

Analysis of task antecedents involves observation of both the training and production settings. In the training setting, those stimuli serving as S^Ds for work behavior should be identified. In the production setting, two sources of information are important: 1) whether or not the relevant stimuli in the training setting are also available in the production setting, and 2) whether or not stimuli that only occur in the production setting control off-task behaviors. It is our belief that careful analysis of antecedent stimuli in the training and production settings is important in programming for transfer of skills from one setting to another. As will be detailed below, we view such transfer as directly related to stimulus control variables.

The Training Setting

A worker who is performing accurately in the training setting has "learned" the task at hand. The requisite response topographies are under stimulus control. Those stimuli whose presence affects the probability of correct responding are *relevant* to work completion. Those stimuli that can vary substantially without affecting worker performance are *irrelevant*. The procedures discussed in Step Training and Chain Training are designed to ensure that stimuli provided by the task become relevant to work performance, that is, affect the probability that specific behaviors will be performed. Frequently, however, workers learn in addition that stimuli that should be irrelevant, such as the presence of a specific trainer, time of day, presence of peers, or position in the room, are relevant. That is, a change in these stimuli affects work accuracy or rate. It is important to recognize that the stimuli defined by a trainer as relevant may only be a subset of the stimuli the worker is treating as relevant. Analysis of antecedents in the training setting focuses specifically on the stimuli the worker is treating as relevant and irrelevant.

Central to this analysis is recognition that the onset of a chain or the performance of a particular step in the chain can be under control of more than one stimulus. In natural environments, the behavior of human beings is seldom under the control of a single stimulus. More likely, several stimuli must be present before a response will be performed. In previous chapters we have described responses as being controlled by specific stimuli (i.e., the response, "picking up the screwdriver" was controlled by the stimulus, "a screw in a threaded hole"). In a static training setting this may be true. When the screw is in a hole where the worker picks up the screwdriver, and when it is not the worker does not pick up the screwdriver. If those same task parts were presented in a different setting, however, the response might not occur. This suggests that the simple stimulus-response relationships we have been discussing so far are limited in the breadth with which they describe the worker's behavior.

This limitation rests in the model of a single stimulus controlling a single response. In the above example a worker may have learned that "reaching for the screwdriver" should occur only when a screw is in a threaded hole, a particular trainer is present, and work is being done at a particular work station. To oversimplify this relationship we might hypothesize that the response was controlled 70% by the presence of the screw in the hole, 20% by the presence of a particular trainer, and 10% by being at a particular work station. Variation in any of these stimuli would affect the probability of the response. The degree of the effect would depend on both the degree of variation and the degree of control exerted by that stimulus. Each of these three stimuli, however, would be relevant for correct performance of the response.

In analyzing the training setting to identify relevant and irrelevant antecedent events, consider both physical and social stimuli. Aspects of the physical surroundings include general location, availability of supplies, noise and lighting conditions, etc. Some physical stimuli do provide relevant information, signaling whether or when tasks should be performed. For example, in jobs requiring the performance of multiple tasks, such as the food service positions described by Sowers, Thompson, and Connis (1978), relevant stimulus dimensions usually cue the worker about *which* chain is appropriate (e.g., bussing tables, stacking dishes, or sweeping). Other physical stimuli, however, do not provide relevant information. The same dichotomy is true with social stimuli. The presence, proximity, or behavior of supervisors and counselors usually should not provide relevant information in routine assembly tasks, but in many jobs social stimuli are quite important. For example, the customer's asking him to wash the windshield is relevant to a service station employee regardless of the physical condition of the glass. Analysis of which of these stimuli are being treated as relevant by the worker will involve identifying those stimuli that, when modified or removed, result in change in work behaviors.

The Production Setting

Once a trainer has defined those training stimuli that the worker is treating as relevant to work performance, analysis of whether these stimuli are also present in the production setting should be made. If the stimuli that control responding in the training setting are not present in the production setting, some decrement in worker responding should be expected. We cannot assume that just because a behavior occurs in one setting it will occur in another (Stokes and Baer, 1977). A behavior will transfer from one setting to another if stimuli controlling that behavior are present in both settings.

Production setting stimuli usually are different from training setting stimuli. Even if the same physical location is used for both training and production, trainer presence and attention during training will add many stimuli not available during production. Training often is done, however, in a physical location apart from the production setting. In these situations it is important to determine which stimuli in the production setting are not present in the training setting (i.e., noise level, presence of co-workers, several supervisors). It is possible that even if all the relevant training stimuli are provided in production, the worker will be unproductive because of the presence of novel stimuli that serve as S^Ds for off-task behavior (i.e., gazing, talking, watching a supervisor). To avoid this problem the last few trials of training actually should be conducted in the production setting. This is done to increase the probability that the worker will learn to treat novel production setting stimuli as irrelevant.

A final factor defining production setting antecedents is an analysis of the range of variability in irrelevant stimuli present during production. For example, if noise level should not affect performance, noise level variation should be noted, so that the worker can be taught to perform the task at any noise level that might occur. Similarly, if the presence of any specific supervisor should not affect task performance, it will be useful to note how many different supervisors may be assigned responsibility for the worker, and how much variation exists in the presence and absence of each during the work day. In each case, documenting the range within which irrelevant stimuli vary involves specifying the extent of the changes that might occur in the physical or social working environment that should not affect performance.

CONSEQUENCES OF WORK

Analysis of work consequences means observation of those stimuli that occur as a result of, or contingent upon, worker behaviors. The consequences for worker behaviors are generally the reinforcers a worker receives for work completion. Additional stimuli, such as social praise for being on-task, attention from co-workers for screaming, or eating food stolen from another worker, are also consequences that can follow worker behavior. An emphasis on consequences is focused on the objective of maximizing the maintenance of those skills learned during training. From a Setting Training perspective two subobjectives emerge: 1) to ensure that the type, amount, and schedule of reinforcement used in the latter stages of training will be similar to those found in production, and 2) to minimize the effect that production setting consequences for off-task behavior will have on a worker's productivity.

The consequences most appropriate in the final stage of training will be dictated largely by the kind, amount, and schedule of reinforcement available in the production setting. The assumption is made here that any environment in which individuals are asked to be productive will be managed in such a way that reinforcers are available for work completion. In those situations where reinforcement for work completion does not occur, is delivered at a minimal level, or is delivered long after the behavior is performed, there should be no expectation that vocational skills learned in training will be maintained.

It is unlikely, however, that consequences in the production setting will be delivered at the magnitude or frequency used in the early phases of training. All too frequently a worker who has learned a skill within a training setting that provided high levels of praise and reward for work performance is immediately placed in a production setting that offers low levels of reward for work completion. Not surprisingly, the worker's performance suffers. Training should not be considered complete until the worker is maintaining accurate performance on the same, or nearly the same, schedule of reinforcement that s/he will experience in the production setting. To reach this objective the consequences for work behavior in the production setting should be assessed, and the consequences in the training setting should be gradually made to approximate this naturally occurring level.

In addition to assessing production setting consequences for work-related behavior, the consequences for non-work behavior should be noted. There usually is more potential reinforcement for socializing and other off-task behaviors in production settings than in training. By attempting to determine what inappropriate behaviors will be reinforced in production, the trainer can identify potential problem areas and attempt to create learning situations that will minimize their occurrence.

SETTING TRAINING PROCEDURES

The objective of training is to provide a worker with vocational skills that will be useful to him/her in a production setting. Training variables, as defined in Setting Training and Chain Training, must be flexible. The performance of the worker is the index that guides modification of training procedures. In Setting Training we suggest that training variables also be guided by the demands of the production setting. Specifically, a trainer should be aware of the antecedent stimuli and consequent stimuli a worker will experience in the production environment. While the early phases of training can be markedly different from production, the latter stages should closely approximate production setting antecedents and consequences. In fact, much of Setting Training should be conducted in the production setting itself with continued individual attention from a trainer. When ultimate production is expected in several locations, Setting Training should occur in a representative sample of these locations. To achieve this objective without decrement in worker performance the following training guidelines are suggested:

1. *Identify antecedents and consequences that differentiate the training and production settings.* Differences usually will relate to the components discussed above: antecedents that cue the worker when to perform the chain, irrelevant setting characteristics that will vary but that should not affect work performance, reinforcement contingencies for task production, and contingencies of reinforcement and punishment for behaviors incompatible with work. Identification of these discrepancies between the training and anticipated performance settings provide the basis for Setting Training procedures.

2. *Begin varying irrelevant antecedent stimuli as soon as the worker is expected to perform any group of steps independently.* A worker learns that a stimulus is relevant if it consistently and systematically sets the occasion for reinforcement following a requisite response. A stimulus will be treated as irrelevant if its presence does not affect the probability that responding will be reinforced. By varying the dimension and presence of different stimuli across training trials, the worker learns that these stimuli are not S^Ds for work behavior. Their absence in production thus will be less likely to affect work behavior.

   In varying irrelevant stimuli, ensure that the entire range of expected natural variation is sampled. For example, if amount and volume of distracting conversation were an identified irrelevant dimension, and if natural variation were expected to range from quiet conversation among two people to boisterous group exchanges, the trainer should ensure that the worker had experienced Setting Training situations that included both these extremes and some intermediate levels. These experiences in training should substantially increase the probability that accurate work behavior will be performed in the presence of production conversations.

   One of the most important setting characteristics that a trainer will usually need to vary is the presence and apparent attention of the trainer himself or herself. Thus as the worker begins to perform a group of steps reliably, the trainer may begin stepping a few feet away, engaging in conversation with someone else, or performing other activities while the worker is expected to continue through the task. This teaches the worker that trainer proximity and activity should not provide information that is relevant to task performance. Of course, it is critical that alert, covert attention be maintained constantly so that any task errors can be consequated immediately, and that reinforcement be provided if the worker does in fact continue through the task. It is also useful to alternate among trainers during Setting Training, to ensure that presence of a specific individual is not treated as a relevant stimulus for the worker's task completion behaviors.

3. *Provide differential reinforcement for higher response rates.* Reinforcement for work behaviors seldom is provided in natural production settings unless work rate is adequate. Therefore, an important focus of setting training is development of work rate on a newly learned task so that production expectations can be met. Rate-building contingencies often are more efficient during Setting Training than in the production setting, because the trainer

usually can provide more immediate consequences than production supervisors, who have responsiblity for a group of workers. Further, focusing on rate during training prevents inappropriate work rates from coming under control of task-provided stimuli.

To provide differential reinforcement for higher rates, the supervisor should note both the facility with which individual steps are performed as well as the time required to complete an entire task. Reinforcers can be delivered during the assembly sequence for improvements on specific responses. We have found it helpful to use a stop watch to time each complete assembly during later training trials. This gives the trainer an indication of changes in rate over time and provides a basis for giving more reinforcement for those assemblies that are completed more rapidly than usual.

4. *Fade reinforcement for step and task completion to the level expected in production.* Since task performance ultimately should be maintained by events in the natural setting, the trainer should gradually attempt to change reinforcement procedures used in training to approximate naturally occurring reinforcement type, amount, and schedule. One of the most frequent natural contingencies in sheltered workshops is akin to a higher order schedule of reinforcement, in which each chain of behaviors is treated as a single response and reinforced on an interval or ratio schedule. Changing to such a schedule in training involves gradually requiring the worker to perform more and more work before a reinforcer is delivered.

   It also is important to ensure that the type and amount of reinforcement available in production is used during Setting Training. A worker who has been trained with edible reinforcers should not be expected to maintain performance if tokens (a novel reinforcer) are all that are used in the production setting. If tokens are used in production, Setting Training should include a systematic pairing of edibles and tokens to facilitate the development of tokens as conditioned reinforcers (Kelleher and Gollub, 1962).

5. *After the worker begins to perform the task independently, conduct training sessions in which those reinforcers available for off-task behavior in production are accessible.* This will usually involve moving the worker into the actual production environment. The stimuli cuing off-task behavior and the natural reinforcer for those off-task behaviors will be available. If stimulus control for on-task behavior is well developed, the worker will perform the task. If stimulus control for on-task behavior is not adequately developed, or if stimulus control for off-task behavior is strong, the

worker will not perform the task. By including this phase of training, however, the trainer will be able to intervene immediately if work behavior breaks down. The trainer can then provide the assistance necessary to regain appropriate responding. Conducting Setting Training in the production environment serves both to evaluate the efficacy of training and to provide a safeguard against the worker's completely losing the skills s/he gained during training.

SUMMARY

Once a worker has acquired the skills needed to perform a task independently in training, careful consideration should be given to the differences and similarities between antecedents and consequences of worker behavior in the training setting and antecedents and consequences in the production setting. The trainer's attention to antecedent variables should focus on 1) identifying those stimuli in the training setting that control task-appropriate responding, 2) determining if those relevant stimuli are also present in the production setting, and 3) identifying stimuli that are only present in the production setting and are likely to control off-task behavior. Trainer attention to consequence variables should focus on ensuring that the type, amount, and schedule of reinforcement the worker will experience in production are similar to those used in the latter phases of training and identifying consequences in the production setting that may act as reinforcers for off-task behavior.

To maximize the probability that skills learned in training will transfer to production, five training guidelines are suggested: 1) identify antecedents and consequences that differentiate the training and production settings; 2) vary irrelevant antecedent stimuli; 3) provide differential reinforcement for faster work rates; 4) gradually fade reinforcement type, amount, and schedule to those expected on the job; and 5) expose the worker to the competing stimuli and reinforcers s/he will experience during production.

PART IV

PRODUCTION SUPERVISION

chapter 10
THE PRODUCTION ENVIRONMENT

The production environment is that aspect of sheltered work programs that distinguishes them from other therapeutic endeavors. In the production environment, materials and information are transformed through work into goods or services that have economic value. To accomplish this the production environment imposes specific demands, structures, and objectives that distinguish resulting work behavior from other activities (Neff, 1968). For the severely retarded workshop employee, these environmental characteristics usually relate to sustained, accurate, and rapid performance of operant chains required by contracted work. Therefore, the production environment should be organized so that these work behaviors are facilitated. Our discussion of the production environment will focus on definition of production goals, required staff skills, and procedures for production planning and organization.

PRODUCTION GOALS

Production supervision procedures should be designed to accomplish three objectives: 1) maximizing the productivity of each worker, 2) teaching and maintaining at appropriate rates the social and general work behaviors expected in a production setting, and 3) maintaining an overall production system that is economically feasible. The first of these, maximizing individual productivity, has long been accepted as an important outcome in vocational facilities (Whitehead, 1978). It is our contention that with appropriate supervision, most severely retarded individuals can attain productivity levels comparable to those observed in industry, and thus earn non-trivial incomes (Bellamy, Peterson, and Close, 1975; Bellamy, Inman, and Yeates, 1978). Since production rates provide the basis for individual remuneration and for program classification and funding, low work rates may prevent many retarded adults from entering into many work situations. There is also some indication that individual productivity is related to the more general evaluations of supervisors, on the basis of which employment decisions may be made (Chaffin, 1969). Moreover, individual productivity may be related to several factors, including characteristics of the individual worker, the task to which s/he is assigned in the production setting, and the behavior of the supervisor. In discussing procedures that facilitate productivity, our focus will be on those factors over which a supervisor has the most immediate control: the work setting, the supervisor's behavior, and the adaption of these to individual characteristics of workers. (For reviews of available research, the reader should consult Bellamy, Inman, and Schwarz, 1978; Gold, 1973; and Martin and Pallotta, 1978.)

The second objective of production supervision relates to behavior in the work setting that is *not* task specific. In any production environment a class of behaviors can be identified that facilitates worker performance and promotes independence. Conversely, another class of behaviors can be identified that is likely to preclude or even terminate work opportunities if these behaviors continue to occur in the production situation. The first group of behaviors may include such things as obtaining assistance when it is needed, maintaining a neat work area, using time clocks, returning to work on time from breaks or meals, and getting parts or tools when needed. The second group of behaviors could include such things as disruptive social interactions with co-workers, temper outbursts, stealing, leaving the work area at inappropriate times, and some forms of self-stimulation. An effective production supervision system should facilitate acquisition of the first group and reduce the incidence of the second, while maintaining high productivity levels.

The third objective, maintaining an economically viable production system, reflects an emphasis of many work-oriented rehabilitation facilities. By increasing the commercial income of a shop through sound business practices and production management, a facility can and should become less reliant on income from social service agencies. As more and more severely handicapped people request vocational habilitation services from agencies that are already fiscally strained, it seems that business income and expense will need to play a more significant role in facility planning. Therefore, our sugestions for production supervision procedures are designed to be compatible with sound business management (Horner and Bellamy, 1978a; Whitehead, 1978).

The supervision procedures suggested in the following chapters address these three objectives. The procedures emphasize careful design and preparation of the work setting so production supervisors can interact primarily with workers rather than with materials. The procedures reflect an interest in efficient work flow in the production setting. The procedures also derive from unique characteristics of workshops, which often have more supervisory staff than is found in comparable competitive industrial settings. Along with the public funding that supports this additional staff comes the need to conform to requirements of a variety of regulating and certifying groups. Our procedural recommendations for production are compatible with normal program requirements associated with the Wage and Hour regulations (Federal Register, 1974) and the Commission on Accreditation of Rehabilitation Facilities (1978). Depending on characteristics of the task, task design, and workers, it should be possible to implement our suggestions with a production supervisor-to-worker ratio of up to one to ten in programs for the severely retarded.

STAFF SKILLS FOR PRODUCTION SUPERVISION

Effective production supervision requires skill in managing both *work* and *workers.* As with training, management of *workers* requires that the supervisor have at his or her disposal a variety of skills from which specific techniques can be selected and applied to given individuals and situations. Management of *work* requires detailed knowledge of both task characteristics and production requirements.

1. *Supervisors should be able to define and implement contingency rules that specify the temporal relationship between worker behavior and significant events in the production environment.* Contingency rules are guidelines for staff behavior that specify what environmental events (if any) will occur as a consequence of defined behaviors. The supervisor can control the timing or occurrence of a variety of events in the work environment, including such things as work breaks, supervisor assistance, attention, correction, change of work assignment, and proximity to particular co-workers. By determining when such events will occur relative to individual worker behavior, the supervisor often can increase rates of task performance and decrease rates of undesired behaviors. Doing this effectively requires many of the same skills described in Chapter 5. The supervisor should be able to identify reinforcers, define behaviors to be reinforced, establish and follow contingency rules, and increase the informational value of reinforcers. Similarly, recognizing the effects of unintended reinforcers is also important.

In discussing the reinforcement skills required for training we suggested that the primary criterion for selecting among potentially reinforcing events was effectiveness. Because of the expense of individual training, it seems prudent to use the most powerful reinforcers available in order to decrease total training time. However, some additional considerations are appropriate for selection and use of reinforcers in production. Because of the long-term nature of production work, values pertaining to the normality of the work environment assume greater importance. Not only should reinforcers delivered in production be effective, we believe they should also be age- and situation-appropriate. Individuals in vocational programs are adults, not children. They are engaged in productive work, not preschool activities. Therefore, if effective reinforcers can be found that reflect socially normal adult tastes, these seem preferable to using coloring books, artificial affection, and children's toys. Work breaks, choice of assignments, compliments from supervisors, and money are more natural reinforcers in most work settings. When snacks or edibles are used, scheduling consumption during breaks is clearly more normal than providing such reinforcement on the job.

2. *Supervisors should be skilled at evaluating contingency rules through observation of worker behavior.* The assessment skills described for effective training are also relevant to supervision. Flexibility and individual accommodation are keys to effective contingency management. For example, the inappropriate social behavior of one worker might be ignored because the supervisor hypothesized that corrections could be reinforcing. Appropriate work behavior of another worker might be similarly ignored because of the supervisor's observation that task completion had become an effective conditioned reinforcer, and supervisor contact was not necessary to maintain performance.

Like training, production supervision is a pragmatic process in which behavioral observations are used to develop initial hypotheses about effective treatment techniques. The supervisor then continuously evaluates the selected techniques by measuring worker performance against established criteria, and s/he modifies techniques that do not have the intended effect. Ultimately, therefore, the focus of effective supervision is less on a theoretical analysis of what the supervisor "should" do and more on the effects of supervision with respect to worker behavior. Our approach to management of workers in production is consistent with application of contingency management techniques in a variety of settings. (For a review of contingency management skills, see Sultzer and Mayer, 1976.)

3. *The supervisor should know in detail the quality standards and task analysis for each task in production.* This knowledge is essential for quality control of products to ensure delivery according to industrial specification. Immediate quality checks allow the supervisor to recognize errors as soon as they are made. If the supervisor is also familiar with the task analysis, the error then can be translated into a specific assembly step, and any required assistance can be provided on subsequent assemblies. In well-organized shops the contractor might be asked to develop or agree to a written list of quality standards as part of the sales process.
4. *The supervisor should know, for each task, the normal time standard on which workers are paid.* Familiarity with the normal productivity standard provides a clear objective against which the performance of each worker can be compared. Although our recommended evaluation of individual productivity emphasizes individual improvement in comparison to previous performance, knowledge of this final criterion also can be useful if the eventual goal of the habilitation process is to normalize worker income.

PRODUCTION PLANNING AND ORGANIZATION

Production planning and organization include production-related activities for which the supervisor is typically responsible, but which may be done when workers are not present. The purpose of this planning and organization is to increase the ability of supervisors to provide individually appropriate supervision procedures to workers as well as ensuring contract completion. Planning and organization also increase the flexibility of the total production environment, so that it can adapt readily to changing production demands. Guidelines are presented in this section to assist in organizing the production setting and planning individual work assignments.

1. *Designate specific storage areas in the work setting for parts and supplies at each stage of production.* For most workshops, this involves establishing separate areas for storing 1) incoming parts and materials for each job, 2) assembled products ready for quality screening, and 3) products ready for packaging and shipping. By clearly labeling each of these areas the shop can establish standard operating procedures relative to parts location. This minimizes supervisor and worker time required for materials location and handling. It also facilitates control of parts inventories, helps

avoid quality control problems, and makes possible a smooth flow of work through the shop. For example, incoming parts and supplies can usually be organized with respect to either the customer or task. As products are completed, they can be moved to a separate work area where quality checks are performed and any required packaging is done. Storage of packaged products ready for delivery then can be accomplished in an area with easy access to building exits or loading areas.

2. *Design work stations to promote worker independence and efficiency.* Three considerations are important in work station design. First, work stations should be designed so that each individual is responsible for discrete, countable units of work. This provides the basis for continuous measurement of productivity and helps to clarify the precise performance expected of each worker. A second consideration is that, when possible, a physically separate work area should be defined for each worker. This not only facilitates individual independence, but also assists the supervisor in establishing realistic objectives for each individual and implementing supervision contingencies to achieve them. Finally, work stations should be designed so that all parts, tools, supplies, etc., needed by either the worker or supervisor are readily available. For example, in programs with which the authors are associated, individual workbenches are arranged so that tools used in the task are placed on one area of the bench, component parts are arranged sequentially on another, completed products in another, and data sheets used by the supervisor on yet another area.
3. *Maintain a written schedule of tasks assigned to each worker and post it in the production area.* Most vocational programs maintain a standard daily or weekly schedule in which each workday is divided into specific work periods and breaks. As a supplement to this we suggest developing a task assignment schedule for each worker (see Figure 10.1). Such a schedule helps in planning how a shop's resources can be used to meet production demands. Furthermore, publicly posting the schedule in the shop provides clear cues to supervisors about planned worker assignments. This should minimize inconsistencies among staff behaviors and minimize downtime if regular supervisors are absent. Such a schedule can be developed at a regular planning meeting among staff members who are knowledgeable about immediate production demands, worker skills, and supervisor abilities. The best interval between such meetings varies depending on frequency of changes in contracts and workers. Shops that get new production orders or

		#1 Steve Biel	#2 Joe Williams	#3 Betty Davis	#4 Rhonda Johnson	#5 Bobbie Clark	#6 Dennis Thomas
Monday	WP 1	Cam switch # 321	Training	Power Cord	Heat Sinks	Training	Test Adapter
	WP 2	Hand Prep	Sorting Coupons	Power Cord	Heat Sinks	Test Adapter	Test Adapter
	WP 3	Laced Cable #2143	Battery #0033	Hand Prep	Laced Cable # 2143	Test Adapter	Test Adapter
	WP 4	Laced Cable # 2143	Battery Shield	Sorting Coupons	Laced Cable # 2143	Test Adapter	Battery # 0033
Tuesday	WP 1	Hand Prep	Hand Prep	Test Adapter	Training	Hand Prep	Battery # 0033
	WP 2	Laced Cable # 2169	Training	Test Adapter	Laced Cable # 2169	Hand Prep	Battery # 0033
	WP 3	Heat Shield	Laced Cable # 2143	Test Adapter	Laced Cable # 2169	Hand Prep	Laced Cable # 2143
	WP 4	Heat Shield	Laced Cable # 2143	Test Adapter	Laced Cable # 2169	Training	Laced Cable # 2143

Figure 10.1. A weekly schedule of worker assignments with four work periods per day.

supplies on a weekly basis, for example, might find a weekly planning meeting useful.

Of course, the benefits of such scheduling are not limited to severely retarded workers. Planning and posting similar schedules of supervisor assignments or responsibilities is also useful for managing staff. A posted schedule provides useful discriminative stimuli for staff behaviors and acts as a basis for providing precise performance feedback to individual staff members. Cataldo and Russo (1978) have shown that such posting of assignments reliably increased the work output of a group of professional clinic employees. We have observed the same phenomenon in our shop.

4. *Prior to each work period ensure that all necessary materials are available at each work station.* The work station should not become a discriminative stimulus for waiting or other off-task behavior while a supervisor obtains needed supplies. Research has demonstrated that sustained work behavior comes under control of stimuli that indicate that work is expected and will be reinforced (Martin and Flexer, 1975; Screven, Straka, and LaFond, 1971). From a practical standpoint, these results suggest that sustained work behaviors can also come under the control of naturally occurring stimuli, such as the work station itself, if appropriate learning opportunities are provided. This involves ensuring that work behaviors are reinforced in that setting and that all other behaviors are not reinforced in that setting. Our suggestion that work stations be prepared prior to a worker's entry into the production setting is designed to prevent occasions during which a worker will have to wait for needed assistance. In addition, by having work stations supplied before work periods begin, the supervisor can spend most of his or her time managing reinforcement contingencies and performing quality checks, rather than continually organizing materials. The worker's dependence on supervisors is minimized when work stations are well supplied, since everything they need is immediately available.

Procedurally, this involves scheduling organization or set-up time for some supervisors between work periods. During this time, data sheets can be replaced or updated, records can be transferred or graphed, completed products can be removed, parts bins at work stations can be filled according to individual worker assignments, and necessary tools can be placed at each work station. As workers gain experience in the work setting, each of these materials handling activities probably will be the focus of training activities, so that progressively less supervisor time is required to manage materials in the production environment. However, the supervisor should continue to ensure that work stations are properly prepared, so the worker does not learn that the work station occasions behavior other than sustained work.

5. *Establish a production measurement system that gives the supervisor daily information on individual productivity.* Regular feedback about the productivity of individual workers provides the foundation for effective supervision. The major criterion for success of supervision efforts can be stated in terms of production rates. This will mean improvement in production rate unless normal productivity is regularly achieved. When improvement does not occur, a clear indication is available that a different set of supervision contingencies should be tried. Such feedback also can improve supervisor performance. Although published data are not totally consistent, several studies have shown that feedback to program staff about the results of their efforts can improve subsequent performance of assigned duties (Boles and Bible, 1978; Panyon, Boozer, and Morris, 1970; Quilitch, 1975).

    Individual productivity records are maintained in some form by all vocational programs that meet Department of Labor regulations (Federal Register, 1974). While this information may be used regularly in computing payroll or in overall program management decisions, it seldom is organized so that supervisors can monitor the productivity of individual clients. Productivity measures in many programs are obtained only during periodic checks of individual work rate. Whether or not this provides reliable payroll information, it does not give the supervisor regular data for evaluation of supervisor techniques.

    Therefore, one measurement system we recommend relies on continuous measures of productivity, which can supply daily feedback to staff as well as provide payroll and management information. During all production periods the supervisor or worker should record the task, the time work commenced, the time it ended, and the number of units produced. Then, at the end of each workday, an average production rate can be computed. Figure 10.2 illustrates a simple form for recording this information. These data allow the supervisor (and worker) to determine immediately whether a worker's performance is slower or faster than usual. If the supervisor knows a worker's average productivity on an assigned task, performance can be compared to previous levels. The supervisor then can respond differentially to work rates that are slower and faster than usual. This differential responding will be more immediate, more accurate, and more effective than if such data were not available.

Date	Task#	Status	Start Time	Stop Time	Units Completed

Figure 10.2. A simple form to record worker performance.

Of course, this measurement system assumes that all tasks have been designed so that individuals are responsible for discrete and countable units of work. This is extremely difficult, if not impossible, for some tasks. For these, a daily measure of time-on-task (Cooper, 1974; Kozloff, 1971) or time-in-motion (Rusch, Connis, and Sowers, 1977) provides the supervisor with a fair estimate of productivity. When necessary, time sampling can provide a useful measurement, as long as enough samples are obtained so as to be representative.

Another approach, which we employ, involves the use of a timer that emits an audible signal every *n* seconds, the interval being determined by reliability requirements discussed by Powell, Martindall, Kulp, Martindale, and Bauman (1977). At the end of each interval, a buzzer sounds, cuing a supervisor to scan the production environment and record whether each worker is on- or off-task. At the end of each day, the number of on-task intervals can be compared to the total number of intervals and used to estimate percent of time each worker was on-task over the day.

6. *Plan a reinforcement delivery system for the production environment.* Although contingencies of reinforcement for production workers should be individually defined, some aspects of reinforcement delivery nevertheless can be standardized across workers. When this is done, the diversity of reinforcement programs that a supervisor must implement is reduced. As a result, the time required for supervisors to acquire necessary reinforcement skills

also is reduced, as is the supervisor time required for normal reinforcer delivery.

A carefully managed token economy provides an efficient way of standardizing reinforcer delivery. Several other advantages also accrue with the use of a token economy: 1) Tokens can be delivered in production without delay or disruption of ongoing work. 2) The variety of events that can be used as reinforcers is increased, since they need not be present in the production environment. 3) With a token economy, a set of many reinforcing events can be made available. This reduces the probability of satiation and also facilitates the supervisor's job of identifying effective reinforcers. 4) A token economy can be less contrived than other reinforcement approaches to the extent that it involves pay (in tokens or money) for work completed. 5) Token exchange and consumption or enjoyment of reinforcing events can occur in natural settings, such as during work breaks, thus enhancing the normalcy of the entire reinforcement process. Procedures for establishment and operation of token economies have been described in detail in a number of recent texts (Kazdin, 1977; Walker and Buckley, 1974). Rather than repeating those procedural guidelines, we simply will describe some aspects of one token system with which we have worked.

The *partial immediate payment* system in the Specialized Training Program is a token economy designed to increase work rate and accuracy. In the system, task completion behaviors (i.e., production work) are the only responses that are reinforced by tokens. Other behaviors, such as attending, social responses, etc., are consequated in other ways. Money, in the form of coins, is used as the token for productive work. This is treated as an advance on the individual's paycheck for the task just completed and is subtracted from his/her check at the end of the month. Money earned in partial immediate payment can be spent in vending machines, at simulated stores, or in neighborhood commercial establishments during work breaks. Individualized supervision contingencies are used to define the elapsed time and/or number of work units required per unit of pay.

Obviously, an important aspect of this and any token system is the planning of an adequate range of back-up reinforcers for which tokens can be exchanged. As a regular part of the production organization process, therefore, potential reinforcers should be identified and made available. The variety of events available at any one time and across time often determine the overall effectiveness of a token system.

SUMMARY

In most sheltered workshops the production environment is designed to maximize individual productivity, to develop general work behaviors appropriate to the setting, and to operate as an economically sound enterprise. Two critical aspects of planning a production environment that meets these objectives are identification of needed staff skills and development of efficient organizational procedures.

Staff skills important in direct-service management of the production environment are similar to those required for effective training: the ability to define and implement contingency rules for improving worker behavior, the ability to evaluate the effects of contingency rules using behavioral measures, and a detailed understanding of the quality control standards and time standards for every task in the workshop.

Careful planning and organization of the work setting can increase the productivity of each worker. Critical aspects of planning and organization are: 1) definition of efficient work flow by defining discrete storage spaces for tasks at various stages in production; 2) design of individual work stations to promote independence; 3) detailed, regular scheduling of worker and staff assignment; 4) daily materials organization at each work station; 5) development of a system for measuring each worker's daily productivity; and 6) design of a reinforcement delivery system. Attention to each of these aspects of the production setting affects the efficacy with which the direct-service staff can implement supervision contingencies for increasing work rate and improving work behavior.

chapter 11
INCREASING AND MAINTAINING WORK RATE

Concern with increasing and maintaining worker productivity is not limited to sheltered workshops. Since the establishment of modern factories, research projects and management innovations alike have sought ways to increase and maintain both individual and collective work rates. The production management literature is now replete with accounts of successful strategies focusing on design of the work task and work environment, the responsibilities given to individual workers, and the procedures used in supervision and management. It is significant that most popular strategies — job enlargement, establishment of autonomous work groups, use of flexible work weeks, etc. — involve simultaneous attempts to increase productivity and to improve the quality of work life. (For an excellent reveiw of current industrial research, the reader is referred to Cummings and Molloy, 1977.)

Much industrial research is directly applicable to management of severely retarded workers, as our suggestions on design of tasks and work settings imply. However, our research on improving productivity of severely retarded individuals has focused principally on the effects of changes in the immediate work environment and supervision method, rather than on more general characteristics of management style. Our procedural recommendations reflect this direct service focus, with primary emphasis being placed on the immediate production supervisor.

From a behavioral perspective, individual productivity is defined in terms of the rate at which work-related behaviors are performed. Low levels of productivity are not taken as evidence of limited productive capacity, laziness, or inadequate work adjustment. Instead, low productivity is regarded as something that can be improved by changing the antecedents and consequences of work-related behaviors. It is important to note that concern with the quality of individual work life is not lost in this behavioral approach to productivity, since accommodating individual differences and preferences is the foundation upon which an effective behavioral technology is built. It has been our experience that use of the procedures recommended here usually decreases negative interactions between supervisors and workers and increases positive ones.

In improving productivity of workshop employees, the supervisor should function as a contingency arranger and manager. This requires continuous monitoring of individual work rates and on-task behavior. Characteristics of the work setting and the supervisor's behavior then are adjusted as necessary to create effective discriminative stimuli and arrange reinforcing consequences for work behavior. Procedures suggested in this chapter are designed to help the supervisor utilize information about worker performance and to provide a systematic approach to developing supervision strategies that may be effective in specific situations. As with other parts of the book, this chapter's emphasis is empirical: we are suggesting a system for designing and evaluating techniques for individual workers and situations, not a cookbook of procedures that should be expected to apply to all workers in all situations.

1. *Allow an individual to work independently in the production setting only after s/he can perform the task reliably without errors.* Error-free independence is established mainly in the later stages of training, but the initial experiences in the production setting are also very important. The difference between Setting Training and the early phases of production lies principally in the amount of staff attention. Production, as we have defined it, begins when the worker no longer is receiving continuous attention from a trainer. Therefore, stimulus control over work behavior must be transferred from the training situation, in which individual attention is present, to the production setting, where such attention is not present.

   There are several important reasons for requiring that a worker perform a task consistently and accurately before leaving individual training. First, in a group production setting, errors are not likely to be noticed as quickly as in training. If the worker completes a step incorrectly and then is able to continue through the chain, it can be assumed that the opportunity to progress through the task will function as a conditioned reinforcer for the error response. Similarly, behaviors irrelevant to the task, such as ritualistic manipulation of parts, can be reinforced inadvertently by the opportunity to continue through the chain. In individual training this adventitious reinforcement can be precluded by skillful trainer intervention; such intervention is less feasible in a production setting where one supervisor is responsible for several workers.

Second, for the production supervisor's efforts to be efficient, s/he must be able to design reinforcement contingencies for fairly large response units. That is, the worker should be expected to work independently for relatively long periods without contact with the supervisor. One of the easiest ways to accomplish this is to treat the operant chain acquired during training as a *single response* that can be reinforced on some specified schedule (see Chapter 2). The worker's ability to perform the chain reliably and accurately is critical to the success of such reinforcement scheduling efforts.

A final reason for allowing a worker to enter a group production setting only after s/he reliably performs the task relates to the possibility of social reinforcement for error responses. Quality standards on many tasks are such that errors must be corrected immediately in production. As a result, a worker can receive considerable supervisor attention following error responses. The possibility clearly exists that such attention will function as a reinforcer for the worker's errors and thus result in an increase in the frequency of incorrect or incompetent work behaviors.

When an individual has just completed training on a new task, therefore, the supervisor at first should provide a rather high frequency of attention to the worker in production. As is discussed in more detailed later, this attention should include instructions, positive social contacts, praise, and assistance, with each provided as a contingent consequence of work-appropriate behavior. This extra attention then should be faded as quickly as possible without adversely affecting work rate. (Actually, even skillful fading procedures often result in temporary dips in rate; any persistent decrement or trend should be taken as evidence that fading was too rapid.) In fading the extra attention, it may be useful first to provide extra attention at the beginning of each work period, then at the beginning of each day, etc., while contact at other times approximates that received by more experienced workers. Another fading strategy simply involves gradually reducing contacts at all times until the normal level is reached. Whatever fading method is chosen, ensure that accuracy is maintained as attention is reduced. Make sure the worker performs accurately across supervisors.

2. *At the beginning of each work period provide definitive verbal instructions to each worker regarding behavioral expectations and production contingencies.* Although reinforcing appropriate be-

havior and not reinforcing inappropriate behavior are usually reliable methods of communicating expectations to a worker, it is often more efficient to add to this process a simple instruction of what is expected. Empirical support for this suggestion has been provided in a variety of applied habilitation settings (see Ayllon and Azrin, 1964; Gordon, O'Connor, and Tizard, 1955; Huddle, 1967; Zimmerman, Overpeck, Eisenberg, and Garlick, 1969).

Instructions should specify appropriate and/or inappropriate behaviors, describe performance goals, and define relevant consequences or contingencies. For example, a supervisor might say at the outset of a work period, "Janis, when you finish these twelve switches you may take your break." The attention that a supervisor gives to the worker while stating these expectations or rules should be assumed to be reinforcing to many workers. Therefore, we suggest providing instructions when the worker is doing something appropriate, such as coming to work, completing a work unit, or appropriately requesting supervisor assistance. Such instructions usually can be faded out as a worker gains more experience in the production setting. They will be useful primarily when a worker first enters the setting, when something about the setting (behavior antecedents or consequences) has changed, or when the worker's performance has become undesirably variable.

3. *Allow workers to devise alternate methods of assembly in production only if accuracy and production rate are maintained at acceptable levels.* Despite early attempts to identify one best way to perform each work task in factory settings (Gilbreth, 1911), many recent work improvement strategies have stressed the value of letting individual workers determine their own unique work methods. However, the application of this approach in sheltered workshops can pose problems without very careful monitoring. The specific problems relate to what is known from research on operant chains. First, as a worker completes the chain of behaviors required by a task, incorrect performance of one response does not necessarily prevent performance of subsequent responses. Sometimes it results instead in the inability to perform some later response, or in the assembly of an incorrect product. In either case, the reinforcement otherwise available for correct task assembly is missed, and, with repeated instances, it can be assumed that an extinction process would begin. As was noted in Chapter 2, however, extinction of operant chains results in a breakdown of early chain elements, not necessarily in the particular element that was performed incorrectly.

A similar extinction process occurs when the worker performs a step in a unique way, so that the familiar S^D for the next response is not produced. Unless the worker is capable of devising the appropriate response to the new stimulus condition, the usual reinforcement is unavailable for the part of the chain that has been completed. Partial extinction ensues, with the consequence noted above: early steps of the chain begin to break down, regardless of where the error occurred. Therefore, unless it can be assumed that the worker has the problem-solving skills required to identify and correct inaccurate steps independently, the supervisor should intervene before the extinction process begins.

Procedurally, this involves monitoring and assisting the worker on previously incorrect steps, together with preventing progress through the chain until each step has been completed accurately. For example, in many of the tasks in the Specialized Training Program, component parts are arranged in parts bins sequentially in the order of use during assembly (see Figure 3.3). A place-marker is moved in front of each bin in turn as assembly progresses, to provide a distinct cue to the worker about what component should be used next. It is not uncommon for workers in early stages of production to skip those task steps that involve moving the place-marker, with the result that errors often are made later in the chain. When this occurs, the supervisor increases his or her surveillance of the worker, so that assistance or corrections can be provided as needed to prevent the worker from bypassing steps of the task. Of course, after a worker has gained experience in assembly of a product, use of the place-marker often does become unnecessary, and supervisors allow these steps to be dropped from the chain if correct performance is sustained.

4. *Teach workers at least one acceptable way to get supervisor assistance.* Unanticipated needs occasionally arise in most production settings: parts may be absent or defective, breakage occurs, and minor accidents happen. Individual needs also may require that a worker get the supervisor's attention at specific times, as for example, when a detailed quality check must be performed at a critical step in the assembly. Clearly, teaching workers to respond to such situations independently and adaptively is an important goal in most sheltered work programs. However, until independent skills are learned for such occasions, it is important that the worker always be able to get the supervisor's attention when necessary. Systematically teaching a worker to do this assists the worker and it provides a clear discriminative stimuli for staff

responses. Without a reliable strategy for getting a supervisor's attention, a worker often stops working or performs inappropriate responses in unfamiliar circumstances. When the supervisor notices this and corrects the situation, the attention and assistance given the worker often function as reinforcers for off-task or incorrect behaviors, thus establishing the work area and task as S^Ds for non-work behavior.

To obtain supervisor attention a worker may be taught to raise a hand or walk to the supervisor and wait until s/he is not busy. When first teaching the skill it may be easiest to teach a worker to request assistance after each product is completed, so that the supervisor can come, check the product, and deliver a reinforcer for task completion. This situation maximizes the natural reinforcement for requesting staff attention.

Procedures for teaching the skill of obtaining supervisor assistance are not unlike those described earlier for task training. First, define the naturally occurring S^D for the response (e.g., for a quality control check, the S^D often is produced by the last step in the assembly). Provide prompts, directions, etc., to obtain the desired response in this situation, and deliver immediate reinforcement. (Often, the requested attention or asssistance is a suffficient reinforcer.) Over time, fade out the prompts, until the worker responds independently to the naturally occurring S^Ds. This process of teaching skills in the supervision setting is described in more detail in the next chapter.

5. *To the greatest extent possible, ignore off-task and inappropriate behavior. Provide attention and assistance contingent on task-appropriate work behavior.* It is useful to assume that contacts from a supervisor will reinforce most workers in a production setting. Therefore, the supervisor should avoid attending to behaviors that are incompatible with working. For example, verbal directions like "Get back to work" should be avoided, since the result is often a chain of behaviors involving off-task behavior and supervisor contact, followed by on-task behavior and a reinforcer for working. Furthermore, the worker's return to task can function as an immediate reinforcer for the supervisor's instruction, although the long-range effect of this contingency is detrimental: there is an increase in the off-task behavior to which the supervisor attends.

Supervisor attention should occur not just when a worker is attending to task, but when that attention has been sustained for a period of time. For example, Kazdin (1977b) found that reinforcing students for 30 seconds of task attending was more effective when the 30-second period was preceded by additional on-task behavior than when off-task behavior occurred immediately prior to the interval. Again, the concept of chaining is relevant here. The supervisor should avoid reinforcing a chain of behaviors consisting of an off-task period followed by an on-task period. Procedurally, this usually involves waiting for on-task behavior, then delaying for gradually increasing periods before attention is provided. For similar reasons, the supervisor also should avoid consistently pairing reinforcement for on-task behavior with close proximity to a supervisor. Such proximity can become a discriminative stimulus that signals the worker that task attending will be reinforced. When this occurs, the probability of on-task behavior when the supervisor is more distant usually deceases. Calling out praise from across the room is useful in avoiding this situation.

For experienced workers, on-task behavior ultimately should be reinforced by the opportunity to perform more work. That is, the reinforcement available for task completion is obtained only when the worker is on-task *and* performing the required behaviors. Thus, when adequate reinforcers are available for task completion, extra reinforcement for task attending usually can be eliminated.

6. *Check the quality of each product as soon as possible after completion.* Immediate quality control not only increases the reliability of the shop's production, it also allows all reinforcement for task completion to be based on *correctly* completed products. Prior to the delivery of reinforcement, the supervisor should check each part for quality against the defined list of standards for the product. Immediate quality checks also minimize the reinforcement and overlearning of assembly errors. When incorrect products are identified, the supervisor can determine at what step in the task analysis the error occurred and provide assistance on that step in the next assembly. Assistance then can be faded during subsequent assemblies until independent performance is again accurate. Try to provide assistance before the error occurs, rather than as a correction, to avoid the necessity of attending to undesired work behavior.

For more experienced workers whose accuracy is reliable, reinforcement may be scheduled not after a single unit is completed but after several units. Since this increases the possibility that an error that does occur will practiced and reinforced, additional care is necessary in checking quality in such situations.

When errors present a production problem for an individual worker or the shop as a whole, a systematic measurement and recording system should be implemented. This can be accomplished by simply adding a column to the production data sheet (Figure 10.2) in which the supervisor can record when a particular kind of error was corrected either during or after assembly. Remediation efforts usually involve one of three strategies. First, the consequences for task completion can be changed, so that more effective reinforcers follow accurate performance. With workers who are experienced in the functioning of a token economy, addition of a cost contingency for inaccuracies may also be useful (Walker, Hops, and Fiegenbaum, 1976). Changing the consequences for accurate task completion may be ineffective if correct performance is very infrequent or if the worker is failing to make some critical discrimination in assembly, resulting in randomly correct and incorrect products.

The second strategy involves increasing the general supervision level, so that errors are precluded during the assembly process by supervisor assistance. This assistance, then, is faded gradually over time, until the worker again completes the chain independently and accurately. Of course, some errors occur with such frequency and unpredictability that the supervisor cannot anticipate them and provide assistance. In these situations, the third strategy, individual retraining, usually is better than relying on corrections in production. In individual retraining, the worker receives individual attention and training, as described in earlier chapters, until performance is again accurate.

7. *Define individual supervision contingencies for each worker.* So far, our production guidelines have focused on procedures that could be standarized across workers. The purpose of this standardization is to increase the efficient use of staff, so that time is available for implementing individual contingencies for all workers. Individualized contingencies of reinforcement in the production setting represent an effort to maximize the productivity of each worker.

   Supervision contingencies are rules that specify what environmental events will follow the work and work-related behaviors of an individual in the production setting. Work behaviors of primary interest in efforts to improve productivity are task-completion responses (that is, performance of the final step in an assembly chain) and task attending, or appropriate orientation toward and engagement with task components and tools.

   The environmental events of primary interest in supervision contingencies are those that can be scheduled effectively by the supervisor, so that they occur only as specified in contingency rules. The list of such events is a lengthy one for creative supervisors: allowing an individual to choose preferred work tasks, to work beside a favored co-worker, or to leave early for work break; providing supervisor praise, proximity, or conversation; giving paycheck advances or contingent access to background music; and allowing individuals to record and monitor progress toward some goal. For useful ideas, the reader is referred to studies reviewed by Martin and Pallotta (1978) and Bellamy (1976). Of course, selection of events to be included in any individual contingency involves identification of functional reinforcers for that individual worker. Other kinds of environmental events automatically follow task-completion responses, regardless of supervisor planning. For example, after each task is completed, the worker often can experience the sight, shape, or feel of a finished product. While such events may be sufficient in some cases to maintain work rates at high levels, supervisor-planned contingencies are often necessary as a supplement to these naturally occurring events. Our attention in this section will be focused on contingencies that are planned and implemented by work supervisors.

Events that are controlled by the supervisor can occur according to either response-dependent or response-independent contingencies. In response-independent contingencies, the event occurs regardless of what the worker does. A work break at 10:00 a.m. each day and a paycheck every Friday exemplify response-independent contingencies. In response-dependent contingencies, the chosen consequence occcurs only after a behavioral criterion is met, such as in piece-rate payment, or work breaks scheduled after completion of ten units of work.

The most useful contingencies for improving productivity in sheltered vocational programs are response-dependent contingencies. Clearly, this suggestion differs from long-standing goals of organized labor movements, which have worked diligently to replace piece-rate wages with hourly rates. This is understandable, since experiments with animals have demonstrated that carefully managed response-dependent contingencies can maintain such high response rates over long periods that organisms seriously injure themselves (Skinner, 1953). However, as yet such dangerously high work rates have not presented grave problems in sheltered workshops. Rather, productivity is so low that a nationwide program now exists for individuals whose "productive capacity" is assumed to be "inconsequential" (Federal Register, 1974). The use of response-dependent schedules seems warranted in assisting individuals in sheltered vocational programs to

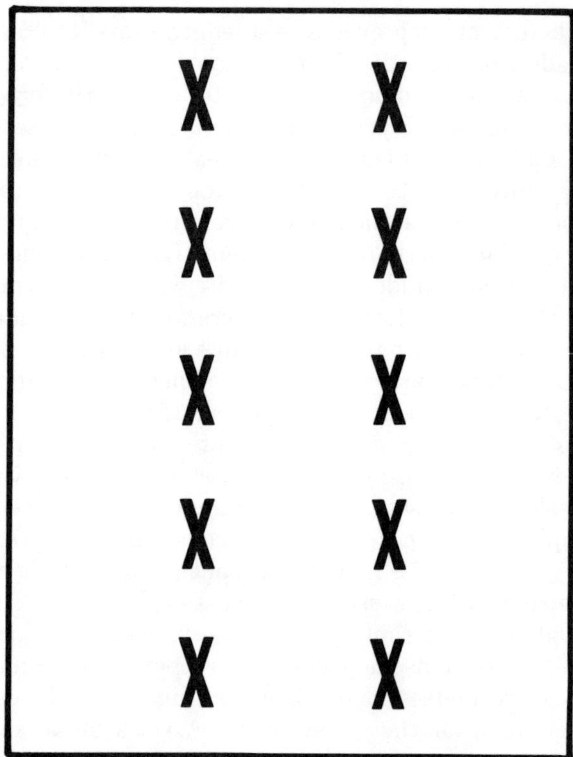

Figure 11.1. A card kept at a work station. The worker places a completed unit on each X. When the card is filled the worker receives a reinforcer.

achieve normal productivity levels. After this level is achieved, it may be possible to maintain it with response-independent contingencies.

There are two basic response-dependent contingencies that are useful in supervising production: ratio schedules of reinforcement and interval schedules of reinforcement. In ratio schedules, the reinforcing consequence is scheduled to occur after a defined number of responses has been completed. This may involve delivery of reinforcement after each response (labeled continuous reinforcement) or after a fixed or variable number of responses. For example, in the Specialized Training Program, several workers receive partial immediate payment after placing completed units on a fixed number of Xs on a card that is placed on the workbench (see Figure 11.1). The size of the fixed ratio can be increased simply by putting more Xs on the card. (For other examples of ratio schedules the reader is referred to Evans and Spradlin, 1966; Koegel and Rincover, 1977; and Schroeder, 1972.)

In interval schedules reinforcing events are scheduled so that they follow the first response after a defined time interval has elapsed. Interval schedules differ from response-independent contingencies in that occurence of the consequent event is determined by both time passage and response emission whereas in response-independent contingencies the consequence is contingent only on the passage of time. In supervising production in sheltered workshops, interval schedules are particularly well suited for reinforcing on-task behavior. For example, in our shop we have found it useful to reinforce defined periods of on-task behavior (such as 20 seconds during which the individual works continuously) only *after* a specified time period, such as 10 minutes, has elapsed.

Martin and Pallotta (1978) suggest a useful combination of ratio and interval schedules: supervision contingencies can be designed so that task completion is reinforced on a ratio schedule conjunctively with an interval schedule of reinforcement for on-task behvior. For example, a worker might receive a paycheck advance of 25¢ each time ten products are completed. At the same time the worker's on-task behavior could be praised at variable intervals that average five minutes in length. Of course, as the worker becomes more proficient, both reinforcement schedules could be gradually thinned, so that progressively more productive behavior would be required. Thus, the immediate pay for ten units might be reduced to 5¢ or the number of units increased to 50. Similarly, supervisor praise for on-task behavior might be reduced to occur at intervals of 15 to 20 minutes.

The specific contingencies that are feasible in any production setting will be determined to some extent by staff skills, type of work, available equipment, ease of counting work units, and many other factors. It has been our experience, however, that useful individualized contingencies can be implemented in practically every sheltered work setting with resulting increases in productivity of most workers. There are several sub-rules related to implementation of individual contingencies:

(a) *Carefully define the contingency.* To ensure accurate implementation, each supervision contingency should be defined so that the worker behavior, setting, consequent events, and schedule are specified clearly. Figure 11.2 illustrates one way to write such definitions. By looking at the figure one can determine that Fred is an experienced worker who assembles 10 circuit boards before receiving the chosen consequence for task completion, which is a 10¢ advance and social praise. Staff members attend to him as a consequence

Worker	Setting	Behavior	Consequence	Contingency
Fred	Production Assembly of Circuit board No. C-073	1. Completion of board, (stuffing and crimping leads)	10¢ paycheck advance plus staff attention and praise	Every 10th board.
		2. Task attending (looking at task and appropriately manipulating tools or components) maintained w/o interruption for 30 seconds	staff contact (praise, proximity or touch)	At approximately 20 minute intervals

Figure 11.2. A specification of contingency rules for one worker.

for on-task behavior only about every 20 minutes, and only when attention to task has been sustained without interruption for at least 30 consecutive seconds.

(b) *Ensure that all staff use the contingency consistently.* Accurate implementation of supervision contingencies can be facilitated in several ways: 1) Allow all staff to participate in the definition of contingencies. 2) Keep written accounts and publicly post all current contingencies where they will be seen by all supervisors. 3) Build in worker responses that cue staff when attention is appropriate. In the example in Figure 11.2, Fred could be taught to raise a hand to signal a supervisor each time ten circuit boards were completed. 4) Arrange for regular, non-punitive observation and feedback for staff as to the adequacy of program implementation.

(c) *Try out the supervision contingency for an adequate period of time.* There are few supervision contingencies that workshop supervisors have not tried at least once. It has been our experience that many potentially powerful contingencies are rejected in such trials on the basis of very short implementation periods in which the contingency may or may not have been used consistently. Although rapid behavior change may be observed occassionally, most supervision contingencies should not be expected to affect worker behavior immediately. Unless real decline is noted, a contingency's effects should be monitored for at least one week before alterations are considered.

(d) *Make sure the worker experiences the reinforcer.* If work rate is very low, attention to task very infrequent, or reinforcement schedules too intermittent, it often happens that the worker never receives the planned reinforcer. Clearly, the contingency cannot be expected to affect behavior in these instances. Plan contingencies so that the worker can be reinforced at least two to four times in each work period. If productivity is so low that this does not occur naturally, the worker might be guided physically through the task, as in training, a few times during each period.

(e) *Arrange for feedback to workers about their productivity.* Feedback about work performance with graphs, illustrations, or simple comments functions as a reinforcer for many workers (Loos and Tizard, 1955; Jens and Shores, 1965; Levy, 1974). For example, one might keep daily graphs of total production or average production rate as compared with industrial standards, and display these graphs within view of the worker. More immediate feedback procedures that assist the worker in monitoring his or her performance in relation to contingency requirements may be helpful with severely retarded workers. For some workers, the effectiveness of fixed ratio schedules can be enhanced by adding a "counting" method to the task arrangement. If a contingency specifies that quality checks and token reinforcers will be delivered after every five completed units, a card or box for completed units could be designed with five marked areas for placement of completed products (see Figure 11.1). Similarly, when contingencies specify a time interval in which each product must be completed, a timer that provides discriminable cues as to elapsed and remaining time is sometimes useful. For example, we found a simple kitchen timer helped two workers significantly increase their work rate by providing them a method to compare production time per unit with their own previous average on a complex cable assembly. In this case, they tried to beat the bell that sounded when the timer ran out. If they succeeded, they received twice as much partial immediate payment as they did if they did not beat the timer. In both cases, the contingency led to a work rate that was commensurate with the industrial time standard of 17 minutes. Moreover, this normalized work behavior was maintained over an extended time period (Bellamy, Inman, and Yeates, 1978).

8. *Use daily production data to evaluate contingencies used with each worker. Modify supervision contingencies as necessary.* The best guess of an experienced supervisor about effective reinforcers and contingencies for an individual's work behavior often will be wrong; that is, implementing the selected procedures will not change work rates as expected. Even when changes do occur, it should not be assumed that the improved productivity will persist. The chosen consequence suddenly may stop functioning as a reinforcer, or other available reinforcers for alternate behaviors may become more powerful.

Therefore, an integral aspect of production supervision is the monitoring of individual work rates to evaluate supervision contingencies. Daily averages of time required to complete a unit of work provide a means that is sensitive to practical changes in rate. By carefully noting when a supervision contingency was implemented on a continuing record or graph, the supervisor can estimate quickly the effects of every contingency. Of particular interest will be three aspects of performance, each of which can be discerned in a simple graph: 1) Has overall rate improved? That is, is the average time required to complete a unit less than before the contingency was implemented? 2) What trends are apparent? Is the worker gradually improving over time, gradually getting slower, or is there no change discernable in the graph? 3) Has the worker's performance become less variable from day to day? Stability and predictability generally are characteristic of valued employees. (For a detailed discussion of issues in such visual analysis of single subject data, the reader is referred to Hersen and Barlow, 1975, and Sidman, 1960.) If daily performance graphs indicate unacceptable variability, trends, or rate, consideration should be given to revision of supervision contingencies. "Unacceptable" refers to anything less than normal factory expectations. To expect less of a severely retarded worker, we feel, simply imposes arbitrary limits on staff effort and worker accomplishment.

In revising unsuccessful supervision contingencies, identify aspects of the contingency that may have been dysfunctional for the individual and generate possible alternatives. Baer (1977) suggested several questions that can be of assistance in this effort:

(a) Was the program implemented consistently? Observations by each staff person should help to identify whether or not the planned contingencies were followed. Observe particularly whether or not the chosen consequences were delivered as scheduled; whether or not these consequences were available at other times as well; and whether or not behaviors incompatible with working were followed by potentially reinforcing events.

(b) Were the reinforcers appropriate to the individual? This always involves a supervisor's guess, since the appropriateness of a reinforcer is demonstrated only when it increases behavior rate. When no effect has occurred, the supervisor simply must guess whether to attribute the failure to the chosen consequence or to other aspects of the contingency. (Suggestions were presented in Chapters 6 and 10 for identifying potential reinforcers.) If a token system is used, particular attention should be given to the variety and novelty of available back-up items, their exchange values, and the worker's exposure to them.

(c) Can schedules of reinforcement be made more appropriate? Ineffectiveness of a contingency can result from consequences being delivered too infrequently or too frequently. More frequent reinforcement is often appropriate when an individual is working on a task requiring greater effort (Schroeder, 1972), longer time periods, or work in a distracting environment.

(d) Can a more specific target behavior be identified? Rate of production is a global measure that is affected by several discrete behavioral components. Sometimes contingencies are ineffective simply because they were applied to the wrong behavior or to one that is too general. For example, work rate is affected by pauses between repetitions of the task chain, by performance of irrelevant behaviors in the work setting, by slow movement, and by irrelevant behaviors that are performed as part of the chain. In a recent study of one worker's behavior in a production setting, Horner (1978) collected data on the rate of four irrelevant behaviors in addition to work rate. Increasing reinforcement levels for work completion improved production rate slightly. As production rate increased, the rate of three of the irrelevant responses decreased, However, the fourth irrelevant response, an unnecessary movement of task materials, increased with production rate. This suggested that the fourth irrelevant response was actually under control of task-related stimuli. A later intervention eliminated this controlling relationship. During the intervention the fourth irrelevant response dropped to a near zero rate level. Simultaneously, the worker exhibited a 300% increase in work rate. The data from this study suggest that care must be taken in defining the target behavior (dependent variable) that is to be consequated. In this study, focusing on production rate as the target behavior was much less effective than focusing on the controlling relationships that maintained the fourth irrelevant response. The choice of the target behavior is of major importance in the success of supervision contingency management. If a particular contingency is ineffective, re-evaluation of the target behavior may be appropriate.

SUMMARY

Increasing and maintaining worker productivity is of critical importance in sheltered workshop programs. In order to improve the productivity of workshop employees a supervisor must function as an efficient contingency manager. This requires supervisors to provide supplemental training, as needed, for individual workers immediately upon entering the production setting. It also requires supervisors to monitor, continuously, the performance of individual workers over extended periods to identify performance problems as they emerge. When performance problems are deemed serious enough to warrant intervention, supervisors should assess the baseline level of the problem behavior, design a tentative intervention program, publicly post the program to ensure that all supervisors know its exact nature, implement the program, and, finally, assess the program's effect in terms of how it alters the frequency and/or duration of the worker's behavior. As in training, supervisors should adjust their behavior to accommodate the idiosyncracies of each individual worker. In other words, effective supervision, like training, is a dynamic process that demands consistency, continuous assessment, and systematic modification.

chapter 12
CHANGING WORK BEHAVIOR

Behaviors not specifically required for task completion often present problems that can significantly reduce an individual's productivity and employment options. For example, workers may engage in frequent disruptive contact with co-workers, respond inappropriately to interruptions or visitors, exhibit periodic temper outbursts, be unable to use time clocks, return late from work breaks, be unable to request assistance from supervisors, or exhibit unacceptable variability in dress and hygiene habits. Changing such behaviors, which are incompatible with adequate work performance, is accepted as a responsibility of sheltered work programs.

Many excellent descriptions of techniques for changing vocationally relevant behaviors are now available. The reader is referred to Gardner (1971) for a procedural overview and to Kazdin (1975) and Kanfer and Phillips (1970) for related discussions of behavior modification applications. The detailed techniques suggested in these texts will not be repeated. Rather, the purpose of this chapter is to focus these techniques on the decisions that direct-service staff persons are required to make in managing a work environment. Each of the following guidelines has contributed to improved work performance in at least some of the work settings with which we have been involved.

1. *Do not make appropriate behavior a prerequisite for vocational training and production opportunities. Deal with inappropriate behavior within the work setting.* Although many individuals enter sheltered workshops with a variety of behaviors incompatible with sustained work, focusing only on changing these undesirable behaviors may be counterproductive. Despite deficits in dressing habits or social courtesy, the vocational competence required for personal status and remuneration seldom is achieved without direct vocational training and supervision. To postpone vocational instruction until other behaviors are changed simply

extends the period of vocational incompetence and prevents access to natural reinforcers for work behavior.

One of the naturally occurring reinforcers for appropriate behavior in the production setting is the opportunity to perform more work and receive more reinforcement for that work. If problem behaviors are changed before vocational skills are taught, it is likely that the new "adaptive" behaviors will require some sort of contrived reinforcement over a long period of time. On the other hand, if task-specific skills are taught first, general work behaviors often can be developed by using the opportunity to work as a reinforcer. This is because many workers learn to value the monetary and social outcomes of specific work behavior. Teaching specific skills first allows the worker to experience success as an employee and provides a natural reinforcer for later behavioral interventions.

2. *Observe the individual's problematic behavior in the situation in which it occurs before defining a specific intervention objective or strategy.* Simple observation of behavior in the work environment often provides information that is critical to the success of an intervention program. Observation may reveal that a problematic behavior is preceded consistently by some event or another behavior, or that the behavior occurs only in the presence or absence of specific supervisors.

When observing problem situations, it often is useful to record each behavioral incident of concern, together with the environmental events that immediately precede and follow it (Bijou, Peterson, and Ault, 1968; Gardner, 1971). From these records, one may estimate the strength and nature of the problem behavior, the antecedent stimuli that probably control the behavior, and the consequences that follow performance of the response.

In identifying a target behavior, the supervisor should index overall rate and variability of the behavior, as well as changes in various stimulus contexts. Techniques are available for remediating skill deficits, for increasing and decreasing the rate of a behavior in a given situation, and for decreasing variability in responses over time or situations. To evaluate antecedent conditions, the supervisor should determine whether or not distinct cues exist in the environment for the desired response, whether or not these cues vary across time or supervisors, and whether or not cues for the desired behavior and possible alternative responses are discriminable to the worker.

The supervisor should also evaluate consequent events to form hypotheses about what maintains the current level of responding:

Is the activity itself inherently reinforcing? Is it maintained by escape or avoidance contingencies? Do specific events consistently occur that seem to function as reinforcers? From these hypotheses about the function of antecedents and consequences of problem behaviors it usually is possible to design intervention programs that are more appropriate to the individual and situation than those that might be designed without systematic observation. (For more detailed information the reader is referred to Lovaas and Bucher, 1974; Sultzer and Mayer, 1972; and Kazdin, 1975.)

3. *Select one or two intervention objectives. Don't work on everything at once.* Observing this guideline has at least two important advantages. First, it increases the probability that a worker will enjoy initial success in the work environment. As treatment objectives are reached one at a time, new behavioral goals are established for which the worker can receive reinforcement. When simultaneous changes on several behaviors are expected, positive interactions between supervisors and workers often decrease, and small gains often remain unnoticed.

   The second advantage of defining only one or two treatment objectives at a time is that this provides clear discriminative stimuli for staff behavior. When a manageable number of programs is to be implemented, the consistency with which each is conducted should be improved. This, in turn, increases the probability that the staff will be reinforced by worker success.

4. *Define the problem operationally and determine how performance will be measured.* The primary purpose for specifying the problem behavior is that this focuses intervention efforts initiated by the supervisory staff. Operationally defining a problem involves specifying a behavior that is observable and measurable, defining the antecedent stimuli that should set the occasion for the response or alter the response frequency, and defining performance criteria in terms of topography, rate, accuracy, etc. For example, after observation, a problem of "disruptiveness" in the work area might be defined operationally as shouting at a co-worker, which occurs whenever the co-worker drops something on the floor, and which is almost always consequated by supervisor attention of some sort. The treatment objective could then be that, given an occasion on which the co-worker dropped a component, the individual would continue working without looking at or talking to the co-worker. (For further discussion of the process and benefits of defining treatment objectives, the reader should consults Short (1974), Becker, Engelmann, and Thomas (1975), and Kanfer and Phillips (1970).

5. *Specify two criteria for each treatment objective: one for successful termination of the program and one for changing the program.* The degree of behavior change desired by the supervisor should be specified prior to defining any particular procedure. That is, it should be clear to the supervisor exactly when the worker has mastered the skill or met the performance objective. Specifying this success criterion saves staff time by ensuring that intervention programs are maintained only as long as they are needed. To continue the previous example, the supervisor might define success as two consecutive weeks in which no shouting is noted, or 20 consecutive instances of parts-dropping that are not followed by the shouting response.

   Specifying a failure criterion, at the achievement of which the program will be changed, ensures that ineffective programs will not continue indefinitely. Defining this criterion prior to development of a treatment program defines staff expectations about how rapidly the problem should be solved and provides a standard against which treatment progress can be compared.
6. *Develop and implement an intervention program.* Intervention involves systematically altering the antecedents and consequences of the target behavior until the desired change is achieved. The literature on applied behavior analysis now is replete with suggested techniques that have been used effectively to change individual behavior in one or more settings (*Journal of Applied Behavior Analysis,* 1968–1978).

   There are several guidelines for applying this behavior change methodology in sheltered workshop production environments:

   (a) *When possible conduct all interventions in the natural work setting, taking advantage of naturally occurring discriminative stimuli and consequences.* There are several reasons for this guideline. First, appropriate behavior ultimately should come under control of naturally occurring events in the environment. For example, the worker should learn to punch a time clock when entering the work area or return to work when a break is completed, not just perform these activities when instructed to do so. Second, the naturally occurring stimuli that signal that a response is appropriate often vary from one time to another. This variation may be lost in simulated instructional situations. Finally, the production environment is a complex system in which a variety of possible reinforcers are available for several different responses. An intervention procedure that was effective in a more controlled environment might not be effective when such reinforcement for competing responses is available (Gollub, 1977).

A useful technique for production-setting interventions is to change the frequency with which the naturally occurring antecedent occurs. For example, assume that the intervention objective is to reduce the frequency with which one worker shouted "Phone" when the telephone rang. To ensure repeated presentation of the S^D (telephone ringing) a supervisor might arrange to be called throughout one or two workdays at frequent, pre-arranged times. Instructions to work quietly just before each ring might be sufficient to occasion appropriate silence that could be reinforced. The delay between these instructions and the ring could then be gradually increased and the instructions eliminated altogether if appropriate responding were maintained with the chosen reinforcer. The use of naturally occurring consequences in intervention programs often decreases disruption of the production environment. Staff attention, opportunity to work, selection of work assignments, and contingent breaks usually involve less special arrangement than other possible consequences.

(b) *In general, avoid the use of negative consequences.* Aside from the legal and moral issues surrounding civil rights and protection of human subjects, there are two major reasons why we recommend against using predominantly negative consequences to eliminate or reduce undesirable behaviors. The first is that punishment procedures often simply teach workers to avoid punishment by not exhibiting certain behaviors in the presence of staff members who implement the punishment program. It is almost always the case that in the absence of these same staff members the behavior reoccurs. The second major problem with the use of punishment is that it usually works in the sense that an undesirable behavior is suppressed immediately. Of course, this is not bad in and of itself, but the immediate effect certainly makes it more likely that supervisors will employ similar punishment techniques in the future. The ultimate result is a contingency system that focuses on behaviors that should not occur rather than behaviors that are appropriate. Such a system, if it works at all, teaches workers to *not* behave inappropriately rather than to behave progressively more appropriately. We believe habilitation is facilitated when retarded adults learn to enjoy learning new and adaptive skills.

(c) *Evaluate the procedure using measures of the target behavior, and make appropriate modifications when the failure criterion is met.* As with all other techniques suggested in this text, changing individual behavior in the production setting should be viewed as a pragmatic process. The essential characteristic of the behavioral approach lies not in the use of a particular technique or procedure, but rather in the evaluation of any selected procedure on the basis of actual behavior change.

SUMMARY

In addition to improving work rates, most sheltered workshops attempt to improve each employee's general work behavior. This not only increases the possibility of successful vocational placement outside the workshop, but also may decrease the staff and equipment costs associated with the workshop's production.

In applying behavior change techniques in the production environment, it is useful first to observe the problem behavior in its natural context. One or two specific objectives then can be identified, the behaviors defined operationally, and treatment procedures implemented and changed according to subsequent worker behavior. Useful procedures in most workshops will be those that can be implemented by the normal production staff without long-term disruption of the setting. The use of naturally occurring antecedents and consequences in interventions often facilitates program effectiveness.

PART V

CONCLUSIONS

chapter 13
IMPLEMENTING THE TECHNOLOGY

Given current training procedures, many severely retarded individuals can become vocationally competent participants in the economic life of their communities. Denying these individuals entrance into vocationally oriented facilities no longer can be justified either on the assumption that their productive capacity is inconsequential (Federal Register, 1974) or that necessary service methods are unavailable. If the vocational potential of severely retarded individuals is to be realized, however, sheltered workshops will need to play a critical role. This role will require continued procedural development to meet the unique employment challenges presented by these individuals.

Two important characteristics of the procedures we have recommended should be re-emphasized. The first is that, taken together, the procedures do comprise a *technology*. As such, they utilize not only the techniques suggested in previous research, but also the research methods themselves. This means that while behavioral principles form the basis of the technology of habilitation, the technology is by no means limited to the results of previous research behavior analysis. We incorporate findings from concept learning research (Becker, Engelmann, and Thomas, 1975), task analysis (Davies, 1973), and organizational management (Cummings and Molloy, 1977) with the requirement that the effectiveness of each procedure, regardless of its origin, be submitted to ongoing evaluation. As this evaluation process continues, no doubt many techniques we have not identified will emerge and be added to the technology of habilitation. In view of this, we contend that our approach to habilitation is pragmatic, rather than dogmatic. Allegiance to particular phrases or techniques in reinforcing or correcting a learner is directly contradictory to the functional, scientific approach we have outlined. Measurement of individual progress is the key to this pragmatism. Any chosen procedure should be evaluated in terms of its observable effectiveness with a particular individual in a given situation, not in terms of its theoretical foundation, its popularity, or its utility in other programs.

The second important characteristic of habilitation procedures we have described is an emphasis on *direct service.* Careful attention to the details of day-to-day interactions between a trainer or supervisor and each severely retarded worker is critical in effective habilitation. The three components of direct service — task planning, vocational training, and production supervision — require precise organization and implementation of individualized habilitation procedures. We have tried, throughout this text, to specify objectives for each of these components and delineate procedures that will facilitate attainment of those objectives. The objectives in task planning are to: 1) identify a maximally feasible design for task completion, 2) acquaint the trainer with the particular response demands and discriminative stimuli of the task, and 3) construct a data sheet that will facilitate consistency in training and provide a convenient method of collecting training data. The procedures through which these objectives are met involve design and analysis of each task, with careful attention to both the demands of the job and the skills of the particular worker(s) who will learn it.

The objective of vocational training is increased competence on the part of the worker. Following training a worker should be able to perform the task independently, accurately, and quickly. Worker deficiencies in any of these three categories belie the adequacy of training. The objective of training *is not* that the trainer follow a prescribed routine of procedures, or that the worker be exposed to experiences designed to improve his/her "work attitude;" the objective of training is to increase the vocational competence of the particular severely retarded individual being trained. The exact procedures through which this is achieved will vary across workers and tasks. In general, however, the process will require that trainers are able to assess, assist, and reinforce worker responses. The range of training demands typically encountered with severely retarded people will involve application of these skills to 1) teaching the particular response demands for individual steps of a task and bringing these under control of task-produce stimuli, 2) modifying training procedures when particular steps prove difficult, 3) teaching the stimulus response relationships that raise a sequence of responses to the level of an adaptive response chain, and 4) teaching the worker to maintain a high, accurate rate of independent performance when s/he leaves the training setting and enters production.

Many variables will affect how a worker behaves once s/he leaves training and enters the production setting. It should be recognized that the way in which the latter stage of training is conducted can facilitate production performance. The contingencies present in the production setting, however, will have by far the greater impact on a worker's behavior. As such, a focus on the objectives and procedures of production supervision is necessary. The objective of production supervision is to maintain or improve the worker's high, accurate, independent performance. The procedures accomplishing this objective will involve 1) planning and organizing the physical layout of the production setting, 2) defining functional reinforcers and building these into contingency rules, 3) implementing these contingency rules in an attempt to improve work rate and minimize inappropriate work behavior, 4) re-implementing training procedures when the worker's performance decreases, and 5) maintaining a data collection system that affords systematic monitoring of each worker's progress over time.

The direct service technology of vocational habilitation that we have discussed is still in its infancy. Much of the empirical verification necessary to raise the procedures discussed in this volume to the level of acceptance remains unavailable. As the technology is implemented and elaborated, we urge that three major areas of focus be maintained: 1) careful analysis of ethical considerations, 2) attention to the quality and type of work involved, and 3) systematic improvement of the technology.

ETHICAL CONSIDERATIONS

The need to safeguard the rights of participants in social service and research programs has been emphasized repeatedly during the last few years (Friedman, 1976; Horner, in press). In the vocational rehabilitation network a legal mechanism now exists to ensure that appropriate safeguards are implemented: individual habilitation plans are to be developed with the participation and informed consent of the person to whom they apply (Rehabilitation Act of 1973). This legal mandate reflects several earlier discussions of value and ethical issues in the application of behavioral analysis. Bandura (1969), Kanfer and Phillips (1970), and others have argued that value issues arise primarily in the definition of treatment *objectives*, (i.e., in the identification of specific behavioral goals for an individual entering a treatment or educational setting). The ethical safeguard usually proposed is that the client be the final arbiter in selection of all treatment objectives.

Neither these suggestions for professional ethics nor the available legal safeguards, however, provides a meaningful protection of the rights of severely retarded adults. Although some participation in program planning may well be possible for these individuals, their significant behavior and language deficits make it unlikely that consent that is legally or ethically valid can be given to any treatment alternative

(Friedman, 1975, 1976). Naturally, this difficulty applies to all programs serving severely retarded individuals, not just those that label their methods as "behavior modification" or those that identify research as well as service objectives. As habilitation services are extended to severely retarded individuals, new mechanisms will be needed to safeguard clients' rights. In the absence of an effective mechanism for obtaining informed consent of severely retarded adults, a concerted effort is needed to develop procedural guidelines for defining individual habilitation objectives. Of central concern will be a recognition of the value judgments brought to the treatment setting by service providers.

Our focus throughout this text has been on detailing efficient and effective ways of providing severely retarded people with useful vocational skills. We are well aware, however, that the technology we advocate does not exist in an ethical void. Central to the provision of vocational services are two major ethical issues: 1) Is vocational competence an appropriate goal for a severely retarded adult, and 2) Are the means suggested in this text for teaching vocational competence acceptable within the moral and ethical framework of our present society?

Vocational Competence as a Habilitation Goal

A behavioral technology does not dictate which behaviors an individual should perform. From a behavioral perspective all responses are viewed in terms of their topography, frequency, and stimulus context, not their desirability. Yet, when decisions are made concerning *which* behaviors of a client should occur (or occur more frequently) and *which* should not occur (or occur less frequently) emphasis shifts from one of technology to one of ethics. In many settings serving the retarded, the individuals who administer treatment are the same individuals who define treatment goals. This often makes the distinction between technology and ethics all too obscured.

The objectives of any treatment or habilitation plan are centered around defining behaviors that the client "should" be exhibiting. The definition of such objectives is based typically on certain value judgments, or assumptions, about how that individual "ought to" behave. It is likely, therefore, that the designation of vocational competence as a treatment goal will be grounded in the assumption or value judgment that vocational behavior is important and "appropriate" for the client.

From our perspective the current trend toward vocational training with retarded individuals is based on three general value judgments or assumptions: the importance of normalization, a focus on deinstitutionalization, and a belief in maximizing personal independence. Wolfensberger (1972) championed the principle of normalization, which states that the retarded should be trained with normal teaching techniques to perform normal behaviors in normal settings. As stressed throughout this text, we feel severely retarded people require better than normal teaching. The normalization principle does suggest, however, that when determining treatment objectives for a client, care should be taken to ensure that the objectives are congruent with the behavior of normal, same-aged individuals. Adults in our society place great importance on, and expend exeptionally large amounts of time performing, work (Turkel, 1972). Therefore, if normalization is a value held by the individual(s) constructing habilitation objectives, it is likely that vocational competence will be considered as a viable treatment goal for severely retarded adults.

This line of reasoning is closely paralleled if deinstitionalization is perceived as an important value or assumption in serving the severely retarded. The institution offers treatment in isolation from society. Advocates of deinstitutionalization suggest that a more appropriate approach to habilitation lies in community-based treatment centers. Severely retarded adults entering community settings, however, frequently lack the skills valued by members of that community. To be accepted members of a community, retarded individuals may need to demonstrate self-help, eating, social, language, and vocational skills. Within such a context, the treatment objectives for retarded adults may be influenced by those behaviors valued by their non-retarded peers. Once again the value attributed to vocational competence by most communities in our society suggests that vocational skills be considered as one treatment goal.

Yet another value held by many individuals in our society is the importance of personal independence. This value extends to economic independence. Generally, it is considered "appropriate" for adults in our society to be self-supporting. By developing vocational competence, retarded individuals should become less dependent on others in the community. Gold (1975) has suggested that acceptance of the severely retarded will in part be related to their ability to demonstrate competence in valued skill areas. Vocational competence would both meet this criteria and function to decrease the economic dependence of the retarded person.

The social value attributed to normalization, deinstitutionalization, and personal independence suggests that vocational competence is a habilitation goal worthy of consideration with severely retarded adults. It would a be major error, however, to assume that vocational training should be incorporated automatically into the habilitation plan for *all* retarded adults. A central concern of ours is that availability of a technology for vocational habilitation should not result in an emphasis on vocational objectives for every individual. More appropriately a variety of alternative treatment objectives should exist in community service programs, and each objective should be evaluated in light of its impact on the lifestyle of individual clients. A focus on independent living skills, on development of leisure and recreational abilities, on academic skill development, on vocational skills, or on harmonious domestic living might be differentially appropriate for different individuals. Since none of these objectives can be defended adequately as prerequisites for others, the relative emphasis given to each reflects the skills, assumptions, and value judgments of those defining habilitation objectives. A danger is created by the availability of a technology for vocational habilitation, that being the possibility that the relative emphasis on work skills in individual programs will reflect the abilities of staff members rather than the habilitation needs of individual clients.

Techniques for community living, self-help, language, and other intervention objectives are developing rapidly. However, in many instances the complexity of the required technology will be greater than that required for vocational training. For example, effective residential programming in group homes and effective community living skill training involve many more complex issues of stimulus control than have been addressed in our account of the vocational habilitation technology. It is a reflection of our own assumptions and value positions that we view vocational skills as central to normal lifestyle in our society. Alternate program emphasis can be equally well justified in terms of the assumptions and values of other persons responsible for programming. Our caution is simply this: the availability of techniques for vocational development should not preclude efforts of parallel technologies in other service areas, nor should it automatically result in a primary emphasis in vocational objectives for all severely retarded individuals.

Ethical Implementation of the Technology

A second ethical issue relates to the application of the procedure described in the present volume. If the decision is made to define vocational competence as a habilitation goal, the behavioral guidelines suggested here should be evaluated as to their ethical acceptability. Here again the final decision rests with the values of the decision-maker. Our emphasis in developing the guidelines in the text has been on pragmatism and accountability. Habilitation implies change in behavior. If service providers intervene in the life of an individual, that intervention should produce observable effects. Habilitation goals focus on behavior that will allow the "client" to more easily adapt to his/her environment. Habilitation methods should bring the worker closer to this goal. A major ethical issue for service providers is demonstration that the services they provide do actually have a habilitative impact on the people they serve. This will require that a system for empirically documenting behavior change be tied to the treatment procedures. Collecting data on response frequences, rates, or topographies is more than an approach developed for research purposes; it is a system intimately connected to effective treatment. Documentation of worker or client behavior affords the service provider invaluable information from which to direct his/her delivery of services.

A second major ethical consideration is that the methods used to reach habilitation goals be accountable. From our perspective this requires that the least restrictive or least intrusive treatment option be used to meet habilitation goals. The doctrine of least restrictive alternative has been applied to education of handicapped children (Education for All Handicapped Children's Act, PL 94-142; *Pennsylvania Association for Retarded Children* v. *Pennsylvania*, 334 F. Supp. 1257 (1971)), and to the treatment of clients in institutions. It focuses on the liberty and privacy rights of handicapped individuals, and recognizes that any intrusion of those rights should be tied to a worthwhile goal and be designed in minimally restrictive manner. In some instances value decisions related to even the least restrictive treatment procedure may make this treatment option unacceptable.

The issue of using the least restrictive treatment alternative is of special importance when serving severely retarded adults who can neither consent to entering treatment nor provide meaningful information if they want to terminate treatment. The fact that the people for whom the technology of vocational habilitation is designed are severely handicapped puts an added burden on service providers and community advocates to clearly specify the values that contribute to both the objectives and procedures used in treatment.

A NEED FOR WORK IMPROVEMENT

In addition to focusing on the objectives and procedures of vocational habilitation and the ethical considerations guiding these objectives, concern must be directed toward the type of work that severely retarded people will be trained to perform. In his review of issues currently facing sheltered workshops in this country, Whitehead (1978) focused on work improvement as an urgent need that could affect the continued existence of workshop programs. Workshops simply need more work that is adequately priced so that their employees can earn non-trivial wages in a dignified manner. Whitehead's (1978) suggestions for improvement include a variety of strategies to increase industrialization. The suggestions read much like an organizational chart of a successful company: innovations are needed in management, sales, finance, engineering, and production methods.

As we noted earlier in this text, such improvement in the quantity and price of work in sheltered workshops will be critical to effective habilitation of many severely retarded adults. Although competitive employment options do exist and should be pursued (Cook, Dahl, and Gale, 1977), extended employment at high wages in an industry-like workshop is now a more realistic vocational objective than competitive employment. Therefore, it seems possible that unless the work improvement advocated by Whitehead is actively pursued, welfare alternatives to vocational habilitation increasingly will be suggested for the more severely disabled (Levithan and Taggart, 1977).

It is unlikely, however, that work improvement alone will automatically result in an extension of work opportunities to severely retarded individuals. In fact, there is some evidence that exactly the opposite can occur. Work improvement in sheltered workshops often results in fewer opportunities for severely retarded individuals, not more opportunities. Scott's (1967) historical account of workshops for blind individuals supports this concern. During World War II, when national production demands resulted in considerable work expansion in workshop programs, Scott (1967) found evidence of an increasing reluctance of workshops to include more severely handicapped individuals. The recent proliferation of "activity centers" and "development centers" for moderately and severely handicapped individuals may also relate to this possibility. As many sheltered workshops have become more commercially sucessful, they have included more mildly handicapped individuals while the severely disabled were increasingly relegated to "pre-work," activity or educational programs. The availability of the habilitation technology described in this text suggests that such stratification is unnecessary. Yet, an active effort by those concerned with severely retarded adults seems necessary to ensure that work improvement in sheltered workshops results in more, not fewer, work opportunities for these individuals.

An additional impact of work improvement is frequently an exacerbation of the conflict between the rehabilitation and production goals of the workshop program. That is, competitive job placement of effective workers according to individual rehabilitation plans is often detrimental to workshop's ability to deliver quality products to industrial customers. As production demands increase, the need for rehabilitation and placement efforts is felt more acutely in the service program.

The direct-service technology of habilitation may offer some assistance in this conflict, since it raises the possiblity that severely retarded adults can become the stable employees whose productivity is central to the workshop's commerical success. A more extensive community placement effort, such as that described by Sowers, Thompson, and Connis (1978) could then be designed for mildly handicapped participants. In effect, the technology presented in this text raises the possibility of switching popular program emphasis for mildly and severely handicapped individuals: a production focus for the more severely disabled could allow them to earn significant wages in extended employment, while an educational emphasis with mildly handicapped persons might increase placement possibilities.

Work improvement in sheltered workshops appears critical to the vocational success of many severely retarded adults. However, without adequate intervention, work improvement could decrease, rather than increase, work opportunities for severely retarded people. The technology of habilitation could facilitate inclusion of these individuals as work is improved, and may also help to ameliorate traditional conflicts between rehabilitation and production needs in sheltered work programs. If this technology is to have optimal impact on services delivered to the severely retarded, continued efforts must be made to update, improve, and expand the techniques we currently have available.

NEED FOR TECHNOLOGICAL IMPROVEMENT

As we noted at the outset of this text, an empirical basis is not yet available for defining a comprehensive set of habilitation techniques. Research is needed that refines the principles on which techniques are based, expands the set of available techniques, and defines useful procedures for broader aspects of workshop operation.

The basic principles on which our procedural suggestions have been based derive from extensive research in the analysis of behavior. Nevertheless, performance of people in vocational contexts raises some issues that this research has addressed only marginally. In the critical area of operant chain performance, for example, much of the available research has been completed with animals. Performance of long heterogeneous chains by humans has received little research attention, and the applicability of animal research findings remains in question. The same is true to a lesser extent when research on schedules of reinforcement (Ferster and Skinner, 1957) is applied to the work behavior of severely retarded adults. Predicted effects of various schedules have been only partially observed when severely retarded individuals served as experimental subjects (Weisberg, 1971). The basic principles on which the habilitation technology is based thus require continued evaluation. Research is needed that asks basic research questions in applied vocational settings.

In addition to this research on behavioral principles, there is a need to identify and elaborate alternative techniques for task planning, training, and production supervision. The procedures used as examples in our presentation represent only a small subset of techniques that could result in competent vocational performance. Identification and description of a larger group of procedures for each of the problem areas we discussed could assist direct-service staff persons in defining individually effective procedures for their employees. More efficient data collection systems, more varied means of providing reinforcement and assistance in training, and more creative supervision contingencies are all needed.

Technological improvement is also needed at a more global level. As effective procedures are identified, an important question is whether or not these will be used systematically in day-to-day facility operation. Research is needed on organizational, staffing, and environmental design characteristics that result in implementation of effective procedures. The work of organizing infant day-care centers (Herbert-Jackson, O'Brien, Porterfred, and Risler, 1977) and evaluating the structure of group homes for delinquent adolescents (Phillips, Phillips, Fixsen, and Wolf, 1974) provides models for the needed research. If this organizational research is to be effective in workshops, it will be necessary to integrate the procedural technology we have presented with techniques from many other disciplines, especially management, sales, engineering, and finance. Little will be gained if a habilitation technology is successful in creating competent workers for whom no work is available.

Closely related to this need for organizational and environmental design is the need to develop an outcome-oriented approach to program evaluation. Currently popular evaluation systems focus primarily on the process through which services are provided, with emphasis on staff characteristics, filing systems, and documentation of other treatment processes (Commission on Accreditation of Rehabilitation Facilities, 1978; Joint Commission on Accreditation of Hospitals, 1973). Research is needed to identify equitable measures of program *outcomes,* so that effectiveness can be assessd more pragmatically, without imposing rigid procedures of uncertain validity. In such an outcome-oriented evaluation, the use of multiple measures should be a critical feature. Irvin, Crowell, and Bellamy (1978) suggest that a multiple-evaluation strategy has several advantages over single-instrument approaches: 1) Several different results are important. For example, sheltered work programs typically strive to increase individual productivity and earnings, to place workers in competitive jobs, to change community attitudes, to increase commerical revenue, and to provide services to all who can benefit. Using several measures increases the ability to assess these multiple outcomes. 2) Several different decision-makers need program evaluation data, but their information needs are quite different. The direct-service staff person, workshop director, funding agency, contracting industry, state legislature, and general public are all involved in decisions that affect program operation. Each could benefit from particular kinds of evaluation information. 3) Use of multiple measures reduces the probability that error, which is associated with any measurement method, will distort the results. Concurrence of two or more measurement methods, which are susceptible to different sources of error, provides more useful and more reliable information to decision-makers. Therefore, in planning outcome-oriented approaches to evaluation, it will be important to avoid the easy reliance on a single rating scale, test, or site visit as the primary data source, and to develop instead an array of methodologically sound instruments that assess important outcomes.

SUMMARY

The ability of severely retarded individuals to learn complex vocational tasks has been documented in research efforts for over two decades. The involvement of severely retarded people in meaningful employment situations, however, has been minimal. One reason for this is the difficulty of incorporating isolated habilitation techniques into existing rehabilitation procedures. For techniques that have been used successfully in research or demonstration projects to have impact on the current service system, they will need to be synthesized into a workable procedural package. The present text combines task planning, training, and production supervision guidelines in a first step toward such a synthesis.

The task planning guidelines discussed in Chapters 3 and 4 enable workshop staff to determine quickly and effectively the optimum production design and to construct a task analysis. The procedures discussed under task planning are designed to help workshop staff meet both their habilitation and business objectives while working with severely retarded people.

The vocational training guidelines emphasize the variety of procedures that have been used effectively to train severely retarded adults. Research to date clearly indicates that these procedures can make a difference. With careful, systematic training severely retarded individuals can acquire complex vocational skills. These skills will be of ecological significance, however, only if they result in greater worker productivity and earnings. The production guidelines in Chapters 10, 11, and 12 are designed to maximize the ability of severely retarded workers to use their vocational skills over long time periods.

Many individuals have contributed via research or practical experience to the development of the procedures and guidelines we suggest. Over time this body of knowledge has developed into a new technology: a technology of vocational habilitation. Much work still needs to be done, however, if this technology is to increase vocational opportunities for severely retarded people. It is, in fact, a substantial understatement to say that we need more empirical verification of planning, training, and production supervision techniques currently available. This vertification should come from day-to-day changes in the behavior of severly retarded adults in working situations.

The time for conjecture, deliberation, and isolated research is past. The impetus for future development rests with researchers and service providers working together. Many people have shown that severely retarded workers can learn. We need now to demonstrate that this learning potential can result in viable incomes. It is time to turn the learning demonstrations of the past into earning demonstrations.

REFERENCES

Ayllon, T., and Azrin, N. 1964. Reinforcement and instructions with mental patients. J. Exp. Anal. Behav. 7:327–331.

Antes, W., Honeycutt, J., and Koch, E. 1973. The Basic Motions of MTM. The Maynard Foundation, Naples, Florida.

Baer, D. M. 1977. Prepared remarks at the meeting of the American Association for the Advancement of Behavior Therapy, Atlanta, December.

Ball, T. S. 1971. Itard, Seguin and Kephart: Sensory Education— A Learning Interpretation. Charles E. Merrill, Columbus, Ohio.

Bandura, A. 1969. Principles of Behavior Modification. Holt, Rinehart and Winston, New York.

Bandura, A. 1977. Social Learning Theory. Prentice-Hall, Englewood Cliffs, New Jersey.

Barker, G. 1963. The Stream of Behavior. Appleton-Century-Crofts, New York.

Becker, W. C. 1971. An Empirical Basis for Change in Education. Science Research Associates, Chicago.

Becker, W., Engelmann, S., and Thomas, D. 1975. Teaching 2: Cognitive Learning and Instruction. Science Research Associates, Chicago.

Bellamy, T. 1975. Habilitation of the severely and profoundly retarded: A review of research on work productivity. In T. Bellamy (ed.), Habilitation of Severely and Profoundly Retarded Adults: Reports from the Specialized Training Program. University of Oregon Center on Human Development, Eugene, Oregon.

Bellamy, T. (ed.). 1976. Habilitation of Severely and Profoundly Retarded Adults: Reports from the Specialized Training Program. University of Oregon, Eugene, Oregon.

Bellamy, T., Horner, R., and Inman, D. (eds.). 1977. Habilitation of Severely and Profoundly Retarded Adults: Reports from the Specialized Training Program, Vol. II. University of Oregon, Eugene, Oregon.

Bellamy, T, Inman, D., and Horner, R. 1978. Design of vocational habilitation services for the severely retarded: The Specialized Training Program Model. In G. Hamerlynck (ed.), Applied Behavior Analysis Techniques for the Developmentally Disabled. Brunner Mazel, New York.

Bellamy, T., Inman, D., and Schwarz, R. 1978. Vocational training and production supervision: A review of habilitation techniques for the severely and profoundly retarded. In N. Haring and D. Bricker (eds.), Teaching the Severely and Profoundly Handicapped, Vol. 3. Special Press, Columbus, Ohio.

Bellamy, T., Inman, D., and Yeates, J. Evaluation of a procedure for production management with the severely retarded. Ment. Retard. In press.

Bellamy, T., Oliver, P., and Oliver, D. 1977. "Operations" in vocational training for the severely retarded. In C. Cleland, J. Schwartz, and L. Talkington (eds.), Research with the Profoundly Retarded, Vol. 3. The Western Research Conference, Austin, Texas.

Bellamy, T., Peterson, L., and Close, D. 1975. Habilitation of the severely and profoundly retarded: Illustrations of competence. Educ. Train. Ment. Retard. 10:174–186.

Bellamy, T., and Snyder, S. 1976. The trainee performance sample: Toward the prediction of habilitation costs for severely handicapped adults. AAESPH Rev. 1(4):17–36.

Belmont, J. 1966. Long-term memory in mental retardates. In N. R. Ellis (ed.), International Review of Research in Mental Retardation, Vol. 1. Academic Press, New York.

Belmore, K., and Brown, L. 1976. A job skill inventory strategy for use in a public school vocational training program for severely handicapped potential workers. In L. Brown, N. Certo, K. Belmore, and T. Crowner (eds.), Madison's Alternative for Zero Exclusion, Vol. VI. Madison Public Schools, Madison, Wisconsin.

Bensberg, G. (ed.). 1965. Teaching the Mentally Retarded: A Handbook for Ward Personnel. Southern Regional Education Board, Atlanta.

Berkson, G., and Landesman-Dwyer, S. 1977. Behavioral research on severe and profound mental retardation (1955–1974). Am. J. Ment. Defic. 81: 428–454.

Bijou, S. W., Peterson, R. F., and Ault, M. H. 1968. A method to integrate descriptive and experimental field studies at the level of data and empirical concepts. J. Appl. Behav. Anal. 1:175–192.

Boles, S. M., and Bible, G. S. 1978. The student service index: A method for managing service delivery in residential settings. In M. Berkler, G. Bible, S. Boles, D. Deitz, and A. Repp (eds.), Current Trends for the Developmentally Disabled. University Park Press, Baltimore.

Brolin, D. 1976. Vocational Preparation of Retarded Citizens. Charles E. Merrill, Columbus, Ohio.

Brown, L. 1973. Instructional programs for trainable-level retarded students. In L. Mann and D. Sabatino (eds.) The First Review of Special Education, Vol. 2. Journal of Special Education Press, Philadelphia.

Brown, L., Bellamy, T., and Sontag, E. 1971. The Development and Implementation of a Public School Prevocational Training Program for Trainable Retarded and Severely Emotionally Disturbed Children. Madison Public Schools, Madison, Wisconsin.

Browning, R. M., and Stover, D. O. 1971. Behavior Modification in Child Treatment. Atherton, New York.

Cataldo, M., and Russo, D. 1978. Developmentally disabled in the community: Behavioral/medical considerations. In G. Hamerlynck (ed.), Applied Behavior Analysis Techniques for the Developmentally Disabled. Brunner Mazel, New York.

Chaffin, J. 1969. Production rate as a variable in the job success or failure of educable mentally retarded adolescents. Except. Child. 35:533–538.

Clark, A., and Hermelin, F. 1955. Adult imbeciles: Their abilities and trainability. Lancet 269 (1):337–339.

Commission on Accreditation of Rehabilitation Facilities. 1978. Standards Manual for Rehabilitation Facilities. Commission on Accreditation of Rehabilitation Facilities, Chicago.

Conley, R. W. 1969. The Economics of Mental Retardation. Johns Hopkins University Press, Baltimore.

Cook, P., Dahl, P., and Gale, M. 1977. Vocational Training and Placement of the Severely Handicapped: Vocational Opportunities. The American Institute for Research in the Behavioral Sciences, Palo Alto.

Cooper, J. A. 1974. Measurement and Analysis of Behavior Techniques. Charles E. Merrill, Columbus, Ohio.

Crossman, E. K. 1971. The effects of fixed-ratio size in multiple and mixed fixed-ratio schedules. Psych. Rec. 21:535–544.

Crosson, J. 1966. The experimental analysis of vocational behavior in severely retarded males. Doctoral dissertation, University of Oregon 1966. Dissert. Abst. Int. 27:3304.

Cummings, T. G., and Molloy, E.S. 1977. Improving Productivity and the Quality of Work Life. Praeger Publishers, New York.

Davidson, P., Clark, F., and Hamerlynck, G. 1974. Evaluation of Behavioral Programs in Community, Residential and School Settings. Research Press, Champaign, Illinois.

Davies, I. 1973. Competency Based Learning: Technology, Management and Design. McGraw Hill, New York.

Dokecki, P. 1964. Reviews of the literature relative to the behavior potential of the severely retarded. Train. School Bull. 61:65–75.

Donnelly, G. H., Gibson, J. L., and Ivancovich, J. M. 1975. Fundamentals of Management. Business Publications, Dallas, Texas.

DuRand, J., and Neufeldt, A. H. 1975. Comprehensive Vocational Service Systems. National Institute on Mental Retardation, Downsview, Ontario, Canada.

Dunham, P. 1977. The nature of reinforcing stimuli. In W. K. Honig and J. E. R. Straddon (eds.), Handbook of Operant Behavior. Prentice-Hall, New Jersey.

Edmonson, B. 1974. Arguing for a concept of competence. Ment. Retard. 12:14–15.

Evans, G., and Spradlin, J. 1966. Incentives and instructions as controlling variables of productivity. Am. J. Ment. Defic. 71:129–132.

Federal Register, May 17, 1974, 17509. Chapter V, Part 525: Employment of handicapped clients in sheltered workshops.

Ferster, C., and Skinner, B. 1957. Schedules of Reinforcement. Appleton-Century-Crofts, New York.

Fisher, M., and Zeaman, D. 1973. An attention-retention theory of retardate discrimination learning. In N. Ellis (ed.), The International Review of Research in Mental Retardation, Vol. 6. Academic Press, New York.

Friedman, P. 1975. Legal regulation of behavior modification. Ariz. Law Rev. 17:39–100.

Friedman, P. 1976. The Rights of Mentally Retarded Persons: The Basic ACLU Guide to a Mentally Retarded Person's Rights. Avon Books, New York.

Gardner, W. I. (ed.). 1971. Behavior Modification in Mental Retardation. Aldine Publishing Co.,Chicago.

Gilbreth, F. 1911. Motion Study. D. Van Nostrand, New York.

Gold, M. 1972. Stimulus factors in skill training of the retarded on a complex assembly task: Acquisition, transfer and retention. Am. J. Ment. Defic. 76:517–526.

Gold, M. 1973. Research on the vocational habilitation of the retarded: The present, the future. In N. Ellis (ed.), International Review of Research in Mental Retardation, Vol. 6. Academic Press, New York.

Gold, M. 1975. Vocational training. In J. Wortis (ed.), Mental Retardation and Developmental Disabilities, Vol. VII. Brunner Mazel, New York.

Gold, M. W., and Barclay, C. R. 1973(a). The effects of verbal labels on the acquisition and retention of a complex assembly task. Train. School Bull. 70:39–43.

Gold, M., and Barclay, C. 1973(b). The learning of difficult visual discriminations by the moderately and severely retarded. Ment. Retard. 11:9–11.

Goldfried, M., and Davison, G. 1976. Clinical Behavior Therapy. Holt, Rinehart and Winston, New York.

Gollub, L. 1977. Conditioned reinforcement: Schedule effects. In W. Honig and J. Staddon (eds.), Handbook of Operant Behavior. Prentice-Hall, New York.

Gordon, S., O'Connor, N., and Tizard, J. 1955. Some effects of incentive on the performance of imbeciles on a repetitive task. Am. J. Ment. Defic. 60:371–377.

Greenleigh Associates. 1975. The role of the sheltered workshop in the rehabilitation of the severely handicapped. Report to the Department of Health, Education and Welfare, Rehabilitation Services Administration, New York.

Grossman, H. (ed.). 1973. Manual on Terminology and Classification. American Association on Mental Deficiency, Washington, D.C.

Gruneberg, M. 1976. Job Satisfaction. John Wiley, New York.

Herbert-Jackson, E., O'Brien, M., Porterfred, J., and Risler, T. R. 1977. The Infant Center: A Complete Guide to Organizing and Managing Infant Day Care. University Park Press, Baltimore.

Hersen, M., and Barlow, D. 1975. Single Case Experimental Designs. Pergammon Press, New York.

Honig, K. (ed.). 1966. Operant Behavior: Areas of Research and Application. Appleton-Century-Crofts, New York.

Honig, W., and Staddon, J. (eds.). 1977. Handbook of Operant Behavior, Prentice-Hall, New York.

Horner, R. H. 1977. Stimulus control, transfer and maintenance of upright walking posture with a severely retarded adult. In T. Bellamy, R. Horner, and D. Inman (eds.), Habilitation of Severely and Profoundly Retarded Adults: Reports from the Specialized Training Program. University of Oregon, Eugene, Oregon.

Horner, R. H. 1978. Stimulus control of chained responses: Implications for vocational training and supervision of severely retarded workers. Unpublished dissertation, University of Oregon.

Horner, R. H. Accountability in habilitation of the severely retarded: The issue of informed consent. AAESPH Rev.

Horner, R. H., and Bellamy, G. T. 1978(a). Long-term structured employment: Productivity and productive capacity. In G. T. Bellamy, G. O. O'Connor, and O. C. Karan (eds.), Vocational Habilitation for Developmentally Disabled Persons: Contemporary Service Strategies. University Park Press, Baltimore.

Horner, R. H., and Bellamy, G. T. 1978(b). A conceptual analysis of vocational training with the severely retarded. In M. Snell (ed.), Systematic Instruction of the Moderately, Severely, and Profoundly Handicapped, Charles E. Merrill, Columbus, Ohio.

House, B., and Zeaman, D. 1960. Transfer of a discrimination from objects to patterns. J. Exp. Psychol., 59:298–302.

Huddle, D. 1967. Work performance of trainable adults as influenced by competition, cooperation and monetary reward. Am. J. Ment. Defic. 72:198–211.

Hunter, J., and Bellamy, T. 1977. Cable harness construction for severely retarded adults: A demonstration of training technique. AAESPH Rev. 1(7):2–13.

Inman, D. 1978. Gaining control over tension in spastic muscles. In G. Hamerlynck (ed.), Applied Behavior Analysis Techniques for the Developmentally Disabled. Brunner Mazel, New York.

Inman, D. P., and Cheney, C. 1974. Functional variables in FR pausing with rabbits. Psychol. Rec. 24:193–202.

Irvin, L., and Bellamy, T. 1977. Manipulation of stimulus features in vocational skill training of the severely retarded: Relative efficacy. Am. J. Ment. Defic. 81:486–491.

Irvin, L., Crowell, F., and Bellamy T. 1978. Multiple assessment evaluation of programs for severely retarded adults. Ment. Retard.

Jacobs, J. 1976. Retarded persons as gleaners. Ment. Retard. 14(6):42–43.

Jens, K., and Shores, R. 1965. Behavioral graphs as reinforcers for work behavior of mentally retarded adolescents. Educ. Train. Ment. Retard. 4:21–26.

Johnson, S. M., and Bolstad, O. D. 1973. Methodological issues in naturalistic observation: Some problems and solutions for field research. In L. A. Hamerlynck, L. C. Handy, and E. J. Mash (eds.), Behavior Change: Methodology, Concepts and Practice. Research Press, Champaign, Illinois. p. 7–67.

Joint Commission on Accreditation of Hospitals. 1973. Standards for Community Agencies Serving Persons with Mental Retardation and Other Developmental Disabilities. Joint Commission on Accreditation of Hospitals, Chicago.

Kanfer, F., and Phillips, J. 1970. Learning Foundations of Behavior Therapy. Wiley, New York.

Karan, O., Wehman, P., Renzaglia, A., and Schutz, R. 1976. Habilitation Practices with the Severely Developmentally Disabled. University of Wisconsin, Waisman Center on Mental Retardation and Human Development, Madison, Wisconsin.

Karan, R., Eisner, M., and Endres, R. 1974. Behavior modification in a sheltered workshop for severely retarded students. Am. J. Ment. Defic., 79:338–347.

Kazdin, A. E. 1975. Behavior Modification in Applied Settings. Dorsey Press, Homewood, Illinois.

Kazdin, A. E. 1977(a). The Token Economy. Plenum Press, New York.

Kazdin, A. E. 1977(b). The influence of behavior preceding a reinforced response on behavior change in the classroom. J. Appl. Behav. Anal. 10:299–310.

Kelleher, R. T. 1966. Chaining and conditioned reinforcement. In W. Honig (ed.), Operant Behavior: Areas of Research and Application. Appleton-Century-Crofts, New York.

Kelleher, R. T., and Gollub, L. R. 1962. A review of positive conditioned reinforcement. J. Exper. Anal. Behav. 5:543–597.

Koegel, R. L., and Rincover, A. 1977. Research on the difference between generalization and maintenance in extra-therapy responding. J. Appl.

Behav. Anal. 10:1–12.

Kozloff, M. A. 1971. Measuring Behavior: Procedures for Recording and Evaluating Behavior Data. CEMREL, Inc, St. Ann, Missouri. 1-63.

Krasner, L., and Ullman, L. (eds.). 1965. Research in Behavior Modification. Holt, Rinehart and Winston, New York.

Laski, F. 1977. Entitlement to services for persons who are developmentally disabled. Unpublished manuscript prepared for Developmental Disabilities Center, Temple University, Pittsburgh.

Lent, J. 1974. How To Do More: A Manual of Basic Teaching Strategy. Edmark Associates, Bellevue, Washington.

Levithan, S., and Taggart, R. 1977. Jobs for the Disabled. Johns Hopkins University Press, Baltimore.

Levy, J. 1974. Social reinforcement and knowledge of results as determinants of motor performance among EMR children. Am. J. Ment. Defic. 78:752–758.

Loos, F., and Tizard, J. 1955. The employment of adult imbeciles in a hospital workshop. Am. J. Ment. Defic. 59:395–403.

Lovaas, I., and Bucker, B. 1974. Perspectives in Behavior Modification with Deviant Children. Prentice-Hall, New York.

Lynch, K., and Graber, P. 1977. Survey of Michigan rehabilitation facilities: Implications for the developmentally disabled. Research Monograph, ISMRRD, University of Michigan, Ann Arbor, Michigan.

Mager, R. 1962. Preparing Instructional Objectives. Fearon Publishers, Palo Alto, California.

Martin, A., and Flexer, R. 1975. Three Studies on Training Work Skills and Work Adjustment With the Severely Retarded. Monograph No. 5, Texas Tech Unversity, Rehabilitation Research and Training Center in Mental Retardation, Lubbock, Texas.

Martin, G., and Pallotta, A. 1978. Behavior modification in sheltered workshops and community group homes for the retarded: Current status and future considerations. In G. Hamerlynck (ed.), Applied Behavior Analysis Techniques for the Developmentally Disabled. Brunner Mazel, New York.

Martin, J. 1969. Attending behavior of mentally retarded males during a fading procedure. Unpublished doctoral dissertation, University of Oregon.

Meichenbaum, D. 1977. Cognitive-behavior Modification: An Integrative Approach. Plenum Press, New York.

Mercer, C. D., and Snell, M. E. 1977. Learning Theory Research in Mental Retardation: Implications for Teaching. Charles E. Merrill, Columbus, Ohio.

Merwin, M. 1974. The effect of pre-training upon the training and transfer of circuit board assembly skills of retarded adults. Doctoral dissertation, University of Illinois. Dissert. Abstr. Int. 35(12):6136B.

Millenson, J. 1967. Principles of Behavior Analysis. Macmillan, New York.

Mischel, W. 1968. Personality and Assessment. John Wiley and Sons, New York.

Neff, W. 1968. Work and Human Behavior. Atherton, New York.

Nirje, B. 1969. The normalization principle and its human management implications. In R. Kugel and W. Wolfensberger (eds.), Changing Patterns of Residential Services for the Mentally Retarded, pp. 179–195. President's Committee on Mental Retardation, Washington, D.C.

O'Neill, C., and Bellamy, T. 1978. Evaluation of a procedure for teaching saw chain assembly to a severely retarded woman. Ment. Retard. 16(1):37–41.

Panyon, M., Boozer, H., and Morris, N. 1970. Feedback to attendants as a reinforcer for applying operant techniques. J. Appl. Behav. Anal. 3:1–4.

Paul J., Stedman, D., and Neufeld, R. 1977. Deinstitutionalization: Program and Policy Development. Syracuse University Press, Syracuse, New York.

Perske, R. 1972. The dignity of risk and the mentally retarded. Ment. Retard. 10(1):24–26.

Phillips, E. L., Phillips, E. A., Fixsen, D. L., and Wolf, M. M. 1974. The Teaching-Family Handbook. Research Press, Champaign, Illinois.

Pierrel, R., and Sherman, J. 1963. Train your pet the Barnabus way. Brown Alumni Monthly February:8–14.

Potter, J. T., Biacchi, A. J., and Richardson, E. A. 1977. Simulating real-life situations in a classroom setting: The Montgomery County training module. In E. Sontag (ed.), Educational Programming for the Severely and Profoundly Handicapped. Council on Exceptional Children, Reston, Virginia.

Powell, J., Martindale, B., Kulp, S., Martindale, A., and Bauman, R. 1977. Taking a closer look: Time sampling and measurement error. J. Appl. Behav. Anal. 10:325–332.

Prill, N. 1977. Evaluation of a procedure for teaching generalized tool use skills to a severely retarded person. In T. Bellamy, R. Horner, and D. Inman (eds.), Habilitation of Severely and Profoundly Retarded Adults: Reports from the Specialized Training Program, Vol. II. University of Oregon, Eugene, Oregon.

Quilitch, H. R. 1975. A comparison of three staff-management procedures. J. Appl. Behav. Anal. 8:59–66.

Rilling, M. 1977. Stimulus control and inhibitory processes. In W. K. Honig and J. E. R. Staddon (eds.), Handbook of Operant Behavior. Prentice-Hall, New York.

Rincover, A., and Koegel, R. L. 1975. Setting generality and stimulus control in autistic children. J. Appl. Behav. Anal. 8:235–246.

Roos, P. 1975. Remarks, Conference on Research Needs Related to the Education of the Severely Handicapped. Educational Testing Service, Princeton, New Jersey.

Rosen, M., Clark, G., and Kivitz, M. 1977. Habilitation of the Handicapped. University Park Press, Baltimore.

Rusch, F., Connis, R., and Sowers, J. 1977. Withdrawing a response cost token economy in an experimental restaurant setting: A case study. Paper presented at the Oregon Conference, University of Oregon, February, Eugene, Oregon.

Saunders, R. R., and Koplik, K. 1975. A multi-purpose data sheet for recording and graphing in the classroom. AAESPH Rev. 1:1–8.

Schneider, B. 1976. Staffing Organizations. Goodyear Publishing Company, Pacific Palisades, California.

Schoenfeld, W. N. 1970. The Theory of Reinforcement Schedules. Appleton-Century-Crofts, New York.

Schroeder, S. 1972. Parametric effects of reinforcement frequency, amount of reinforcement, and required response force on sheltered workshop behavior. J. Appl. Behav. Anal. 5:431–441.

Schusterman, R. 1967. Attention shift and errorless reversal learning for the California sea lion. Science 833–835.

Scott, R. A. 1967. The factory as a social service organization. Soc. Probl. 15:160–175.

Screven, C., Straka, J., and LaFond, R. 1971. Applied behavioral technology in a vocational rehabilitation setting. In W. Gardner (ed.), Behavior Modification in Mental Retardation. Aldine Publishing Co. Chicago.

Short, J. 1974. Measurable objectives for educational programs. In R. Ulrich, T. Stachnik, and J. Mabry (eds.), Control of Human Behavior, Vol. 3. Scott, Foresman and Company, Glenview, Illinois.

Sidman, M. 1960. Tactics of Scientific Research: Evaluating Experimental Data in Psychology. Basic Books, New York.

Sidman, M., and Stoddard, L. 1967. The effectiveness of fading in programming a simultaneous form discrimination for retarded children. J. Exp. Anal. Behav. 10:3–15.

Skinner, B. 1948. "Superstition" in the pigeon. J. Exp. Psychol. 38: 168–172.

Skinner, B. 1953. Science and Human Behavior. Free Press, New York.

Skinner, B. F. 1968. The Technology of Teaching. Appleton-Century-Crofts, New York.

Skinner, B. F. 1969. Contingencies of Reinforcement: A Theoretical Analysis. Appleton-Century-Crofts, New York.

Sowers, J., Thompson, L., and Connis, R. The food service vocational training program. In: T. Bellamy, G. O'Connor, and O. Karan (eds.), Vocational Habilitation for Developmentally Disabled Persons: Contemporary Service Strategies. University Park Press, Baltimore. In press.

Spradlin, J. E., Girardeau, F. L., and Corte, E. 1965. Fixed ratio and fixed interval behavior of severely and profoundly retarded subjects. J. Exp. Child Psychol. 2:340–353.

Staddon, J. E. R. 1977. Schedule-induced behavior. In W. K. Honig and J. E. R. Staddon (eds.), Handbook of Operant Behavior. Prentice-Hall, New York.

Steers, R. 1976. Organizational Effectiveness: A Behavioral View. Goodyear Publishing Company, Pacific Palisades, California.

Stokes, T. F., and Baer, D. M. 1977. An implicit technology of generalization. J. Appl. Behav. Anal. 10:349–367.

Striefel, S. 1974. Behavior Modification: Teaching a Child to Imitate. H & H Enterprises, Lawrence, Kansas.

Sultzer, B., and Mayer, R. G. 1972. Behavior Modification Procedures for School Personnel, Holt, Rinehart and Winston, New York.

Terrace, H. 1963. Discrimination learning with and without "errors." J. Exp. Anal. Behav. 6:1–27.

Terrace, H. 1966. Stimulus control. In W. Honig (ed.), Operant Behavior: Areas of Research and Application. Appleton-Century-Crofts, New York.

Touchette, P. E. 1971. Transfer of stimulus control: Measuring the moment of transfer. J. Exp. Anal. Behav. 15:347–354.

Touchette, P. E. 1975. What the researcher is giving the practitioner. Presentation at the American Association on Mental Deficiency, Annual Convention, June, Portland, Oregon.

Turkel, S. 1972. Working. Pantheon Press, New York.

Ullman, L., and Krasner, L. (eds.). 1976. Case Studies in Behavior Modification. Holt, Rinehart and Winston, New York.

Walker, H. M., and Buckley, N. K. 1972. Programming generalization and maintenance of treatment effects across time and across settings. J. Appl. Behav. Anal. 5:209–224.

Walker, H. M., Hops, H., Fiegenbaum, E. 1976. Deviant classroom behavior as a function of combinations of social and token reinforcement and cost contingency. Behav. Ther. 7:76–88.

Weisberg, P. 1971. Operant procedures with the retarded: An overview of laboratory research. In N. Ellis (eds.), International Review of Research in Mental Retardation, Vol. 5. Academic Press, New York.

White, O. R. 1970(a). An investigation of complex chains in the adult, retarded male. Unpublished master's thesis, University of Oregon.

White, O. R. 1970(b). A Glossary of Behavioral Terminology. Research Press Co., Champaign, Illinois.

Whitehead, C. W. 1978. Sheltered workshops in the decade ahead: Work and wages or welfare. In G. T. Bellamy, G. O. O'Connor, and O. C. Karan (eds.), Vocational Habilitation for Developmentally Disabled Persons: Contemporary Service Strategies. University Park Press, Baltimore.

Williams, P. 1967. Industrial training and remunerative employment of the profoundly retarded. J. Ment. Subnorm. 13:14–23.

Wolfensberger, W. 1972. (ed.). The Principle of Normalization in Human Services. National Institute on Mental Retardation, York University Campus, Downsview, Toronto, Canada.

Zeaman, D., and House, B. 1963. The role of attention in retardate discrimination learning. In N. Ellis (ed.), Handbook of Mental Deficiency. McGraw-Hill, New York.

Zimmerman, J., Overpeck, C., Eisenberg, J., and Garlick, B. 1969. Operant conditioning in a sheltered workshop. Rehab. Lit. 30:326–334.

index